THE ENGLISH SOUL

The English Soul

Faith of a Nation

Peter Ackroyd

REAKTION BOOKS

Published by
REAKTION BOOKS LTD
Unit 32, Waterside
44–48 Wharf Road
London N1 7UX, UK
www.reaktionbooks.co.uk

First published 2024
Copyright © Peter Ackroyd 2024

Printed and bound in Great Britain
by TJ Books Ltd, Padstow, Cornwall

A catalogue record for this book is available from the British Library

ISBN 978 1 78914 845 9

Contents

AUTHOR'S NOTE

THIS BOOK DESCRIBES the spirit and nature of English Christianity, as it has developed over the last 1,400 years. It was the presiding faith of the people and has been the reflection, perhaps the embodiment, of the English soul. I am aware that in this undertaking I have not included other powerful and significant faiths that have influenced the religious sensibility of this nation. Judaism, for example, has been an important element in English life since the eleventh century, and the nation now harbours the second-largest Jewish population in Europe. But although it is an important part of English religious history, it does not characterize it. The same may be said of Islam. There were more Muslim than Christian subjects of the British Empire by the end of the nineteenth century, and Islam has become the second-largest religion in England. But although its adherents have contributed to our present understanding of the English soul, they did not create it. Islam is not of native origin or of native inspiration. Hinduism, similarly, is a powerful force for faith, but it is not of indigenous growth. These other religions are not pertinent to the nature and spirit of the present enquiry, and are the material for another book. This study is an account of the Christian English soul, which accepts the fact that Christianity has been the anchoring and defining doctrine of England. The reader should bear in mind, however, that most people of other religions in this country would consider themselves both English and of sincere faith.

The Venerable Bede, illumination from a manuscript of Bede's *Homilies on the Gospels*, 1143–78.

One

Religion as History
The Venerable Bede (673–735)

B ede's *Historia ecclesiastica gentis Anglorum* or *Ecclesiastical History of the English People* is an illustrious example of piety combined with scholarship. It is the book he was destined to write. From the age of seven he was attached to the 'twin' monasteries of Monkwearmouth and Jarrow, seventh-century foundations close to the northeast coast of Northumbria; the two foundations were seven miles apart, and Jarrow was established two years after Monkwearmouth, but these were the permanent centres of his intense contemplation. It is supposed that he came from a well-born or even noble Saxon family, and was by traditional account born in the village of Monkton near Jarrow, but nothing is certain; he once referred to the fact that the family house eventually became part of the monastic domain and that he was born 'in the territory of this monastery'.

From approximately the age of nine, in fact, Bede became associated with the scriptorium and library of Jarrow, together with its daily round of prayer, chant and meditation. From that time forward he wrote, in an autobiographical fragment, that he spent the rest of his life in the monastery, and 'amidst the observance of monastic rule, and the daily charge of singing in the church, I always took delight in learning, or teaching, or writing.' He had also to act as author, scribe and copyist. In this triune vocation he persisted, and by the end of his life he had composed some sixty separate volumes, of which he considered the *Ecclesiastical History* to be his last.

It is the fitting culmination of a lifetime's meditation on biblical exegesis, orthography, science and metre, on computation and chronology, on the lineaments of the natural world, on the meaning of time, on the fate of saints and martyrs. Bede also wrote homilies, hymns and poems. He was a pioneer of modern learning, replacing the classical texts of Romanized Britain with the spiritualized and Christianized studies of the new dispensation. Nothing, sacred or human, was alien to him. He left the bounds of his monastery on few occasions, but the world of learning came to him. He mentions in passing two mentors and one instructor, but he was essentially self-taught and self-disciplined. He would have been trained to comprehend Latin, as well as undertaking early studies in chronology, but he seems to have taught himself Greek and a little Hebrew. That is what might be expected of one who considered himself to exist at the 'edge of the world' in a land that was only partly civilized and that possessed no truly literate culture. In the eleventh century the monk and chronicler Simeon of Durham recalled that visitors were shown the little stone hut or cell where the love and labour of Bede's life were undertaken, but this may be pious fantasy. Bede's period, however, was one in which wood or thatch was giving way to stone.

Of course, the libraries of the 'twin' monasteries contained a wealth of learning from a variety of sources, from chronicles to commentaries and from cosmology to grammar. Bede would also have had access to the monastic libraries of York, Hexham and Canterbury. But his true mentors were the Bible, the first Christian poets, and the Fathers of the first and second centuries who established the doctrinal tenets of the Christian faith. His knowledge of Latin and Greek was based on the understanding that these were the languages with which he might converse with God.

Bede's great work is in spirit and substance a history of *gens Anglorum*, the English people, in distinction to the native British inhabitants, who were sometimes classified as Celtic in origin. It was a phrase that he himself coined in order to mark the passage of years from Celt to Saxon. It is perhaps one of his major contributions to historiography. He acquired much of his information from the sacred texts produced in the scriptoria of major foundations where the laborious work of transcription was undertaken, but also from the testimony of those who had heard or witnessed the significant events of the English world. Jarrow itself, at the centre of the English realms, was much favoured by visitors, who brought their own stories and histories with them. Their words might be inscribed on slate, on tablets of wax or clay, or ultimately on parchment. Out of these diverse origins Bede fashioned a foundation story of Christianity in England. That was the source and origin of his appetite for history and, to that end, he considered historical texts or anecdotes in the same manner as he considered those of scripture. He elicited their meaning with a variety of interpretations both practical and spiritual, allegorical and anagogical. His was called an 'ecclesiastical history' because faith and history were not to be separated.

This was not a new revelation. In the sixth century a British monk, Gildas, had composed a short treatise entitled *On the Ruin of Britain* in which the sins and errors of the British people lead ineluctably to disorder, ruin and eventual conquest by the Saxons, who, although pagan, were the instruments of divine wrath. God's punishment on what he described as an 'indolent' and 'stubborn' people in effect destroyed post-Roman Britain. Gildas composed what was both a religious and political polemic, in an age when there was no distinction between the two. Bede himself knew *The Ruin* very well, and borrowed its eschatology to emphasize the failure of the British race in its confrontation with the Saxon invaders. In a letter to Acca, Bishop of Hexham, he suggests that 'in all holy

books one should ascertain what everlasting truths are there inti-
mated, what deeds are narrated, what future events are foretold.'
The wisdom of the past might thereby be preserved for later generations. There were morals to be adduced from close scholarship.
Bede also introduced the sense of continuity in human affairs, so
that, for example, 'the letters of blessed Peter were written to us
as well as to them [Peter's contemporaries].' Bede was perhaps
the first English historian to suppose that there were patterns and
repetitions even in the crudest chronological account, so that past
and present are locked in a mutual embrace. This was for him a
spiritual truth that was also, as he put it to Acca, 'true history' or
'*vera lex historiae*', the true law of history.

The *Ecclesiastical History* may be the last of Bede's works, but
it does not represent the culmination of his labours. For Bede himself the prize of devotion and learning should be awarded to his
interpretation of the scriptures. But the *History* has been generally
considered the most significant text, largely because of the English
affection for historical writing itself, and has led to his honorific as
'the father of history'. He is also the first and only 'Doctor of the
Church' in England, and is known as 'Anglorum doctor'.

The structure of the completed work is determined by theology as much as by history, being divided into six ages that
correspond to the six days of Creation. Bede was concerned with
numerology, therefore, which offered true vision; the forty days
of the Flood, for example, symbolize the Ten Commandments
multiplied by the four Gospels. In his chronology, too, Bede follows Augustine's account of the six ages of world history, divided
by the Creation, the Flood, the advent of Abraham, the time of
David, the Captivity of Judah and the birth of Christ. To these
Bede appends the gradual revelation of England's destiny. It is in
large part the history of the conversion of a nation.

The first age, for example, begins with the birth of the sea and
land, in a simulacrum of Genesis, which allows Bede to give a

survey of the nation to which he belonged. It was the prelude to the history of the English, who for Bede represented the new people of God, or a new generation of believers, and his ecclesiastical history was designed to outline the ways of God's providence and the local manifestations of God's revelation. The gate had been opened.

The second age begins with the mission of Augustine, at the request of Pope Gregory, to convert the pagan people of the far-flung island. In the third age the apostasy of the Northumbrians is revealed, but much of the country receives the new faith as exemplified by the Synod of Whitby, when the date of Easter is secured and the true monastic tonsure is established. In the fourth age, literature and learning have reached this distant shore. This was aligned with the illustrious reign of King David, which became known as 'the golden age of Israel'. The 'twin' monasteries of Jarrow and Monkwearmouth were in Bede's lifetime part of this great revival, since the learning from the Anglo-Saxons, the Irish and Welsh, the Romans and Gauls all converged there.

The presence of other scholars and teachers, such as Theodore of Tarsus from Asia Minor and Hadrian from North Africa, 'attracted a concourse of students into whose minds they daily poured the streams of wholesome learning'. Schools and monasteries, among them Bede's own Jarrow, flourished in the new dispensation. In this enterprise the layers or levels of time – biblical, Judaic and English – are reconciled in the light of eternity. In the fifth age the English direct their missionary zeal towards the nations closest to them, and the narrative of the sixth age concludes with an examination of the English Church in 731. This was the year in which the *History* was completed.

At the end of his preface Bede reveals the humility of the scholar in his exhortation:

I humbly beg the reader if he finds anything in these books which I have written which is other than truthful, he will not blame me who have zealously laboured, as the true law of history requires, to transmit in simple fashion those things which I have collected from common report for the instruction of posterity.

He himself wrote in limpid and lucid Latin, a token of his clarity of mind. The true law of history permits him to relate those stories and anecdotes that have by common consent been judged to be authentic. These in large part consist of miraculous healing and blessed deaths, which were part of the fabric of life in eighth-century England. He could no more disbelieve or discredit them than his own faith.

Two episodes from the *History* have been justly awarded the merit of consistent praise. The first compared the life of a man to the brief transit of a swallow in a lighted hall. In 627 one of the principal councillors of Edwin, king of Northumberland, pro-pounds the story of the bird escaping the winter's storm by flying in through an open door before leaving through another.

Whilst he is within, he is safe from the wintry tempest; but after a short space of fair weather, he immediately vanishes out of your sight, passing from winter into winter again. So this life of man appears for a little while, but of what is to follow or what went before we know nothing at all.

This may or may not be of Bede's own composition, but it is com-parable to the most majestic and powerful Anglo-Saxon poetry. And why should it not be so? The sensibility of the true historian is close to that of the poet or dramatist, and Bede sets the tone for the English veneration of the past.

The second memorable episode was concerned with the first known English poet, Caedmon, who 'by God's grave received the free gift of song'; he had never been taught to sing or recite verse, and, whenever the harp was passed to him after a banquet, he would rise from the table and return home. He slept one night in the stable at Streonæshalch, now known as Whitby, since it was his task to take care of the cattle there, when a spirit appeared beside him.

'Caedmon, sing me something.'
'I cannot sing, and for this reason I left the banquet and retired here, because I could not sing.'
'Nevertheless you must sing to me.'
'What must I sing?'
'Sing the beginning of creation.'

So Caedmon sang in this sleep, or dream, and on the following morning he recalled his words. He recited them to the leader of his township, who took him to the abbess of Whitby, whereupon she asked him to turn a passage of sacred history into verse. On completing this it became clear that he was blessed by God, and so it came to pass that he would be recognized as a divinely inspired poet to whom all other English poets owe their origin. This is an example, perhaps, of history as high chant. Despite his predilection for the practical and the purposeful, Bede never loses touch with the Saxon past of minstrel or *scop*.

Bede said that he had taken care 'to become acquainted with the actions and sayings of former men of renown, especially of our own nation', so that 'the attentive reader is excited to imitate that which is good.' To this end he collected his material from observers and contemporaries, from libraries and archives; on their return from Rome, scholars would bring him documents and letters, while the manuscripts of Canterbury, Hexham and other centres of learning were carefully examined for the truths 'which we have received from a past generation'.

Bede himself believed that he was living in 'the sixth age of Christ', but, despite this universal attribution, he devoted himself to the 'Church of our nation and race', which existed now and in England. This would be succeeded, at an unknowable date, by the seventh age of the kingdom of God. Yet for him the nation was already a place of prophecy and of miracles, of martyrs and of battles, of apostasy and reunion, of miraculous healing and divine inspiration, of hermits and holy places, of sprits and demons. Bede faithfully recounts the manifold instances of miracles and the deeds of the English saints without distorting the historical record as it was known to him. Even the disputes and controversies of the time, however, were not devoid of 'spiritual significance' or 'inner signification'. That is what gives the *History* its coherence and abiding purpose.

Although it concludes with an encomium on 'these favourable times of peace and prosperity', the *History* also contains a warning for Bede's contemporaries about the frailty of human endeavour. The seven kingdoms of England were not then vying for supremacy, and were united in a common faith supervised from Canterbury and Rome, but the dangers of tyranny, conflict and even invasion were always present. In a letter to Egbert, Bishop of York, written in 734, Bede condemned in the strongest terms the religious condition of the age in words very different from the relatively benign conclusion of the *History*. The sixth age would be concluded at the end of time, but that terminus was unknown and unimagined. At the present juncture, all is in disorder. Bede wrote,

> it is noised abroad concerning some bishops, that they have no men of religion or continence near them; but rather such as indulge in laughter and jests, revels, and drunkenness and other temptations of an idle life, and who rather feed their bodies with carnal food than their minds on the heavenly sacrifice . . . I briefly alluded to the calamity under which our country is suffering most severely, and I earnestly beseech you to strive to rectify what you see done amiss.

He was in particular incensed by the laxity of some great monasteries, which were under the control of the nobility and their families. The monks were often married, and their abbots or abbesses were no more than the secular elite with all its shortcomings. Even the churches might be built as a replica of a nobleman's great hall. The Church was a comfortable annexe to the existing social and political structure. Bede therefore delivered a polemic against greed, sexual licence, intemperance and all the sins that came under the head of '*luxus*' or luxuriousness, which were destroying the strength of the nation and the Church. It was as if he were anticipating the first Norse invasions of the North of England in 793 and 794, together with the sacking of the monasteries, which included Monkwearmouth and Jarrow; but he never claimed to be a prophet. He was aware only that the seventh age would represent the new Jerusalem and the eternal Sabbath of God's kingdom.

The *Ecclesiastical History* itself evinces an abiding interest in near-contemporary saints and sainthood, as Bede recounts what he had heard or read concerning Abbess Hilda or Aidan, Cuthbert or Oswald. With these he could trace the line of faith from ancient to modern times. His list of their virtues and attributes might now seem platitudinous, but it was not so at the time. Of Hilda he wrote that she exemplified 'justice, devotion, chastity, but above all else . . . peace and charity'; of Aidan he invoked 'his love of peace and charity, temperance and humility'.

Bede was at one with his literate contemporaries in their nostalgia for the past and in their reverence for the remnants of churches or dwellings where the ruins still stood as a remembrance of time past. Of a stone church in Lincoln, built at the behest of Paulinus, the first Bishop of York, he remarks that 'walls are to be seen still standing and that every year miraculous cures are wrought in that place.' This was an example of chorography, or the spirit of place.

The British have always possessed a strong inclination for historical knowledge that is combined with the sense of sacred space.

In John Webster's *The Duchess of Malfi* (*c.* 1612/13), Antonio claims that 'I do love these ancient ruines:/ We do never tread upon them, but we set/ Our foot upon some reverend history.' The presence of ruined walls seems to provoke inward delight and to release natural fervour. The association with religion is deepened by the romantic delight in ruined abbeys, and the Shakespearean association with 'bare ruined choirs'. But a more pertinent analogy can be found. In the early eighth century, in the period Bede was writing his *History*, one of the most powerful Anglo-Saxon poems was being composed. It has been entitled 'The Ruin', and laments the prospect of a fallen Roman city, supposed by some to be Bath, with its broken walls and crumbling pillars: 'Roofs are fallen, ruinous towers.'

The Anglo-Saxon imagination had always been powerfully affected by the past, a nostalgia fuelled by fatalism and melancholy. The Anglo-Saxon word *aergod* means literally 'as good as the beginning', so that for Bede himself the past was of pressing social and religious significance; the poetry of his nature, and the inward poetry of the *History*, persuaded him to write of earthworks and walls, and of ruined churches. This melancholy is present both in Gildas and in the monk William of Malmesbury's twelfth-century *The Deeds of the English Kings*. One was a source for, and precursor, of Bede's *History*; the other was deeply indebted to the manner and method of Bede's religious narrative.

In fact William of Malmesbury himself conceived of his work as a continuation of Bede's narrative, with the invading Normans portrayed as restoring true religion. 'I think I have made plain', he wrote, 'how great was the disgrace, how grievous the sickness brought upon England, by the eclipse of education and the depravity of wicked men.' It is the same note sounding through the centuries. He combines visions, miracles, saints and prophecies with transcribed letters and treaties. Legends, sagas and folk tales are placed within what is essentially a true chronology. Bede himself is invoked on numerous occasions as a guide and exemplar, and is sometimes known only as 'the historian'. In the same period as William, Geoffrey of Monmouth tried partly to reverse this theocratic tendency by his portrayal of Arthur and Merlin in *The History of the Kings of Britain*, completed in approximately 1136, but he added to the imagination and folklore of the nation without contributing much to its history.

It may be mentioned that Bede was perhaps the first to portray himself as an Englishman; previously the inhabitants of the island were known separately as 'the men of Wessex', 'the men of Mercia' or 'the men of Northumbria' (which itself had been divided into Deira and Bernicia). Indeed, the tribal boundaries were so strong that the organization of the ecclesiastical dioceses was established upon them. The abbot became essentially a tribal chieftain, whose power was inherited. But for Bede the various peoples had become collectively *Angli* – Englishmen – of which race or *natio* he was pleased to be an example.

Moral and religious intent did indeed shape Bede's historical imagination. History was fundamental to his piety. The past became a repository of stories and legends that confirmed Christian revelation and fashioned Christian eschatology. This tradition established by 'the father of history' was continued in a multitude of forms, so that history itself is considered to be holy and a source of enlightenment. It could also be read as a form of allegory; in this sense the evangelists are understood to be true historians. In those origins lies the power of the English historical tradition, from Gildas in the sixth century to John Milton in the seventeenth century; it stretches even further forward in the Whig version of history, exemplified by Thomas Babington Macaulay and William Stubbs, who in the nineteenth century traced the line of social and constitutional progress in English history so that even the 'Whig version' of history followed Bede's precept of recording 'good things of good men'. The emphasis of much eighteenth- and

nineteenth-century history is in fact to interpret the past in homiletic or didactic fashion, which is not so different from the saints'
lives adduced by Bede, and in which the exemplary patterns of
the past are of the utmost significance. When in 1873 the English
historian James Anthony Froude declared the central principle of
historiography to be the intimation that 'the world is built somehow on moral foundations,' he was echoing Bede's belief in the
divine plan that sustains human life.

During Bede's lifetime his reputation for learning spread
beyond the boundaries of the island that he had come to cher-
ish, and as late as the thirteenth century St Bonaventure, born in
the central Italian region of Viterbo, described his death as the
occlusion of a bright and burning light. Bede's works, whether
concerned with history or with scripture, had their place in every
cathedral or monastic library. He was quite simply the foundation
of the understanding of the Middle Ages, and was constantly compared to Ambrose, Jerome, Augustine and Gregory the Great. For
the last two he had the greatest veneration, and it is not unjust that
he should be called the fifth Father of the Church.

Bede's death was as quiet as his life. According to Cuthbert,
a disciple or follower, he had fallen sick 'with frequent attacks
of breathlessness but almost without pain'. On Tuesday 24 May
735 his breathing became more laboured and he suffered swelling
of the feet. Towards the close of his life he was preparing for the
scriptures to be translated for the first time into the newly written language of Anglo-Saxon, and was working on the Gospel of
St John. He was dictating to a scribe, a boy named Wilberht, and,
despite spending the night awake in prayer, he continued the following day. At three o'clock, according to Cuthbert, he asked for
a box of his to be brought, and distributed 'a few treasures' of his
among the priests of the monastery, including 'some pepper, and
napkins, and some incense'. On the following day, the Feast of the
Ascension, Thursday 26 May, he was laid on the floor of his cell,

where he sang 'Glory be to the Father and to the Son and to the Holy Spirit.' It is a reminder of the pleasure and inspiration that he derived from the music of the liturgy. That night Bede dictated a final sentence to the scribe and died soon afterwards.

Statue of Julian of Norwich, west entrance of Norwich Cathedral.

Two

Religion as Revelation
Julian of Norwich (1343–1416)

A fourteenth-century traveller might venture from Conisford Gate, guarding one southern entry to the city of Norwich, and proceed along Conisford Street; taking this path the traveller would pass the church of St Julian Timberhill on the left-hand side of the road, and might note a small barred window at street level. This would be covered by a black cloth with a white crucifix woven or embroidered upon it, through which the daylight might reach the interior. Many who came there were asking for prayer or exhortation, advice or blessing, since this was the window into the cramped dwelling of the mystic who came to be known as Julian of Norwich. She is the first named female author to write in English. As a result her two devotional texts, known together as *Revelations of Divine Love*, mark further progress in the illumination of the English soul.

Very little is known of Julian, no doubt in accordance with her wishes. She might have been married or she might have been a widow; she might have been a Benedictine nun, or she might have been a mother. She may have come from Norwich itself, although some scholars have detected traces in her writing of a more northern dialect. Such details were unnecessary for one who learned to transcend the confines of time and space. Her life as an anchoress in her cell, or anchorage, was primarily one of solitude and prayer.

When Julian had been deemed fit by the bishop to endure this life of lasting penance, the burial service was pronounced over her and she entered the small space from which she would never depart in this life; as in other such enclaves, there may have been an adjacent room for a servant to use, and perhaps even a small garden for recreation. There was often a small parlour, too, where favoured visitors might enjoy more prolonged discourse. Another small window looked down into the church, from which vantage Julian could watch the ritual of the Mass. A narrow bed, a small altar, a stool and a table made up her meagre furniture. Here she spent more than twenty years, or her remaining life. In the summer she may have worn a black gown and mantle, in the winter she would have supplemented it with an outer garment of wool or fur. Her diet consisted of soup, nuts, fish, bread, fruit and garden vegetables, without the addition of meat.

The events of the external world did not impinge upon Julian's existence. The dreadful devastation of the Black Death, which in 1349 destroyed the larger part of the population of Norwich, is not described by her except, perhaps, in her vivid accounts of the suffering Christ. There were no fewer than five 'great pestilences' that descended upon Norwich during her life, so that the stench of death was everywhere. The rage and incendiary fury of what has become known as the 'Peasants' Revolt' are not mentioned. Many summers of heavy rain, which turned the streets into rivers, pass her by. The interminable war with France, and the 'great schism' of the papacy, are unreported. She was so burning with love and desire for the invisible world that she could not see through the flame.

The mystical tradition can be traced in powers that cannot be summoned or ignored, and in experiences that cannot be understood or explained; they fill the mind and body with sensations and perceptions deeper than any known before, and which were believed to emanate from some divine source that commanded absolute trust and certainty. It was for Julian eternity, or an overwhelming sense of the sacred breaking through time, in which all things became whole. That is perhaps why the English mystics tend to dwell on the Incarnation, when eternity entered time. These revelations came not from wisdom or piety, but by means of absolute and overwhelming intuition. The definitive term of 'mystic' is first recorded for 1692, but the power and longing are far earlier than that date. In England alone, throughout earlier centuries, there was an efflorescence of mystical activity among the British and the Anglo-Saxons. The names of Wulfric, Godric, Leofric, and Christina of Markygate frequently occur in the history of contemplation.

Julian's consummate theology and the lyrical cadences of her recollections in *Revelations of Divine Love* must indeed have come from somewhere. There were in fact manuals of meditation, devotional tracts, psalters, gospels, collections of sermons and of course the Bible itself to nourish and inspire her. The vivid familiarity of her spiritual 'shewings', however, did not necessarily spring from the sermons she heard or the devotional manuals she read. She may have been born with the gift of vision. The fourteenth century was an age of spiritual imagery, sometimes of the most visceral kind. The figure on the Cross writhed in agony, his head punctured with thorns and strips of flesh hanging from his body; it was an aspect of the affective piety that was pre-eminent in the century, when passionate intensity and sympathetic suffering were the twin emblems of true devotion. This was a piety through which the believer was exhorted to see Christ as friend, lover and spouse. And who can see the agony of their beloved without weeping? The community of the faithful, many of whom were anchoresses such as Julian, were urged to place themselves by the manger in Bethlehem, to hold Christ's hand in his agony at Gethsemane, to weep at the foot of the Cross, to stand in silence at the tomb, to rejoice with the shepherds and sing with the angels, to pity the agonies of Mary or lament the wounds of Christ.

In her younger years it is likely that Julian of Norwich attended the mystery plays or 'pageant plays' that were organized in Norwich itself, with each guild performing one episode of sacred history in wagons that trundled through the cobbled streets. They may be considered living tapestries representing the sacred world. The wagons, approximately 7 metres (23 ft) in height, moved on from 'station' to 'station' in a preordained route as the crowds assembled to watch them. There were more than a hundred areas of East Anglia where such dramatic performances were conducted. A living art can be found here, just as we can identify the lineaments of the 'East Anglian school' in the unmatched liveliness of outline in religious imagery and illuminated capitals. The visions of Julian may thus have been prompted in part by early experience of sacred performance. In her 'shewings', for example, she imagined herself to be present as a witness to Christ's suffering, weeping and groaning beside his mother.

There were two written versions of Julian's experiences. A shorter version was set down in the late 1370s or 1380s, and a longer one composed a decade or so later; this interval allowed her to revive or redefine her instinctive responses to what was for her the manifestation of the spiritual and supernatural in her earthly existence. She revised her text two or three times, perhaps softening or sharpening her oral delivery to an unknown amanuensis, who was responsible for their compilation.

In her later and longer text Julian declared that 'this revelation was shewed to a simple creature unletterde.' This in fact may imply not that she was illiterate, but that she did not understand Latin, the language of theological discourse; in fact, she spoke or wrote in Middle English and was one of the earliest, if not the first, to engage in what has become known as 'vernacular theology', addressed to 'mine evenchristen', or her fellow Christians. In any case, she was God's 'creature', a common enough phrase for the lowliness of being enclosed in 'deadly flesh'.

The first visions or 'shewings' may not have been granted in her confinement, but in the setting of her family and of her previous life. In the opening sentence of her earlier account Julian records that she begged to be granted three gifts: the first was 'a bodily sight' of the Passion so that she might witness the agonies of the Crucifixion and suffer all the physical pains of that excruciating ordeal; her second was 'an urgent desire to have of God's gift a bodily sickness . . . so hard that I might die from it', accompanied by all the attendant suffering and fear, so that all would despair of her; her third wish was to receive three wounds, which embraced 'the wound of contrition, the wound of compassion, and the wound of an earnest longing for God'.

Then, on 8 May 1373, in her thirtieth year, Julian's trinity of wishes descended upon her. She lay grievously sick, hovering between life and death for three days and three nights; she was given the last rites, and trusted that she would die. But death was not granted to her, and half-paralysed she lingered until, on the fourth day, her parish priest arrived with words of comfort to ease her passing. The crucifix was put before her face and all around her became dark except light, or daylight, emanating from the figure on the Cross. At that moment her sickness was lifted from her, and she knew at once that her body had been healed. Her second wish had been granted, but she did not rejoice at the peril passed. She was, if anything, sorrowful that death had not embraced her. The priest and his acolyte had departed, leaving the crucifix at the foot of the bed. This prompted her first 'revelation', or 'shewing', or mystical vision. The various words or phrases cannot describe the glimpse of intuitive truth that dazzled her. She saw or glimpsed, in a flash that might have seemed to her to be eternity, 'the red blood trickle down' from the crown of thorns.

Julian would later distinguish her visions as the various manifestations of 'bodily sight', 'ghostly sight' and 'more ghostly sight', which might be roughly translated as physical presence, imaginative apprehension and contemplative truth. But these configurations are unstable. Within the same vision in which she saw the blood running from the thorns, she had a less palpable understanding of divine love that wraps and protects us like a cloth or clothing, winds around and encloses us like a garment; this is an image that might occur naturally to an inhabitant of Norwich, with its trade in cloth and textiles, but here it is understood as a spiritual sight to convey divine love. Thus 'al thing shal be wele'; this phrase, used as a motif by Julian, had been previously uttered by Pontius Pilate in one of the pageant plays and repeated in Walter Hilton's fourteenth-century *The Scale of Perfection*. It may have been a common expression, its homely use concealing a sacred meaning.

There was also a specific revelation from Christ himself: 'And in this [vision] he showed a little thing the size of a hazel-nut, lying in the palm of my hand, and to my understanding it was as round as any ball.' Julian wondered, 'What may this be?' The answer came, 'It is all that is made.' She marvelled at the size and fragility of the nut, but it was said to her that 'it lasts and ever shall last for God loves it. And so all things have their being through the love of God.' The essence or, in medieval terms, the 'substance' of the nut is love. This is a genuine moment of vision, if only because it confirms and corroborates the perception of other mystics, who, in William Blake's words, are permitted 'To see a World in a Grain of Sand' and 'Hold Infinity in the palm of your hand'.

On that one day in May Julian was granted fifteen visions, or revelations; they began at approximately four o'clock in the morning, and ended at about three in the afternoon, one passing into another like the cadences of one melody. But those eleven hours endured for a lifetime. The visions were in large part devoted to the Passion, and to the vista of human redemption. In the twelfth revelation she believed that Christ spoke to her directly: 'I it am. I it am. I it am that is highest. I it am that thou lovest. I it am that thou likest. I it am that thou servest. I it am that thou longest. I it am that thou desirest. I it am that thou menest. I it am that is alle.' That sense of completeness is amplified by her statement that 'we arn in God, and God in us.' For in us is 'his endlesse dwellyng'. It is the node of English mysticism.

These fifteen visions were followed by a night of derangement, during which Julian believed that she was attacked by the devil. Then, in the final (sixteenth) vision, on the following night, she envisioned her soul as a fair city where 'the godhede sitteth at rest'; she was also comforted and reassured by the revelation that 'al thing shal be wele.' This is followed by a short sentence: 'And sone after all was close, and I saw no more.' For Julian of Norwich the revelations were over, but they were not completed. She meditated upon them for the rest of her life, puzzling out their meaning. Fifteen years of contemplation did not resolve the central mystery, until her conclusion in the 86th and final chapter of *Revelations of Divine Love*:

> I was answered in gostly [spiritual] understonding, seyeng thus: 'What, woldest thou wit [know] thy lordes mening in this thing? Wit it wele, love was his mening. Who shewed it the? Love. What shewid he the? Love. Wherfore shewed he it the? For love.'

This level of awareness is described by her as 'knowing'.

Yet Julian's visions tend towards the local and circumstantial. Even her lyrical prose is filled with material imagery and with specific, almost humble, detail. The hazelnut is an example. That is why she trusts in visual detail, in colour and in shape, so that the reader can see the world as Julian sees it. The English soul was mediated through homely images. She describes vividly the blood on the agonized visage of Christ, which dropped upon his face like rain dripping from the eaves of a dwelling after a storm;

some of these drops were as round as the scales of a herring. 'And after this I saw God in a pointe – that es, in mine understanding – by whilke sight I sawe that he es in alle thinge.' The most intimate and familiar detail is here married with the most profound mystical insight. Julian invites us to contemplate this one point, since in a circle smaller than a mustard seed Infinity may be found. The Creation, the Fall and the redemption – time past, time present and time future – are all contained within this point, and can be understood simultaneously. In similar fashion the sorrowful mysteries of Christ's Passion are as close to us as the tangible world. His dying body was 'lyke a dry borde', and he was hanging 'in the eyre as men hang a cloth to drye'. The inference may be that this crucial suffering and death are always happening. The penitent must labour as the gardener, 'delvyn and dykyn, swinkin and sweten, and turne the earth upsodowne'.

It is appropriate here to repeat the evident truth that Julian was the first woman to write in English whose name we know, and that her femaleness informed the nature and quality of her narrative. It may have been transcribed by a male amanuensis, but a female nature inspires it, with the claims of physical experience and sensation overpowering doctrinal matters. The Wife of Bath, in Geoffrey Chaucer's *The Canterbury Tales*, declares, 'By God! If wommen hadde writen stories', to which in the same century Julian of Norwich replies, 'botte for I am a woman, schulde I therefor leve that I schulde nought telle yow of the goodenesse of God?' It ought to be emphasized, perhaps, that in *Revelations of Divine Love* Julian renews the concept of God as the Mother. She also invokes 'Mother Jesus' vouchsafed in 'tendernes of love', since 'oure saviour is oure very moder, in whome we be endlesly borne.' It was precisely this trust in the truth of feeling that made many male clerics so unsympathetic to female mystics.

It has been surmised that Julian was herself a mother, but such reductionism does not alter the fact that she outlines the theology of the divine mother in her account of creation, salvation and spiritual nourishment. In the fourteenth century the visionary experience allowed occasion and place for the manifestation of female sensibility; mystical revelation is a sacred area where the privileges of a male hierarchy do not apply, and where female authority can be asserted. Just as the anchoress is poised between life and death in her sealed cell, so she can mediate between time and eternity.

Julian's revelations end with a paean to 'hevenly joye' in a vision of love and salvation. In an earlier chapter she even draws close to the conclusion that 'we be mightly taken out of hell and oute of the wrechednesse in erth, and wurshipfully brought up into heven.' This was contrary to most religious texts, which dwell on the pains of hell and the unending torments of sinners, and of course a rebuttal of the orthodox doctrines of the Church. She leaves the promise, as it were, in the air. Nevertheless it is consistent with her mystical belief that there is no blame or anger within God, and that 'sinne is nought' beside the infinite mercy and goodness of the divine. When God showed her sin in vision, he affirmed to her that 'al thing shal be wele.' *Revelations of Divine Love* embodies an entire mystical theology in which the contemplation of joy is the ground of being.

✠

THE FOURTEENTH CENTURY, in which Julian lived and prayed, has been often described as the most significant period of English mysticism. From this turbulent era emerged such seminal works as Richard Rolle's *The Fire of Love*, Hilton's *The Scale of Perfection*, *The Cloud of Unknowing* by an unknown author, and Margery Kempe's spiritual autobiography; all in turn manifest a common inheritance in their earnest spirituality matched by a certain spirit of optimism, in their tendency towards individualism and their distaste for regimentation or excessive display. This spiritual pragmatism may be described as the *via media* of English piety, with a sanity and discretion that instinctively avoid obsession or excess. There has never been in England a tradition of theological speculation, or of devotional concepts divorced from practice, and the short handbooks or manuals for mystical growth are the only equivalents to the great *summa theologica* of European faith. They combine characteristic individualism with professions of orthodox faith.

These English mystics also share certain persuasive insights. They desire to be 'homely' with God. That word appears in all their writings. Whether they want to be at one with God, or to feel God, or to know God, or, in one instance, to be married to God, they all desire to have him as their warm hearth. It is a deeply English notion. At some point, too, all these writers express a reserve, a gentle but firm reticence concerning the 'privities' of contemplation. All are witness to a secret that cannot be expressed in words. They are also in dialogue with one another. Hilton is in dialogue with Rolle and the author of *The Cloud of Unknowing*. The author of *The Cloud* is in dialogue with Rolle. Kempe is in dialogue with them all. Only Julian, perhaps, speaks individually to the world, needing no other authority than her own experience.

There are, however, important differences. We may observe a distinction between the male and female mystics. For the male writers, the body is at best a servant, at worst an irrelevance. For Julian and Kempe, the body is ever present, whether as object or as hindrance. The entire relationship is quite different, insofar as it is a relationship at all. For the two women, the flesh is a daily reality. The male writers often write as if they were disembodied minds. They regard the body as an unhelpful influence or as an unreliable guide to spiritual realities, not as gift, blessing or instrument. Except as a source of temptation, it is seen as inert. We are in the realm of fallen but hopeful intellects.

What would later be termed *certitudo salutis*, 'assurance of salvation', appears most strikingly in Julian's writing, but it is everywhere present. And this brings us to the central paradox of the mystical journey. The mystic is enjoined to trust God and the salvation won for him or her, yet never to take it for granted. All has been done for them, yet they must do all in response. All has been offered by divine grace, yet all must be answered by human will. Only God can stretch out the hand, but only man can take it. The cup does not 'earn' the wine poured into it, yet the cup must be pure and clean to receive it.

Charity, of course, was the supreme salvific virtue. Even the salvation promised to the studious mystic was contingent on this. The authorities invoked are strikingly few. The composer of the Psalms, St Paul, St Augustine, St Gregory, Richard of St Victor, St Bernard and St Bonaventura are almost the only authorities quoted or paraphrased. The audience for these texts of piety must also be considered. They seem principally to be addressed to women, who may have been regarded as more susceptible to devotional practice. Even if this had become merely a tradition, that is itself revealing; it had become understood that the devotees of books on spiritual matters were female. It would be frivolous and reductive to say that the spiritual manual was for women of the fourteenth century what the novel became for women of the nineteenth, but it would not be entirely inapt.

THE FIRST OF THE fourteenth-century English mystics (or at least of those with whom we are acquainted) was Richard Rolle, whose principal text is entitled *Incendium amoris* or *The Fire of Love*. Rolle has been described as 'the true father of English literature', and at the least he may be acclaimed as an eminent figure in its development. He was born around 1300 in the village of Thornton-le-Dale or Thornton Dale in the Ryedale district of North Yorkshire, close to the moors. He must have shown some early sign of ability, since he was sponsored at Oxford by the patronage of Thomas Neville, who later became archdeacon of Durham; Rolle did not progress to a degree, suggesting that he left the university of his own choice, but returned to his father's house in Thornton Dale. It was there that, after what he once described as a 'longis inspiracion of god, undirstandynge, wysdome and syghynge', he determined to become a hermit or 'solitari', devoted fully to contemplation.

According to a hagiography composed by some pious nuns in 1381 or 1382, the *Office for Richard Rolle*, Rolle asked his sister to bring two of her 'over-dresses', one white and one grey, to a nearby wood, together with a 'rain-hood'; she obeyed his instructions, but was astonished to see him strip naked, cut off the sleeves of the white tunic and clothe himself with it before donning the grey garment and the rain-hood. With this transformation he hoped and believed that he might resemble the hermit whom he sought within himself. His sister cried out that he had been seized with madness, and he chased her away with threats before himself fleeing the forest. He took refuge in a nearby church and became so wrapped in prayer that he occupied the place usually reserved for the lady of the manor, who, on entering, refused to disturb his devotions.

According to the *Office*, Rolle was still in the church on the following day, when he assisted in the celebration of Mass before mounting the pulpit and delivering a sermon of such beauty and grace that 'the multitude could not refrain from tears.' After that event he was taken up by the squire of the village of Dalton, given more suitable eremitical clothes and granted shelter in the grounds. His patron would conduct visitors to his cell, to whom Rolle would extend blessing and 'advisement'. The *Office* noted that 'he proceeded to give them excellent exhortations while at the same time never ceasing his writings – and all the while what he was writing was not the same as he was speaking.' He would in later years change cells as his solitary life demanded, until he took up residence at Hampole, near Doncaster, where he supervised the instruction of Cistercian nuns at a nearby priory. It was they who compiled the *Office* to celebrate his life of isolation and devotion. He was also believed to possess the gift of healing. He was venerated as a saint, although he was never canonized, and his grave at Hampole Priory became a site of pilgrimage after his death in 1349.

Rolle wrote originally in Latin, but returned to English in the latter years of his life with a powerful and idiosyncratic idiom. It may be worth noting that, both in Latin and in English, Rolle trusts the line of alliteration to convey his meaning. The alliterative line itself is a native English measure and part of the alliterative revival of the century in which emerge *Sir Gawain and the Green Knight*, *Pearl* and *Piers Plowman*. It is marked by a concern for concrete and specific meaning, and could thus be used for texts addressed to a 'lewed' or unlearned audience. We may also infer the influence of wall-paintings and illuminations, of liturgical plays and stained-glass windows, on his devotional piety. Richard Rolle was of his time, while transcending it.

Song and sweetness are never far from the texture of Rolle's prose, which is filled with polyphony, so that in his solitude he fashions a language of praise and joyfulness. Death and melody are 'all one'. His most celebrated work was *The Fire of Love*, composed in approximately 1340, the most widely read of all mystical texts from the medieval period. In this text he considers himself to be 'a pipe of love'. It is an endearing image, but its meaning is deeper than it may seem. He means – and only he could have conceived this image – that the contemplative must relinquish all selfhood, as commonly understood, so that God's melody can sing through them, clean and clear. He is not a mystic who dwells with the unknowable; he relies on the simple experience of his contemplative life as he proceeded from faith to a 'kynde knowynge' encompassing knowledge of the self and longing for God.

Rolle trusts that he lives in a state of union with the divine, manifested in his perpetual awareness of heat, sweetness and song.

Speech then also becomes a form of song, and prayer is a poem. Or, as he puts it in an early English translation of his Latin, 'thoght turns intil sang and intil melody.' This is the expression of the mystic. Yet the central image of *The Fire of Love* is, naturally or supernaturally, fire. For Rolle that fire is a sensual as well as a spiritual experience in the actual experience of 'burning'.

A translation into more contemporary English successfully conveys Rolle's meaning. In the first sentence of his prologue he reveals that 'I first felt my heart wax warm, truly, and not in imagination, but as if it were burned with sensible fire.' This is the key. He goes on to write of 'heavenly heat' and then of 'the unmeasured flame of love', which for 'many truly is hidden, and to a most special few it is shown'. Here, then, is the seal of the true mystic, who cannot speak of the unspeakable. In the fourth chapter Rolle says of the divine that 'His love truly is fire, making our souls fiery and purging them from all degrees of sin, making them light and burning.' In contrast, the sinner shall 'be burned endlessly by continued fires without any comforter'. Those who are saved, however, will flourish in the flames of 'sweetest love' when 'they are set on fire with the most high fire of love.'

Flame is central to the fourteenth-century imagination. Towns and cities were constantly threatened and submerged by fire; the heretics were chained to the stake and the wood beneath put to the flame; and ever since the fifth century BC it had been implicitly believed that light was a form of fire. Rolle touches upon this fundamental tenet of belief when he reveals that 'the fire of endless love' gives 'light within in mind'. Thus he penetrates to what he believed to be the soul of the universe, where those irradiated by wisdom are 'inflamed by that fire' which 'despises all transitory things'. The 'ghostly' or spiritual heat blazes in them, and 'the love of Christ is in us and burning.' It is hotter than a burning coal and glows redder than any rose. The words of God are themselves a 'burning fire'. In an accompanying poem Rolle beseeches 'good

Jesus' to 'burn me'. In contemplation he is 'loving, burning and singing'. His heart resembles 'godly fire' and 'heavenlike sparkles', and 'the eye of his understanding' is opened to reveal 'the citizens of heaven'. He alludes here to the experience of the mystic and of the rapture that seizes him. The ground of his loving and the ground of his seeking are the ground of his burning. He is outlined by supernatural fire, which is as good as any description of the mystical life. Here is no trace of introversion or dogmatism, but only the unforced utterance of joyful experience.

✠

WALTER HILTON, WHO composed the treatise entitled *The Scale of Perfection*, grew up in the lifetime of Richard Rolle and can be considered his companion in spirit if not in life. He has in a manner sheltered from history, the date and place of his birth unknown and his early life uncertain; it has been surmised that he was an Augustinian canon of Thurgarton Priory, near Southwell in the county of Nottinghamshire, but the rest is darkness until the time of his death in March 1396. We can only assume that he wrote *The Scale* in that priory, and the text itself suggests that its first book was written for the sake of an anchoress similar to Julian of Norwich. The second book is of wider import. From Rolle he borrows, or is inspired by, the image of divine grace as song or melody. The physical body is 'but as an instrument and a trumpet of the soul, in which the soul blows with sweet notes of spiritual lovings to Jesus'. But his principal metaphor is that of a journey or pilgrimage to Jerusalem, anticipating John Bunyan in the seventeenth century, and he is the first English writer to employ it extensively as a progress towards spiritual enlightenment. He advises the pilgrim to repeat, 'I am nought, I have nought, I desire nought, but only the love of Jesus.' With that avocation 'then shall our lord Jesus fulfil thy soul with shinings.' Music and brightness once more fill the texts of mystical longing.

As a canon regular of the Augustinian community, Hilton led a more fixed or circumscribed life than Rolle, a circumstance that may account for his more modest or moderate prescription for the devotional life. *The Scale* is less a meditation on visionary experience than a practical and spiritual guide to holy living and dying. That is why it was immensely popular within his own lifetime. His careful and scrupulous mapping of the journey to everlasting life suggests also that he was trained in canon law, and he was in fact known as 'magister', a doctor in theology. He affirmed the virtues of the 'mixed life', combining the urgency of spiritual preparation with the practicalities of ordinary life in a style that is both intimate and easy.

Yet in his mystical experience Hilton entirely transcends his preparatory training. He knows that 'the least touching of love and the least sparkle of spiritual life sent from heaven into such a soul is so great and so comfortable, so sweet and so delectable . . . that it bursteth and sheweth it out in weeping, sobbing and other bodily stirring.'

✝

OF QUITE ANOTHER character is the unknown author of *The Cloud of Unknowing*, a treatise on mysticism that seems to have been composed by a cloistered monk or a recluse who was deeply imbued with the lessons of the first-century Neoplatonist Dionysius the Areopagite. In this tradition God is beyond description or definition, and thus transcends any attempt to reach him. The cloud to which the title alludes is the dark mist that lies between the yearning soul and the divine object to which it aspires; it is 'the night of the intellect', which cannot fathom a darkness that is the excess of light. The author departs from Rolle in his belief that the fervour of spirit is stronger than any 'boisterousness of bodily feeling', such as heat or warmth, in uniting the soul with God 'in spiritual unity and accordance of will'. When asked about the nature of God, the author can reply only, 'I do not know.' The heaven longed for 'is as near down as up, and up as down, behind as before, before as behind, on one side as on another'. It is unfathomable, and can be defined only by what it is not.

The Cloud of Unknowing is in some respects a challenging work, filled with necessary paradox in its evocation of an infinitely transcendent God who is at once being and not being, light and darkness, comprehended and incomprehensible. He can be known only by unknowing; the intellect, and the imagination, must be silenced. Neither desire nor will may assist the aspirant, but only that which is entirely unknowable. Nowhere bodily is everywhere spiritually. And so he or she must persist 'in this nought and in this nowhere'. The created world must be obscured by 'a cloud of forgetting'. Only in 'divine darkness' can a contemplative possibly be united with God, and this unimaginable union can be attained only by 'a devout stirring of love wrought in the will by God'. Only thus will the dark cloud of unknowing be pierced by 'the sharp dart of longing love'. No more can be said of 'this loving stirring and blind beholding' with 'the blabbering fleshly tongue'. *The Cloud of Unknowing*, then, is not evangelistic in purpose; the author is concerned not with those who beg for salvation, but with those who seek perfection in contemplation.

✠

THE FINAL NOTE of this chapter is reserved for an English mystic who lived in the world. *The Book of Margery Kempe* has the merit of being the first autobiography in English, but Kempe's position as an exemplary writer of revelation and vision might be questioned by some if only for the fact that she conceived fourteen children. She was born in Lynn, a seaport and market town in western Norfolk, in about 1373; at the age of twenty she was married to a successful merchant, John Kempe, but after the birth of their first child she was visited by a severe depression that caused her to break down, until she was healed and comforted by a vision of Christ 'in lykenesse of a man, most semly, most bewtyuows & most amiable'. Middle English may be retained in order to capture her distinctively individual voice.

By Kempe's account Christ asked her, 'Dowtyr, why hast thow forsakyn me, and I forsoke neuyr thee?' This was the first emblem of her spiritual destiny. Apparently by mutual consent, she and her husband ended their sexual union in 1413, and from that time forward she devoted her life to spiritual wanderings, pious visitations and pilgrimages. She was no mild or meek pilgrim, however. At worship she wept openly and constantly; she fainted, or shrieked, or cried out, at any reference to Christ and his Passion. Some, such as Julian of Norwich, recognized her spirituality; she also records her generally amicable meetings with bishops, archbishops, Franciscans, Dominicans and others.

But, for those less sympathetic, Kempe was a nuisance and a burden. Her fellow pilgrims often refused to travel with her. Some priests or monks would not preach if she were a member of the congregation. She interrupted or spoiled meals with her exclusively pious conversation. She wore virginal white, despite her life as a married woman, and was a practising vegetarian in an age when such taste was the mark of extreme eccentricity. She remarks that she was eaten and spat out by the gossip of neighbours as a rat eats a piece of dried fish. But she seemed to invite and embrace slander or malice as a way of coming closer to Christ. She believed she was *worthy* of denunciation and vilification. Abuse is to be her cross, her martyrdom and, eventually, her salvation.

Kempe's travels to the Holy Land and other sacred sites were also occasions of controversy. Her first bout of public crying, or 'the fyrst cry that evyr sche cryed in any contemplacyon', occurred on a visit to Mount Calvary, when the attendant friars expounded on the theme of Christ's sufferings. At this juncture 'sche fel down that sche mygth not stondyn ne knelyn, but walwyd and wrestyd wyth hir body, spredyng hir armys abrode, and cryed with a lowde voys as thow hir hert schulde a brostyn asundyr' – she fell down, so that she could not stand or kneel, but wrestled with her own body, spreading her arms on each side, and crying with a loud voice as if her heart would break. She wept and wailed and cried piteously, losing control of her limbs. She added that 'this maner of crying' lasted for many years; in another place she records ten years of open lamentation, complete with 'lowde cry-ingys and schille [shrill] schrykyngys'. In that sense she fulfilled the traditional role of a fool for Christ.

There were occasions when Kempe was arrested and impris-oned but eventually released; she was escorted from certain parishes or dioceses, and was often forbidden to converse with monks or priests. But she would not deviate from what she described as 'the wey of hy perfeccyon'. It was not simply that she was a woman, and thus often scorned by the male clergy, but that she was pious in a way few contemporaries could understand. People could not entertain a faith that expressed itself so violently. Anyone who seemed too pious might be abused as a 'loller' or Lollard. In Margery Kempe, the devotional practice of the time was whipped within the vessel of a troubled, pious, self-centred but enormously generous soul.

In 1431 Kempe's husband, in a state of advanced senility, died after two years of careful tending from her. It seems that in this same period she began to dictate her spiritual autobiography, and the most likely amanuensis was her own son. She sailed for Prussia two years later, before returning to Lynn in 1434. The last glimpse of her lies in the records of the Trinity Guild of merchants from 1439. It was a busy and unconventional life, but how was it that she was declared by some to be a mystic or visionary? The answer lies in her account of the sensations that overwhelmed her in her visions of the Nativity and the Crucifixion; she did not meditate upon them but, rather, experienced them as if she had stepped bodily into the frame of the holy 'shewings'.

For Kempe the Incarnation was an endless physical reality, and the passion of Christ so much part of her awareness of the world that she could not distinguish between the spiritual and the sensual. It was affective piety, part of the spirituality of the four-teenth century, taken to a degree where she lost consciousness of herself and her natural surroundings. In vision she saw herself, for example, escorting Mary home from the Cross on Golgotha. She believed that Christ spoke to her, and she recorded many conversations with God on the nature both of salvation and of divine grace. She was regarded by some as a holy woman who could perform miracles in God's name, but she never strayed into heresy in an age when heretical tracts were being increasingly read and circulated.

The Book of Margery Kempe is marked by homeliness of address and intimacy of detail; her spiritual journey is concerned with 'the forme of her leuyng', the manner of her living, in a fifteenth-century world that is filled with circumstantial detail as well as vision. The reader can hear the voices. When she left Canterbury Cathedral she was harassed by catcalls: 'Thou xalt be brent, fals lollare!' On her devotional visit to Julian of Norwich, the recluse imparted to her these final words: 'I pray God grawnt you perseuerawns' (God grant you steadfastness). There are many 'Chaucerian' moments, the strange but exhilarating conflation of sacred and secular, of piety and farce. Kempe was, after all, both garrulous wife and mystic visionary, and in that respect she seems as thoroughly English as Noah's wife in the mystery plays. She was one of the first, and greatest, exponents of female perception.

This gift of vision is also celebrated in English verse and song, down to its roots in Anglo-Saxon poetry. In *The Dream of the Rood*, composed at some point between the eighth and tenth centuries, the anonymous writer, or rather dreamer, has a vision of the 'rood' or wooden Cross on which Christ was crucified. Here we are in the realm of the mystical: things are perceived as they truly are, not as they really are. The reader, like the dreamer, is drawn deeper and deeper into a vortex of sympathy. The dreamer feels the wounds of disgrace, then sees the tree bleeding; and the tree in turn feels the wounds of Christ as if they were its own. It trembles within the earth, but may not bend, bearing as it does the Lord of all. And the dreamer, too, trembles at the sight. When Christ is taken down, the tree speaks of being wounded with arrows. It is felled to the earth, and even buried, just as is Christ. What moves and sustains the reader is the shifting vision, and the second sight deployed with all the devotion of Margery Kempe. It is part of the fruitful tradition of English mysticism.

Johann Simon Negges, *John Wyclif*, 18th century, mezzotint.

Three

Religion as Reform

John Wyclif (*c*. 1328–1384)

The position of John Wyclif in the English religious tradition has always been a subject of controversy. Was he a fourteenth-century philosopher and theologian who pursued his conclusions as a matter of faith, or was he the willing agent of those magnates who resented the power of the Church? Was he the 'morning star of the Reformation', as he was described in 1548 by a fervent Protestant, advancing propositions that would be taken up by Martin Luther and John Calvin, or was he instead one of the last medieval scholastics who lived in an Oxford world of analysis and definition? The last is in fact much closer to his truth and the truth of his time.

Wyclif's early life is obscure, with the likely date of his birth set at 1328. It is generally assumed that he came from the village of Wycliff-on-Tees, near Richmond in north Yorkshire, and was thus credited with the stubbornness and self-certainty that, according to popular belief, was associated with Yorkshiremen in general. It is believed that he came from a family of minor gentry under the overlordship of his eventual patron, John of Gaunt, but this is surmise. The first certain record places Wyclif as a probationary fellow of Merton College at Oxford University in 1356, but it is likely that he had previously spent five or six years at the Queen's College there, in the study of law. These early years, however, marked him out, and for most of his life he remained attached to, or associated with, the university.

Wyclif migrated from college to college according to the rungs of academic preferment. In 1360 he became for a short time Master of Balliol College, and in 1366 he was appointed Warden of the newly established Canterbury Hall. There he seems to have quarrelled with the resident Benedictine monks, and this has been taken to be one of the first examples of his animosity towards the monastic orders. After leaving Canterbury Hall he took rooms again at Queen's, a college that had some ties with North Yorkshire itself. In 1372, after some nine years of study, he was awarded a doctorate in theology. In the Merton *Catalogus vetus*, a list of fellows compiled before 1422, he is described as 'a doctor in theology who, as is reported, trusted excessively in his own skill'.

As Wyclif's academic posts changed, so did his appointments to various church benefices (posts or sinecures endowed with an annual income). It was considered helpful, and not unholy, to collect as many benefices as possible. Wyclif himself later condemned the practice, but this did not prevent him from assuming in 1361 the provision of the rectory in Fillingham, Lincolnshire, followed by part of the income from the old church of Aust in Gloucestershire; it also did not deter him from requesting a canonry at York Minster in November 1362, although his plea was not successful. He then exchanged Fillingham for Ludgershall in Buckinghamshire, vacating it in the spring of 1374 for the church at Lutterworth, Leicester, where his game of clerical chairs came to an end. This search for prebends, or livings, was part of any orthodox career in the period; without the additional income he accrued, he would not have been able to pursue his studies at the university.

These studies in turn bore fruit, and by the early 1370s Wyclif had acquired a reputation as one of the most eminent logicians and theologians at Oxford. Theory and debate had no bounds within the privileged world of academic discourse; it has been said that there were no forbidden questions and only a few forbidden answers. The prevailing tone was one of scepticism. It was an atmosphere to which Wyclif's close and even remorseless reasoning was most suited. This was the period in which he completed his formative work on logic and began his intense study of theology. He had also written commentaries on Aristotelian physics and psychology. He was in many respects a medieval scholastic, but he never chose a comfortably secluded stance. As a trained and formidable logician, he never avoided the consequences of his argument, and it was the fury of his mind that led him onwards to challenge the foundations of Church and state. Even as he was being celebrated as 'the flower of Oxford', he manifested a preference for the 'seculars' over the 'regulars', those who were not part of a religious order over those who were monks and friars. The latter had been the source of his trouble at Canterbury Hall, and it seems plausible that, partly as a consequence, he came to despise them.

In the small and tight society of English administration, Wyclif's skills naturally drew him to the attention of Court and Parliament. He was appointed a clerk of the Household in the late 1360s, and under royal auspices he attended the Parliament of 1371; he does not seem to have spoken at that gathering, where it was suggested that the religious orders should bear their share of taxation and that the authorities were entitled to seize their goods at a time of national emergency. But this consorted well with his increasingly bitter attacks on ecclesiastical dominion.

Nevertheless, Wyclif's real course was now set for him in the contested theological atmosphere of Oxford. From 1365 until the early 1370s he was at work on *Summa de ente*, an examination of the nature of being, composed of two books containing thirteen treatises. It is sufficiently complex to prevent any brief explanation, but perhaps the critical point lies in Wyclif's account of 'universals'. This is not a topic that now arouses much interest, but its importance to him is emphasized in his judgement that 'beyond all doubt, intellectual and emotional error about universals is the cause of all sin that reigns in the world.' It was one of the great debates of the fourteenth century.

For Wyclif, divine ideas or 'universals' are the true cause of understanding, and are then reflected in 'particulars'. In this, he was rebutting the fashionable philosophy of Oxford, known as nominalism, which stated that all knowledge came from the experience of particular objects and that abstract knowledge did not exist outside the mind. For Wyclif, however, every particle of knowledge was present in eternity. When human beings exist, it must be presupposed that the idea of humanity already exists in the mind of God.

Wyclif followed this theory of universals and particulars in a variety of ways. If a particular human being is suffused with grace, he must be considered to be as great a lord as any potentate. He has the same relation to the universal. The scriptures are a particular emanation of the Word of God. For that reason they must be made simple and accessible to the devout layperson. God's dominion or lordship over all created beings is a paradigm of civil lordship by a particular anointed ruler. The Bible asserts the necessity for a monarchy with lordship over an independent church-state. Human dominion itself is established upon universal grace. The king must be the pastor of the people and promote the stability of the nation, for example, by expelling heretics, selecting clergy and rejecting papal claims of supremacy. There is a divine hierarchy of being, of which the earthly hierarchy is the shadow. In this we see the source of Wyclif's later pronouncements. The philosopher, or theologian, could become a radical.

(It may be of passing interest to note that Wyclif arranged for a toilet, capable of being locked or bolted, for his own private use. He may have anticipated Luther's connection of inventive thought with defecation, but it is more likely to have been the result of the meat-filled medieval diet; in 2021 a toilet block of the fourteenth century was discovered for the use of monks in Muchelney

Abbey in Somerset. Yet Wyclif may also have desired privacy for contemplation.)

✚

IN APPROXIMATELY 1373 Wyclif moved away from philosophical enquiry to the legal and political consequences of his beliefs. This meant that he was able to address problems of Church and state. In 1374 he was one of the royal officials who met papal representatives at Bruges to consider conflicts of papal authority and papal taxation with the national authorities. The conference came to no certain conclusion, and Wyclif was not appointed again; he may have made his case for secular power too strongly. This was also the period in which he became at least partially involved in the political difficulties attendant upon a dying king.

Edward III had failed in his ambition to reassert control over the duchies and provinces of France that had once been claimed by the English, and, already ailing, had left all military business to his eldest son and heir, Edward of Woodstock, otherwise known as the Black Prince. But the prince also become dangerously ill, and died of dysentery in 1376, just a year before his father. Edward's successor was now the Black Prince's son Richard II, then a boy of ten, but the burden of power and authority passed to the king's younger son, known as John of Gaunt. This was the man who enlisted the support of Wyclif in his continual battle with sections of the Church and with the Pope himself, over the familiar matters of benefices and taxation. By the end of 1372, in fact, Wyclif had entered the service of Gaunt. His anti-ecclesiastical stance, and his conviction that the secular powers could take possession of Church wealth, would no doubt have recommended him to the prince at the beginning of what was in effect his regency.

In this period, of more than eight years, Wyclif also completed fourteen volumes of his *Summa theologiae*, which was concerned with law and lordship as well as the nature of Church government. In this work he formulated what came to be his ultimate conclusions. Ecclesiastical law, for example, forbade clerics from owning property, or, as he said at a later date, 'no cleric may hold civil dominion without mortal sin, and by "cleric" I mean pope, cardinal, bishop, deacon and other priests.' Dominion, or lordship, flowed from grace, not from clerical office. This struck against the practices of the contemporary Church, from the Pope's seizing of territory for the monks' farmlands to the parish priest's glebe or parcel of land. To fulfil their divine role, the clerics must be stripped of all possessions. This was set by the example of apostolic poverty and simplicity.

In the autumn of 1376 Gaunt summoned Wyclif to attend the royal council, the body of nobles and other grandees who were supposed to advise and supervise Gaunt in his administration of the kingdom. Wyclif was never a royal councillor, and the reasons for this summons are unclear, except, perhaps, to provide ideological bolster for Gaunt's arguments or to use Wyclif's technical expertise in some ecclesiastical matter. The politics of the period, during the regency of Gaunt, are in any case confused and uncertain, with a number of parties and factions (royal and clerical) striving for pre-eminence.

In February of the following year, however, Wyclif was summoned by Simon Sudbury, Archbishop of Canterbury, and William Courtenay, Bishop of London, to appear at St Paul's Cathedral in order to answer claims of heresy relating to his attacks on the Church. But Wyclif was not alone. He was accompanied by John of Gaunt and other associates of the duke in order to impress the ecclesiastics who had the temerity to interrogate the duke's ally in Christ. He was, after all, in royal service. The Londoners did not in fact favour Gaunt, on account of his excessive wealth, undue power and rumours of general corruption, so when he threatened to drag Courtenay out of the assembly by his hair, the crowd erupted in protest. The meeting collapsed in chaos and Wyclif was somehow spirited away.

This was only the first attack on Wyclif's probity, but it must have given him some understanding of the public consequences of his theoretical reasoning. As do many academics who dabble in worldly affairs, he may even have relished the attention. It is also believed that in this year he began to preach sermons in London, and in the English language, that assaulted the corruption of prelates and the monastic orders; this may have appealed to Londoners, but perhaps not to the ecclesiastical authorities. Three months after this controversy the reigning Pope, Gregory ix, issued five bulls to Sudbury and Courtenay requesting them to take action against Wyclif and his heretical statements, citing in particular his attack upon papal authority, the Church's ownership of property, and its assertion of superiority over secular claims to lands or goods. The Pope's strictures had some effect, and for a short time Wyclif was confined to the Black Hall in Oxford; this was 'an ancient receptacle for schollers', according to the antiquary Anthony Wood, where they could be watched and supervised,

Early in 1378 Wyclif was brought before the ecclesiastical dignitaries at Lambeth Palace in London. Once again the royal court intervened. A representative of the queen mother, Joan of Kent, arrived before the assembled prelates and informed them that they should not pass a formal sentence on the theologian. As the widow of the Black Prince and mother of Richard ii, Joan was a formidable figure; her intervention suggests that there was a Court party that sympathized with Wyclif's dismissal of the Church's claims to property and power. Wyclif was in fact still questioned at Lambeth by the prelates, who charged only that 'he was to discuss no farther such propositions in the schools or in sermons, for fear of scandalising the laity.'

The chancellor of Oxford University himself had already confessed that the arguments condemned by the Pope, 'though they sounded ill to the ear, were nonetheless true', so there was much sympathy and support for Wyclif's attack on the Church establishment. The royal council even asked for his advice on whether the kingdom could hold back revenues from the Pope in the event of crisis. He duly obliged with assent. The death of Gregory IX brought an end to the fulminations from Rome on Wyclif's 'execrable and abominable folly', at least for the time being. At a later date Wyclif in turn described Pope Gregory as a 'horrible devil'.

In the immediate aftermath Wyclif published at least four treatises elaborating upon his now settled convictions on the nature of the Church, on the primacy of scripture rather than dogma, and on the relative powers of Church and king. In all cases he challenged ecclesiastical teaching and the hierarchy that enunciated it. A good man is more to be believed than a bad bishop, he maintained. A king is greater than the Pope, and must be obeyed just as Christ obeyed Caesar and Pilate. If there is no foundation for Church doctrine in scripture, that doctrine must be cast out. All truth is to be found in the scriptures, whether plainly or allegorically stated. The unwritten tradition, handed down by the Church, is of no value. That is why the Bible must be available to all.

It is clear that Wyclif's concern for scriptural authority indicated or hastened his approval for a proposed Bible translated into Middle English, actually composed between 1382 and 1395, which in later years was wrongly considered to be his greatest legacy. He did not write any of it himself, as far as is known, but he encouraged others to do so. In this period, too, he seems to have begun a series of public lectures in Oxford and London. He had preached sermons in the capital before, and they seem to have received the enthusiastic endorsement of the citizens. Now he began a more organized campaign and may have enlisted the support of those students or masters who were convinced by his arguments. He may not have possessed a charismatic personality, but there was always room at Oxford for an eminent and self-confident master who could lead others forwards with the spell of his learning. The history of the university includes many such reputations. The enthusiastic student is always looking for a leading light.

But events took Wyclif away from his academic haven. In the summer of 1378 two English soldiers were imprisoned for disobeying Gaunt's order to transfer a Spanish nobleman to his custody so that he might gain the ransom; the two soldiers escaped from confinement, however, and fled for sanctuary to Westminster Abbey. The duke's soldiers subsequently invaded the abbey and butchered one of the men, also slaying a priest who was in the vicinity. This violation of sanctuary might have been considered a grievous sin, so Gaunt called upon Wyclif to defend his intervention; Wyclif agreed to provide this service for his royal master, and argued that the laws of sanctuary did not apply in matters concerning the welfare of the nation. This was in line with his general teaching. But it had no doubt become increasingly clear to him that he was being used as a convenient tool of an administration that had no real interest in furthering his programme of ecclesiastical reform.

In 1380, therefore, Wyclif returned to his most important tasks in the elucidation of doctrine and in the continuing assault upon the Church. If the Pope were not poor, he was the Antichrist. The friars themselves were no more than members of a sect. The true Church was composed only of the elect chosen by God, even if their identities could not be discovered in this life. These propositions were not plucked out of the air but rather the closely argued consequences of Wyclif's already stated beliefs. His increasingly radical theses posed a problem for the authorities, made infinitely more complex by the emergence of the papal schism, which set up two rival popes, Urban VI in Rome and Clement VII in Avignon; since the English did not favour the French, their allegiance was granted to Urban, which made it much more difficult to countenance Wyclif's stridently anti-ecclesiastical and anti-Roman tenets. He was on his own.

Wyclif's position was not helped in 1380, when, taking rooms at Queen's College, Oxford, once more, he proceeded to publish his Eucharistic tracts. In these he reverted to first principles. The orthodox theory of transubstantiation asserted that the bread and wine of the Mass were by miraculous means changed into the body and blood of Christ. But Wyclif argued that this was impossible. God could not will any created object into nothingness; this would undermine the foundations of every created being. All things partake of universals that exist eternally in the mind of God, and therefore cannot be annihilated. God does not uncreate, otherwise the sun and other stars might go out, so the bread could not vanish or be displaced. How could Christ then become part of it? It would also follow that in the process of transubstantiation the priest could bring the body of Christ into being, a blasphemous and in fact heretical suggestion. Instead, Wyclif argued for what came to be known as consubstantiation, whereby the body and blood of Christ are truly present in the bread and wine, but the substance of bread and wine remains unchanged. They are not to be annihilated by some whispered words at the altar.

This touched on one of the most significant points of Church doctrine, and as a result alienated many of Wyclif's erstwhile supporters, for whom the denial of transubstantiation was a mortal sin and a heresy. The chancellor of the university set up a commission to investigate Wyclif's conclusions, where by a majority they were condemned. On hearing of the result, Wyclif was reported to have said that 'neither the chancellor nor any of his accomplices could in the least weaken his opinion.' It was also reported that John of Gaunt himself rode to Oxford in order to persuade his erstwhile follower to renounce his belief, but this may be anecdotal. Whatever the truth of the matter, Wyclif left Oxford in the latter half of 1380 and retired to his rectory in the Leicestershire village of Lutterworth. But even there, while concerned with the cure of souls, he was engaged in controversy.

In the summer of 1381 the insurrection that came to be known as the Peasants' Revolt began in Essex and Kent before spreading to London and elsewhere. It was in part led by a radical cleric, John Ball, who before his eventual execution stated that for two years 'he had been a disciple of Wyclif, and that he had learned from him the heresies he was teaching'. This is perhaps too convenient to be true, and the supposed confession was not published until twenty years later, but there is no doubt that many contemporaries associated Wyclif with the popular unrest. He was an easy target for those who maintained the primacy of Church and state. Insurrection of any kind could be blamed on his radical doctrines.

It did not help that Wyclif's bitter opponent, William Courtenay, had been translated from the bishopric of London to the archbishopric of Canterbury. In this exalted position he was able to advance his prosecution of Wyclifite doctrines even though he was not able to catch Wyclif himself. At the beginning of May 1382, Courtenay summoned a council at Blackfriars in London in order to consider propositions taken from Wyclif's writings on transubstantiation and the Mass, on papal authority and priestly power, all of which led to a royal proclamation against heresy and heretical teaching. On the day the council was convened an earthquake disturbed London, a rare phenomenon that was interpreted according to taste; Wyclif considered it to be a sign of God's wrath at his opponents, while Courtenay deemed it an omen of the nation belching out heresy. Wyclif himself was never mentioned during the proceedings, no doubt on the understanding that this might alienate his still-powerful supporters at Court while his influence at Oxford was also still strong.

Wyclif was in any case ensconced at Lutterworth, from where he would never depart. There he composed his last works, *Trialogus* and *Opus evangelicum*, which repeat and explain his now settled beliefs. Even in retreat, however, he was not free from the finger of Rome; in 1384 Pope Urban VI summoned him to the Curia to answer the charges of heresy against him, but Wyclif pleaded that he was now too 'disabled and crippled' to undertake the long and arduous journey.

This complaint of ill health was no exaggeration. Wyclif had already suffered a severe stroke, and while attending Mass at Lutterworth towards the end of December 1384, as the host was elevated, he experienced a second, which left him paralysed and unable to speak. He survived for three days but died on the last day of the year. He was buried in the churchyard according to custom, but 44 years later, after his formal condemnation for heresy, his bones were disinterred and burned, their ashes scattered in a nearby stream.

Wyclif had always denied the charge of heresy and considered himself a true follower of scripture. He was no doubt irascible and argumentative, but his disciplined mind cut through the evasions and accommodations of the time to provide a coherent theology of grace and redemption established on what he considered to be the first principles of faith. It was a persuasive and, for some, an indisputable truth; as a result, he attracted at Oxford a group of strident admirers who were eager to reveal these doctrines to the populace. He was the first reformer who helped to change the nature of English faith.

✝

IT HAS BEEN SUGGESTED that here were the beginnings of the Lollards, and it is significant that the first use of *Lollardi* as a term of abuse was applied to Wyclif's disciples or popularizers. He referred once to 'my brothers' and to a 'fraternity', which may imply a small band of followers spreading his words. Lollardy was a more diffuse and pragmatic movement, however, into which only some of Wyclif's ideas filtered down and took more informal meanings. Yet his reliance on scripture, his disdain for the ecclesiastical hierarchy, and his contempt for monks and their possessions may have become more comprehensible and therefore more popular. His conviction that every man, in a state of grace, is in effect a priest could also have encouraged a spirit of equality. A man in grace is a judge of all laws and prohibitions.

But there is still only a slender thread that connects Wyclif to the Lollards. There is no reason to believe that the participants in the Peasants' Revolt, for example, shared his antipathy to the Church in such matters as liturgy, pilgrimages and the cult of the saints. Only three of that movement's early leaders are known to have been associated with him, and very soon theirs had become the general uprising of which he strongly disapproved. He believed that it was not right, or just, to confront royal authority. He had some sympathy with the Lollards' grievances, but not with their manner of expressing them. He was a scholar and not an activist, but his attacks upon ecclesiastical authority may have found an echo in the motives of the insurgents.

Lollardy itself had first emerged towards the end of 1376, and increased in strength during the following years. The complaints against mercenary clerics, and against papal impositions, were in fact already familiar, but grew in depth and volume throughout the thirteenth and fourteenth centuries. In 1357, for example, *The Lay Folks' Catechism* condemned the laziness and ignorance of 'prelates, parsons, vikers [vicars] and prestes'. Wyclif's fulminations against the monks and the papal hierarchy could be taken up effortlessly by a more general audience. His English sermons, and his support for a vernacular Bible, can only have helped to expedite his influence.

It was said that, in the area around Leicester, every other person you met was a Lollard. This was an exaggeration. Anyone with eccentric opinions might be condemned as a Lollard. The loud tears and sighs of Margery Kempe, an enthusiastic and orthodox Catholic, provoked cries of 'loller!' and demands that she be burned. Anyone who strayed from conventional piety might be suspected. But it was always a political, rather than a religious, movement.

Wyclif cannot even be associated with what might be called court Lollardy, by which is meant a group of Lollard knights who believed in the possibility of a pristine Church that denied papal or ecclesiastical authority. They looked back to an age of chivalric nobility in which they, not the priests, were the guardians of the land and the people. This may in part explain the support John of Gaunt and the queen mother extended to Wyclif during his conflicts with the prelates. The Lollard cause, in its early period, had adherents in London and Leicester, in Bristol and Lincoln, in Northampton and other areas south of the River Trent. But it was not directed or organized in any formal sense; it seems to have been largely confined to specific family groups, so it survived but did not necessarily prosper. The impression is of closed communities tied by marriage and geographical location. There were pockets and small localities of belief, but no general or national movement. It cannot even be described as a sect but, rather, as a tendency that had gradually lost its point and direction by the time of the Reformation.

The law consigning heretics to the fire, *De heretico comburendo*, was promulgated in the Parliament of 1401 under the direction of Henry IV, and must have persuaded many of its adherents to return to the fold of the established Church. The fact that only two Lollards suffered the supreme penalty suggests that there were few victims to be found, and fewer found worthy of death. Where Lollardy persisted it was the faith of artisans, craftspeople and what might be called the 'middling' range of the social hierarchy, who no doubt for the sake of appearances still participated in the orthodox church rituals.

The nature and extent of Wyclif's immediate legacy are not known for certain. His influence on the sixteenth-century Reformation is also unclear. He did write of *reformatio* or a return of the Church to its primitive purity and simplicity, and there are aspects of his thought that seem to anticipate doctrines later espoused by William Tyndale, Miles Coverdale and Thomas Cranmer. Wyclif's desire for a vernacular Bible, and his condemnation of the Pope and of the entire ecclesiastical structure, strike the right note. His strictures against papal indulgences as 'delusions without foundation', for example, anticipate those of Luther. But Wyclif cannot be torn out of his context in the fourteenth century and stuck at the head of a Reforming army. He was not that man, and his was not the right period. He did, however, promote an English faith separated from the hierarchy of Rome, with the monarch at its head, and established both upon the reliance on scripture alone and upon the simple devotion of the individual Christian. It is a compelling theme that, as we shall observe, resounded through the centuries.

Four

Religion as Reformation

William Tyndale (*c*. 1494–1536), Thomas Cranmer
(1489–1556), John Foxe (1516–1587)

It has been said that William Tyndale is the true father of English Christianity, in the sense that he inspired those who wished to read, speak and hear the faith in their native English tongue. It was he who translated the entire New Testament, and some of the Old, thus directing light on what had previously been obscure or obscured. In that endeavour he helped to shape and enhance the language, to the extent that he may be said to rival Chaucer or Shakespeare in his influence on what Ben Jonson called the 'language such as men do use'. In the fire of his newly found Protestant faith, he forged new words and phrases that have endured for five centuries, so he has also been described as the father of modern English.

Tyndale was born and raised in Gloucestershire, most probably in a village on the margin of the Cotswold hills. This was a county known for its associations with small groups of Lollards; one of their concerns was for the promulgation of 'the Wycliffite Bible' in Middle English. Tyndale's own territory may have inspired him. In his only account of his childhood he recalled how he was taught that 'king Athelstane caused the holy scripture to be translated into the tongue that then was in England.' This Anglo-Saxon testament may have inspired his later celebration of the vernacular.

The first public record of Tyndale's existence confirms his status in July 1512 as bachelor of arts from Magdalen Hall in Oxford, no doubt progressing from Magdalen School. This implies that he joined the university at the age of fourteen or fifteen; he became a master of arts in 1515. There he became thoroughly acquainted with Latin, so that he could as easily speak it as read it. He may also have had a passing familiarity with Greek, although it was not yet a favoured subject on the syllabus. It was reported by the martyrologist, John Foxe, that at Magdalen he instructed certain contemporaries 'in the knowledge and truth of the scriptures'; that may be an early indication of his passion for their translation.

It is often stated that Tyndale then moved on to the university at Cambridge. That university was the centre of a small group who imbibed Lutheran writings, so the report would place Tyndale within the history of early Nonconformity. He returned to Gloucestershire after his time at university and became the tutor of two young boys, sons of Sir John Walsh at Little Sodbury Manor. In this relative seclusion he may have improved his Greek for the sake of what would become his determining purpose, to reveal the meaning of the scriptures to all good Christians. But even there he became suspected of Lutheran tendencies by the local authorities of the Church; he wrote later that 'I was so turmoiled in the county where I was that I could no longer there dwell.'

For his removal Tyndale needed a patron and a new haven, and in pursuit of a sponsor he travelled to London. His first call was upon Cuthbert Tunstall, Bishop of London, who had a reputation for an enlightened faith in the tradition of Desiderius Erasmus, the Dutch scholar who had prepared new Latin and Greek versions of the New Testament. Tyndale had hoped that, under Tunstall's auspices, he might find space and time also to translate the New Testament. But the bishop had no room for the scholar in his palace, and turned him away. Even then a full English translation might have proved controversial, since there is no mention of purgatory or the seven sacraments in the scriptures, raising difficult questions about the authority of the Church's teaching. Tyndale wrote that he discovered 'there was no place to do [his work] in all England,' so his attention was drawn to Germany, the home of Martin Luther and the true source of evangelical learning. He would, however, need financial and moral assistance to embark on that journey.

Tyndale stayed for about a year in London, sometimes preaching at the church of St Dunstan-in-the-West on Fleet Street. There he came to the notice of Humphrey Monmouth, a merchant and ship-owner who was already leaning towards the reformed teaching of Luther and his adherents, known as 'Scripture-men'. Monmouth would also have been acquainted with the German merchants who resided at the Steelyard (the trading base in England of the Hanseatic League) on the north bank of the River Thames, just west of London Bridge, who promoted Luther's writings. With Monmouth's aid and provision, then, Tyndale took ship to Germany in the spring of 1524. Before he left England never to return, he told a learned scholiast that 'if God spare my life, ere many years I will cause a boy that driveth the plough [to] know more of the Scripture than thou dost.' He may have been alluding to Piers the Plowman, the Christ-like labourer and eponymous hero of William Langland's poem of the fourteenth century, whose simplicity did not preclude the gift of divine grace. The poem itself is set in Tyndale's native Gloucestershire. He was more intent than ever on translating the Bible into English in order to open the eyes of his countrymen to the spiritual truths of scripture. That had become his mission, and his destiny.

Tyndale's first forays in Germany are unknown, but by 1525 he had settled in Cologne, where, with the help of an assistant, William Roye, he supervised the publication of his translation of Luther's version of the New Testament, to the notes and prologue of which he added passages of his own. Luther's doctrines were by now well known. His belief in the primacy of scripture, his rejection of the sacraments of the Church, his emphasis on justification by faith alone and his denial of transubstantiation were considered enough to consign him to eternal fire. In 1521 the English king Henry VIII had himself published a tract against Luther as a heretic and blasphemer.

Yet Tyndale was not diverted from his overwhelming task. From the beginning his New Testament is notable for the simplicity and clarity of its language; it was a way of seizing the hearts and surprising the minds of its new readers. It bore all the signs of Tyndale's reforming zeal. 'Priest' became 'senior', thus dissolving the spiritual distance from the rest of the faithful; 'church' was 'congregation', removing the need for hierarchy; 'charity' was to be translated as 'love', avoiding the significance of good works in the pursuit of salvation. Salvation was promised by Christ alone as the gift of grace. The sinner does not 'do penance', according to Church practice, but individually repents. Purgatory was not mentioned in scripture, and only two of the seven sacraments were acknowledged. The distribution of the New Testament in English, with its message stripped of conventional pieties, was therefore of great benefit to those intent upon reforming the Church.

At the insistence of Henry VIII and his lord chancellor, Cardinal Wolsey, and of the Holy Roman Emperor, Charles V, whose domain included Germany and the Netherlands, the authorities of Cologne were ready to arrest Tyndale and Roye, and to seize their work. But the two men were in some way alerted by sympathizers in the city, and fled up the River Rhine to Worms. It was there in 1526 that Tyndale completed the publication of the entire New Testament, which was very soon despatched or smuggled into England with the help of the German merchants. It came as a blessing and a revelation to many, and to others a heinous and heretical tract. It has been estimated that there were no more than a thousand fervent Lutherans in the country, but they were considered to be a 'filthy dunghill', breeding corruption. Others, either curious or sympathetic, also took up the book. But the authorities were adamant that the source of this infection had to be removed.

Tyndale is next to be found in Antwerp, which, by the time of his arrival in 1526, had become the leading commercial city of Europe. As a large community of merchants it had no interest in ancient hierarchies, and proved receptive to the anti-papal and anti-ecclesiastical strictures of Luther. This was fruitful soil for Tyndale, and it was there that he spent most of the remaining years of his life. He may well have made his way to the English House of merchants, where he could anticipate a welcome. It was in this city, too, that in the spring of 1528 he published his next work, *The Parable of the Wicked Mammon*, which endorsed Luther's belief in justification by faith alone and in the priesthood of all believers. It also offered a spiritualized version of the Christian commonwealth in terms of human works dependent upon faith. Tyndale argues for a society based on cooperation and mutual belonging, with the injunction 'let every man . . . refer his craft and occupation unto the common wealth, and serve his brethren as he would do Christ himself.' He must do unto others (and here the sovereign reference is to the poor) as he would do unto himself. This social creed may seem some way from Tyndale's work as a translator, but the origins of both are the same. *Sola fide* and *sola scriptura,* through faith alone and through scripture alone, were the two imperatives; religious belief and practice were derived from the scriptures, and not from the Roman Church. The sinner is justified only by faith, without the necessary benefit of good works or the pantomime of confession and absolution. Good works are the flower of faith, but not its root. Tyndale took as his original text a sermon delivered by Luther, but he greatly expanded it with his own commentaries and notes.

The Parable of the Wicked Mammon found its way in a manner of weeks to England, where it confirmed Tyndale's reputation as a reformer in the spirit of Luther. The dissemination of what may be called evangelical teaching had now become a matter of concern, and Wolsey asked the authorities in Antwerp to deliver up Tyndale and Roye as manifest heretics. Thomas More, who succeeded Wolsey as lord chancellor the following year, had described Tyndale's treatise as 'a very treasury and well-spring of wickedness'.

There had already been a pronounced campaign against the new doctrine coming from Europe. To the king, and to the authorities of the Church, the name of Luther was abhorred and abhorrent; the renegade monk seemed likely to destroy all good order and piety. The very pillars of the temple might be under-mined. Copies of his *De captivitate Babylonica ecclesiae* (On the Babylonian Captivity of the Church), assaulting the papacy for its enslavement of the true Church, had already been consigned to the fire in 1521. Between 1526 and 1528 the newly published copies of Tyndale's New Testament had also been ceremonially abjured and burned at Wolsey's instigation. The arrival of *The Parable of the Wicked Mammon* added more fuel and flame. Those who sought out or obtained these two forbidden books were arrested, questioned and often imprisoned.

Yet Tyndale continued his mission. In the autumn of 1528 he published *The Obedience of a Christian Man*, which reaffirmed the right of his countrymen to read the Bible in English and asserted his belief that the king, not the Pope, was the head of the Church in England. It seems likely that an epidemic of the 'sweating sick-ness' was then assailing Antwerp, but, whatever the case, he sailed from that city to Hamburg, where in 1529 he published his transla-tion of the Pentateuch, the first five books of the Old Testament. It is to be celebrated as the first translation of Hebrew into English, and the books of Genesis, Exodus and the others came as a reve-lation to those who had long been left in a mist. Tyndale had also begun to formulate a code of moral law, by which God agrees a 'covenant' with humankind to redeem the elect through the blood of Christ; faith in Christ will be rewarded with eternal life. It is not known for certain when and how Tyndale learned Hebrew, but for him it became a natural companion of English, and he was soon rendering it as fluently as Latin or Greek. On the publication of the Pentateuch he returned to Antwerp.

It was there that in late 1530 Tyndale began composing *The Practice of Prelates*, in which he attacks the Pope and his prelates for their hypocrisy and greed. But, in conclusion, he also argued that Henry VIII could in no sense be separated from his first wife, Catherine of Aragon, simply for the fact that she had been his late brother's wife. He had searched the scriptures but could find no lawful excuse for such an act. At this point it seemed possible that the Pope might grant a divorce to the king for politic and practical purposes, but this only augmented Tyndale's dismissal of that cause. It was of course tactless, and may have hastened his death, but it is proof of his belief in his mission to diminish or deny the power of Rome. He stated that 'if this marriage be of God, the pope cannot dispense with it.'

The timing of these matters is significant. In the autumn or winter of 1528 Henry had been struck by Tyndale's assertion of the king's spiritual ascendancy over the Pope in England in *The Obedience of a Christian Man*, and is reported to have said, 'this is a book for me and all kings to read.' In 1531 he sent an agent to Antwerp to persuade Tyndale to return to the king's service. But Tyndale had heard too much about the persecution of Lollards and Lutherans in his native country to succumb. He knew, too, that *The Practice of Prelates*, with its dismissal of Henry's divorce, would have recently arrived in England. He would not have been secure there. In a short time, certainly, his name became anathema at Court.

Tyndale carried on his work at Antwerp, no doubt at the English House of merchants, and in 1534 he produced the revision of his New Testament. There was always a desire for the scriptures to be augmented and clarified, and Tyndale's command of Greek and Hebrew was complemented by his powerful understanding of the resources of the English language. As a result his New Testament has become the model for all later translations; by far the largest part of the New Testament, as well as the first five books of the Old, in the King James Bible are established upon his work. He might have gone on to finish his translation of the Old Testament, and thus have presented a complete Bible to the world, but he was tricked and betrayed into death.

His capture may have been sought by Henry VIII, and his death authorized by Charles V, and the collusion of these forces was responsible for his arrest and execution. The Catholic authorities in England may also have played a part. A clandestine agent or 'intelligencer' by the name of Henry Phillips was given the money and means to inveigle himself into Tyndale's circle of acquaintance in Antwerp. He came to know Tyndale well enough that towards the end of May 1525, Tyndale took his new supposed friend out to dinner in Antwerp. But Phillips had alerted the authorities to their excursion. Tyndale was a short man, and Phillips walked after him. When they approached the soldiers lying in wait, Phillips pointed him out. He was arrested and taken to the castle of Vilvoorde some 25 miles distant, where he was entirely under the emperor's jurisdiction. He was imprisoned and charged with heresy. The merchants of Antwerp protested, but without success.

Tyndale remained in confinement until August 1536, when he was taken before a commission of seventeen worthies, condemned for heresy, stripped of his priesthood and given over to the secular authorities for punishment. He was condemned to die at the stake, but the punishment of burning was considered to be too ignoble; he would instead be strangled before his body was burned. Just as the rope was fastened about his neck, he is supposed to have cried, 'Lord, open the king of England's eyes!' but, as is the case with many celebrated last words, this may be apocryphal. The words of his translation did endure, however, and were taken up to become part of the language; among them are 'knock and it shall be opened unto you', 'seek and ye shall find', 'let there be light', 'the powers that be' and 'the salt of the earth'.

✠

TYNDALE WAS NOT the first, nor was he the last, of the English martyrs. Under the auspices of Thomas More, who in 1529 took up the role of lord chancellor after Cardinal Wolsey's disgrace, those reformers who espoused Lutheran principles were searched out, interrogated, imprisoned, tortured and often burned. More had the reputation of being an enlightened administrator and a model of juridical practice, but now he had become the hunter of heretics who spent hundreds of hours in their pursuit. It was he who took on the task of replying to heretical tracts in English; he could fight fiery words only in the same vernacular. By the early 1530s such books were pouring into England, promoting Lutheran doctrine, damning the Antichrist who sits in Rome, denying the seven sacraments of the Catholic faith, excoriating the notion of purgatory, dismissing the cult of saints, all of them issuing what More called frantic folly and foaming filth. The fight for the English soul had become earnest. For More the heretics were far worse than criminals, since they threatened the souls of others with eternal damnation. The faggot and the flame were too mild for them.

More's tirade against Tyndale, *The Confutation of Tyndale's Answer*, spent some half a million words in defying him, and has the distinction of being the longest religious polemic in the English language. It represented the heart of the debate in England, outlining the opposing tendencies of the period: communal worship and ritual against inner prayer and belief; good works against private faith; inherited orthodoxy against the direct inspiration of scripture; redemption through the sacramental system rather than through Christ alone. For More there is only one true Church, the visible and orthodox communion of Catholics. It is the permanent and living sign of Christ's presence, sustained by inherited custom and maintained by traditional knowledge. It is an extensive and palpable community, rather than a few 'brethren' or 'new men' gathered in secret rooms. Tyndale, however, was possessed by an alternative vision of private belief derived from scripture, and individual grace established upon true faith. He made the distinction between 'an hystorycall faith' and a 'felynge faith', a traditional faith and an instinctive faith. His was a powerful account of individual redemption that More in turn condemned as the shortest way to pride and anarchy.

It would be wrong to suggest, however, that these opposing tendencies were of equal significance at this date. The vast majority of the English were still orthodox Catholics whose piety was well known throughout Europe; the evangelicals, or 'lollers', or sympathizers with Luther, were a small fraction of that number. But although their adherents were few, they were still influential. It was not a simple social or religious matter; their orthodox opponents truly believed that they signified the imminent advent of the Antichrist, the beast of the book of Revelation.

The earliest-known group of Englishmen who espoused Lutheran teaching was to be found in Cambridge. From a pulpit at the church of St Edward, King and Martyr, and in the recesses of an inn called the White Horse, small groups discussed the new doctrines. Members of Wolsey's new institution at Oxford, Cardinal College (now Christ Church), were also debating them with enthusiasm. And of course the interest had already migrated to London, the home of foreign merchants and a haven for native Dissenters. It was an awakening. The authorities were ready. Tracts and translations were identified as heretical and seized; legal measures were introduced against anyone who sold, purchased or read such banned books. Those who professed the beliefs espoused within them were excommunicated as heretics, and the books burned. But then the burning turned from books to people.

The first victim was Thomas Hitton, who was burned at the stake on 23 February 1530. He was a Catholic priest who, after embracing the doctrines of Luther and the works of Tyndale, became an evangelical 'runner' between Antwerp and London, carrying communications between the evangelicals of both cities and expediting the passage of books. He was found loitering in Gravesend, Kent, and, after being accused by locals of stealing linen cloth drying on a hedge, he was searched; in the secret pockets of his coat were found letters to certain 'evangelical heretics'. When he was brought before the Archbishop of Canterbury he reaffirmed the new doctrines, including the dismissal of purgatory and denial of the Mass, whereupon he was despatched to the secular authorities for burning. He was consigned to the flames at Maidstone. More in fact played no part in his trial or punishment, but described Hitton as 'the devil's stinking martyr', who had gone 'straight from the short fire to the fire everlasting'. Hitton was the first of many.

In the following year the flames reached Thomas Bilney. While studying at Cambridge he opened a copy of the New Testament translated by Erasmus and, when he came to the passage affirming that Christ had come into the world to save sinners, 'immediately I felt a marvellous quietness and comfort, insomuch that my bruised bones leaped for joy.' He was changed. He was a fervent and devoted man who preached the gospel in leper-houses and in prisons; he was known as 'little Bilney' because he was short and slender. He became the centre of the small group of reformers at Cambridge in the early 1520s who were not Lutheran but who inveighed against abuses in the Church. He had already recanted his unorthodox opinions in the time of Wolsey, and had borne on his shoulders the faggot, a bundle of sticks and thorns, as a token of his abjuration.

Bilney had now rejected his previous denial, and was once again preaching against pilgrimages and the cult of saints. Any such relapse meant death. In the summer of 1531 his head was shaved and he was taken to the 'lollards' pit' just outside the bounds of Norwich. He had placed his finger above the flame of a candle, while in prison, to inure himself to the pain. In revenge for his death four men walked 13 miles through Suffolk and Essex, from Dedham and East Bergholt to Dovercourt, in order to burn the shrine and elaborate crucifix there; the Cross was believed to have miraculous properties, and the men tested its power by tearing it down and burning it. This is another example of the scorn that sometimes greeted Catholic ritual. Three of the men were hanged.

The burnings continued, shedding a fitful light on the English soul. Richard Bayfield had imported Lutheran books and distributed evangelical tracts. Thomas Dusgate had been sentenced for posting evangelical preachings on the doors of churches. James Bainham was condemned for relapsing into heresy, and as the flames of Smithfield licked around him he called out, 'Oh, ye papists, behold! ye look for miracles; here now may you see a miracle; for in this fire I feel no more pain than if I were in bed; for it is as sweet to me as a bed of roses.'

John Frith had once been accosted by Wolsey for preaching heresy in Cardinal College itself; he had been consigned with others to the fish cellar there, in which cramped and fetid place several of his colleagues died. They, also, were considered to be martyrs even if they were not bound to the stake. Frith was eventually released and fled to Antwerp, where he worked with Tyndale and published translations of some of Luther's writings. He also composed his own work, and in particular attacked the doctrine of purgatory on the grounds that it had no scriptural basis. To pray for the dead, and to give alms for the suffering souls, was of no consequence; the money would be better spent on the sick and ailing among the living.

On his return to England as an evangelical missionary, Frith spent some time without detection among his fellow believers, but he was arrested and, in October 1532, imprisoned in the Tower of London. From his cell he issued no fewer than five tracts, but he was tried for heretical beliefs in his denial of purgatory and transubstantiation. Even then he knew that the end of his journey was death, and he went to the fire at Smithfield in the summer of 1533.

It would be wrong, however, to consider the sixteenth century as the only era of the stake. For the period between 1400 and 1529, John Foxe mentions approximately fifty Lollards burned for heresy, and it is probable that he missed twenty or thirty others. But the burnings were part of a general condition of unease. The principal aspect of religious sensibility was uncertainty or anxiety about the future life; in the sixteenth century death was believed to be not the end but the beginning of human woes.

✝

THE COURSE AND CAUSE of Reformation were various. Wyclif had lit the torch, but Tyndale had led the way. This does not alter the fact that Wyclif had laid bare the root cause of native discontent with the Roman faith; he had helped to build a fortress in England against the powers of Rome and of Catholic Europe – a fortress that, in one form or another, would endure. But his putative followers, the Lollards, were not so much advocates as quietists, who hid their new faith under a bushel. They had no wish to draw attention to themselves, and even participated in the Church's established rituals.

The edition of the New Testament by Erasmus in 1516, with the Greek and Latin texts placed alongside each other, was another matter. It was intended to exorcise generations of Church commentary and interpretation in order to unfold what the Dutch humanist called the true *philosophia Christi*; his friend and companion Thomas More had welcomed it even though he was to pour venom on Luther and Tyndale for attempting the same. Tyndale himself had begun his work as translator with the *Handbook of a Christian Knight* (1503/4) by Erasmus. The tide of religious affairs, which may be said to have come in during the early sixteenth century, was a slow but not a shallow one.

What became known as 'the Reformation' in England perhaps began with the king's imperiousness and anger, but the new faith was disseminated among some of the clergy and gentry, who disliked Roman encroachment upon English sovereignty and, in particular, detested papal taxation. The educated laity were also dismissive of friars, pluralists who held more than one benefice, and bishops. There were doubts, too, about Catholic doctrine. Those who became instrumental in dismantling papal supremacy during the 1530s were not Lollards but in fact former Catholics.

The successive measures of reform legislation instigated by Henry VIII, from the Submission of the Clergy in 1532 to the Six Articles of 1539, were concerned as much with politics as with theology; they were intended to emphasize and enlarge the king's power. The measures amounted to the replacement of the Pope by the king as head of the English Church, the authorization of scripture in the English tongue, and the prohibition of oaths of allegiance to Rome. The dissolution of the monasteries thus fell into place. Henry believed, or trusted, that the English were more satisfied than not with the monarch as the head of their Church; two of the Anglo-Saxon kings had, after all, been honoured as saints. Regional revolt and rebellion against Henry's legislation, in Lincolnshire and in the North, were serious enough to demand ferocious oppression, but ultimately they failed.

It should be understood that the faith of the English was based not on trust but on obedience. In a similar spirit, the emphasis was not on theology but on morality. The social aspects of religious policy were of greatest importance, and would remain so. By the mid-sixteenth century the majority may in part have been reformed, in external matters, but they were not excessively so. They were not concerned with the absolute primacy of scripture. That was left to the evangelicals. They may have paid lip service to the concept of justification by faith alone, but they were more interested in good works. Ambiguity and compromise were part of the English temper; doctrinal purity was not. The overriding principle was that of a single and centralized nation, free from foreign interference of any kind in theological or diplomatic matters.

In the subsequent battle of the faiths that continued in Europe, therefore, Henry sided with the powers that most suited him at the time; this was not hypocrisy, but statecraft. It could also be convenient. An instance may be found on 30 July 1540, when three Catholics and three evangelicals were executed at Smithfield. This attempt at 'balance' did mean, however, that the religious identity of the nation was never certain. It changed with the times, and thus with alterations in power. After Henry's death in 1547, and the accession of Edward VI, a number of reformers made their way to England with the blessing and guidance of the Archbishop of Canterbury, Thomas Cranmer, who hoped that England might become the beacon of religious reform for Europe. The young king was considered to be another Josiah, a convinced evangelical who would surely lead his country towards redemption. With the tacit approval of his father he was brought up by the leading evangelicals in the kingdom, and at the age of nine he came into his inheritance with the support and enthusiasm of reforming courtiers who might use his accession to change the religious policy of the country.

Within a few months images and statues, considered to be the remnants of superstition, were removed from the churches; the churchwardens were obliged to purchase the *Paraphrases of the New Testament* (1521) by Erasmus, and Cranmer's *Book of Homilies* (1547). The new communion service of 1549, grudgingly noted as 'commonly called the mass', dispensed with the elevation of the host, which had been at the centre of the Catholic rite. Rosaries were no longer to be used. Stained-glass windows were smashed, relics were discarded, and pilgrimages to shrines were forbidden. The bell and the lights of devotion were reduced to a minimum. The new Bishop of London, Nicholas Ridley, ordered that the altars be replaced by simple tables. Evangelicals from Germany and elsewhere came to England with professions of zeal for the newly found faith of the nation.

These evangelicals were often invited and entertained by Cranmer; he had been appointed Archbishop of Canterbury by Henry, but after the death of the old king, his more radical preferences became clear. It was he who drafted the provisions of the revised Book of Common Prayer in 1552, having been responsible for the previous version of 1549. The second text was more amenable to reformed doctrine. It is the simple but resonant introduction to the liturgies, services and beliefs of the new faith, and it may be said that this book was the solid foundation for what became the Church of England. Cranmer also compiled the Forty-Two Articles of faith in 1553, which became the model for the Thirty-Nine Articles as the basis of English practice. The twenty-third of the former declared that 'the doctrines concerning purgatory, pardons, worshipping and adoration as well of images as of relics, and also invocation of saints, is a fond thing vainly feigned.' Cranmer also wrote a preface to the second edition of the Great Bible, with the New Testament translated into English by Tyndale and the Old prepared largely by Miles Coverdale. It was the first full Bible in the vernacular to be authorized for the use and edification of the people, and was sometimes inaccurately known as 'Cranmer's Bible'.

Cranmer had been a fellow of Jesus College, Cambridge, where he had been appointed doctor of divinity, before he was taken into the king's service as an ambassador to the Germanic states and a proponent of the king's divorce from Catherine of Aragon. He was a close associate of the Boleyn family, and had proposed that the king seek the opinions of the European universities on the 'great matter' of the divorce. Here was a cleric fit for a king. His fidelity and labour were rewarded with the unexpected offer in March 1533 of Canterbury, a post that he would then occupy as the king's most significant proponent. The Spanish ambassador warned his masters that Cranmer was 'devoted heart and soul to the Lutheran sect'. He even married a German evangelical, Margarete Osiander.

But Cranmer cannot be classified as a Lutheran or as a committed member of any particular group. He followed his own path between the orthodoxies of the old faith and the precepts of the new; in his composition of the Book of Common Prayer, for example, he employed a variety of contemporaneous sources as well as the Sarum Missal of the Catholics. In practice he found a middle way between tradition and innovation, even though in matters of the greatest importance he inclined towards reform. Holy Communion or the Lord's Supper, once known as the Mass, was, for example, conducted in the vernacular.

Cranmer may therefore be considered one of the fathers of the Reformation, and an emblem of the English religious sensibility in his willingness to introduce foreign principles, his appetite for moderation and his capacity for compromise. In that, he might be said to anticipate the nation. After a period of local revolts immediately after the proposed religious changes, the people eventually proved themselves to be neither hot nor cold but rather mild and compliant, keeping their professions of faith to a minimum. The Book of Common Prayer, which generally retained Cranmer's language after years of detailed revision, is still in use today. It remains a breviary, a missal and a ritual liturgy.

Elsewhere, reform implied many things to various adherents. The name 'Protestant' itself had not emerged until 1529, in the German region of Hesse. But these Protestant movements, as we may now begin to call them, were divided, with the Lutherans opposed to the stricter proponents of change; the sects of Geneva

Thomas Anthony Dean, after Gerlach Flicke, *Thomas Cranmer*, n.d., engraving.

were opposed to those of Wittenberg, the reformers of Zurich against those of Heidelberg. There were divisions and subdivisions, clusters and groupings, among those who were united in opposing the Catholic polity. They were at one when it came to the folly of purgatory and prayers to the saints, of the wicked absurdity of papistry in all its forms, and of the sacramental system. They concurred, too, in the absolute need for a vernacular Bible. But arguments abounded over the Eucharist and transubstantiation, the role of images, the administration of the churches, and the nature of predestination. There was not one reformed faith, but many.

All in England were thrown into confusion, however, by the unanticipated death of the young king and the crowning of his older sister, Mary I, in the summer of 1553. Mary was a devout Roman Catholic who was intent upon reversing the measures of her father and brother. It was her divine mission, she believed, to save the nation from heresy. An Act of Parliament in that same year enforced the religious settlement as it stood in the last year of Henry VIII, thus clearing away the innovations of Edward's reign. The European reformers made their way back to Zurich, Geneva or Strasbourg, together with several hundred supporters of the new faith. Some of the monks and nuns came back to their old establishments. The helter-skelter of policy did not encourage any fervent return to the old religion, however, but bland conformism or indifference.

The queen's first misstep came in her marriage to Philip of Spain, a mistake that was compounded by her inability to conceive a child. She had welcomed the match because of their shared Catholicism, which she saw as a bulwark against Protestant Europe, but on realizing her barrenness Philip left for the Netherlands in 1555. Mary's greatest error, however, came in her policy of condign punishment for those who had supported the innovations of the Edwardian regime. Archbishop Cranmer was put on trial, together with bishops Ridley and Hugh Latimer. The two former bishops were burned together in the autumn of 1555, and Cranmer suffered the same fate in the early spring of the following year. But they were not the first to die, and over the course of Mary's reign of just five years, some three hundred were put to the torch. In this respect she was not unlike her father, but upon her has been loaded the opprobrium of centuries. She has become known as 'Bloody Mary'.

This is largely because of the testimony of John Foxe, whose *Actes and Monuments of these Latter and Perillous Dayes, Touching Matters of the Church* is better known as the *Book of Martyrs*. His narratives of heroic fortitude and bloody martyrdom were the popular foundation of Protestantism in England, bringing to a climax all the scorn and suspicion of papistry. His compendious work became one of the four great books to be chained in the cathedral churches as a memorial and tribute to the birth of English dissent. Foxe has therefore been included among the fathers of the Reformation, with Cranmer and Tyndale. But, like Bede and other English scholars, he was drawn to the writing of history with a moral purpose.

Foxe came from the Lincolnshire city of Boston and entered Oxford, as did many of the young reformers, where in 1538 he was elected to a probationary fellowship at Magdalen College. On leaving the college he was for a while a private tutor while working as a lecturer or preacher in the cause of reform; the accession of Queen Mary sent him to the more favourable cities of Europe, where he found employment as a proofreader and as a chronicler of Church history, by which he meant the 'true' Church of dissent. Soon after the death of Mary he published an account of the English Church 'in the recent dangerous times'. It was the seed of what became his life's work. He returned to England and began working in London with John Daye, an eminent publisher of evangelical persuasion. Foxe was ordained a priest in 1560, and became a popular preacher under the more favourable conditions of the Elizabethan Religious Settlement.

Yet Foxe was already embarking upon his great enterprise, and in 1563 Daye published his *Actes and Monuments of These Latter and Perillous Dayes*, which comprehended 'the great persecutions and horrible troubles' inflicted by the late queen, Mary, and her Romish prelates. With almost 1,800 pages in folio, and more than fifty woodcuts of torture and burning, it supplied the new

Protestant faithful with a foundation for their vision of a national Church purified by suffering and strengthened with courage as well as perseverance in adversity. It had come through.

Foxe's account was so popular and influential that new testimony of earlier burnings was brought to him; his time was now occupied in adding, revising and researching material so that the original volume grew over four separate editions both in size and in importance. *Actes and Monuments* was a work in progress reflecting, for example, Foxe's changing views on the progress of Reformation. It occupied him for more than twenty years, and the edition of 1570 comprised two volumes of 2.5 million words, with 149 woodcuts. These woodcuts, some of Blakean intensity, forged the tortured deaths of the Protestant martyrs within the national consciousness. His prose was sharp and colloquial, almost blunt. Here, for example, are the last moments of John Hooper:

> But when he was black in the mouth, and his tongue swollen, that he could not speak, yet his lips went till they were shrunk to the gums: and he knocked his breast with his hands, until one of his arms fell off, and then he knocked still with the other, [at] what time the fat, water, and blood dropped out at his fingers' ends.

The impact of the whole work was overwhelming, and by the time of Foxe's death, in the spring of 1587, he had become the principal creator and advocate of Protestant identity. It was a national, perhaps even an insular, faith with its own sacred history that stretched back with Wyclif and the Lollards into the English past. The true Church was the primitive Church that had fought the Antichrist of Rome. Foxe even invoked Bede and Gildas in order to emphasize the line of continuity in the nature of the English soul.

Five

Religion as Orthodoxy

Richard Hooker (1554–1600)

At the time of Elizabeth I's accession, in 1558, it was not clear what precisely the Protestant identity of England might be. The cycle of religious change had revolved three or perhaps four times and the supreme governor, as she wished to be known in the new Act of Supremacy, was herself of divided sympathies. She was not Catholic, but neither was she wholly reformed. In that, at least, she might have reflected the temper of the country. It is possible that the majority still surreptitiously supported the old faith, but that is not susceptible of proof. There may also have been deep reserves of cynicism or of apathy.

The queen's first Parliament of 1559 was summoned to keep 'an uniforme order of religion' by means of a third Act of Uniformity. It retained the provisions of the Book of Common Prayer that Cranmer had revised in a reformist direction, but adjusted certain instructions to appease the Catholic interest. The reformed Church of England adhered to Calvinism, with the belief in predestination, in justification by faith alone, and in the primacy of scripture; but it was Calvinism with a difference. It rejected, or ignored, Calvin's most contentious doctrine: that just as some are predestined to eternal life (a point that no Church has ever questioned), so others are predestined to eternal damnation.

In the summer of 1559 Elizabeth issued a series of injunctions on religious observance. It was a set of very English proposals. The

M.ʳ RICHARD HOOKER
Author of the Bookes of Eccle
ſiaſticall Politye.

Obijt. 1600. Aᵒ: Ætatis ſuæ 50:

W: Hollar fecᵗ

Wenceslaus Hollar, *Richard Hooker*, 17th century, engraving.

liturgy was to be recited in English, but church processions were still acceptable; the cults of the saints and prayers for the dead were abolished, but the queen still kept a silver crucifix and candles in her private chapel. She preferred the clergy to remain unmarried, and to wear liturgical vestments of the traditional kind. This last proposal caused much controversy in the mid-1560s, when some of the reformed clergy, otherwise known as the more 'godly' or 'precise', refused to wear the surplice in church or the square cap when walking abroad; they did not believe that clerics should be set apart from, or above, God's people. The more rigorous dissenters were therefore deprived of or suspended from their posts. In the course of this dispute the term 'puritan' was first invoked. By 1581 it was reported in a pamphlet that 'the hotter sort of protestants are called puritans.' They would survive.

The Elizabethan Religious Settlement, as it became known, was practical rather than speculative; it introduced compromise and toleration, as well as a fair amount of ambiguity. Its very lack of clarity saved it. In London the reformers preached predestination and justification by faith alone, while in York the faithful still prayed with their rosaries. All opprobrious names, such as 'heretic' or 'papist', were forbidden. It was declared in Parliament that it was forbidden to 'meddle with any such matters or causes of religion, except it be to bridle all those, whether papists or puritans, who are therewithal discontented'. There was, of course, an international dimension, since the new queen did not wish to alienate the Lutheran princes of Germany or to antagonize the Catholic monarchs of Europe.

The Thirty-Nine Articles of Religion, which formulated these proposals, had been suggested in 1563 but did not become official policy until 1571. There was no development of doctrine or change in ritual, neither of which would be countenanced by the queen. They simply elaborated upon, and stabilized, the settlement. The Mass and the adoration of the Eucharist were forbidden;

the doctrines of transubstantiation and of hell were rejected; the teachings on purgatory and the sale of indulgences were dismissed. Nevertheless, the old liturgies, ceremonies and vestments were largely retained. In 1593 a bill was passed in Parliament that affected Nonconformists and Catholic recusants equally. It was designed to ensure 'better obedience', so that attendance at conventicles or other 'unlawful assemblies' was considered to be as culpable as attending Mass. The nation crept towards Protestantism, at a slow and uncertain pace.

It was guided there by Richard Hooker. He is perhaps the unsung hero of the Reformation, who confirmed and strengthened the middle way of faith that Elizabeth had introduced. He, more than anyone else, helped to fashion the Anglican Communion of a later date. Hooker was born in Exeter in the spring of 1554 and, like many precocious students, advanced from grammar school to university. He spent his formative years at Corpus Christi College, Oxford, where he became a master of arts in 1577, after three years of study. In the summer of 1579 he took holy orders as a deacon before being made a fellow of the college. By all accounts he was a mild and complaisant man, a temperament that would consort well with his published writings; he tended to avoid controversy and promote conciliation.

In 1585 Hooker was appointed Master of the Temple Church off Fleet Street, in the legal quarter of London. It was there that he engaged with one of the leaders of the early Presbyterians, Walter Travers, in a debate that helped to define the nature of the Protestant Reformation. He also delivered a sermon in that year, 'Of Justification', in which he set out his argument against his precise opponent. Of the papists now deemed to be enemies of the state, he remarked, 'God, I doubt not, was merciful to save thousands of them,' and he warned his auditors to 'beware lest we make too many ways of denying Christ.' A cardinal, or even the Pope, 'will not be rejected by a merciful God ready to make the best of that little which we hold well'. He will not be that 'captious sophister [a contemporary Puritan dogmatist] which gathereth the worst out of everything wherein we err'.

It was in this period that Hooker began his great work in defence of the Elizabethan Religious Settlement established 26 years before. This was the first grand philosophical and theological treatise to be written in English, designed as a formal, systematic account of Church polity. The scale and scope of the work were such that he felt obliged to resign his post at the Temple Church and take up the living of St Andrew's, Boscombe, in Wiltshire, where he might write undisturbed. The first four books of his magnum opus, entitled *Of the Laws of Ecclesiastical Polity*, were published in 1594; a fifth volume, as large as the previous four combined, was published in 1597. He was writing in defence of the Church of England as defined and established by the monarch, 'though for no other cause, yet for this,' as he writes in the first sentence of his preface, 'that posterity may know we have not loosely through silence permitted things to pass away as in a dream, there shall be for men's information extant thus much concerning the present state of the Church of God.'

In his preface Hooker asks his readers to 'follow the light of sound and sincere judgement', and to abstain from bitterness 'in a tedious prosecuting of wearisome contentions'; it is clear that his argument here was directed towards what he called 'the Brethren, the Godly and so forth', by which he signified the more extreme reformers. It is better, he says, to rely on history and tradition than to accept new injunctions born out of controversy and dogma. He begins with a general contemplation of the nature of law, both human and divine, before considering particular problems and principles that might arise in its application. The good Christian will of course follow the precepts and authority of scripture, but scripture does not contain everything. Natural law, and the law of Reason, should accompany and complement divine law. Reason itself could be said to be the divining rod of truth. It is foolish to pretend to know or presume God's will, since 'our soundest judgement is to know that we know Him not as indeed He is, neither can know him: and our safest eloquence concerning Him is our silence.'

Hooker also supported the Catholic argument that there is an unwritten tradition deriving from the Apostles. He went on to claim that although the Roman Church was guilty of 'abominations', it should be considered part of 'the family of Jesus Christ'. This was a challenging doctrine. He parted company with the more precise of his brethren, who were at one in condemning 'the Popish dunghill'. Hooker in fact considered the Church in England to be the natural and necessary successor to the Catholic dispensation. The faithful under Elizabeth's guidance had not separated themselves 'from the Church we were of before. In the Church we were and we are so still.' He hoped to convince his godly opponents that 'the present form of Church government which the laws of this land have established, is such, as no law of God, nor reason of man, hath hitherto of force sufficient to prove they do ill.' As for those called 'Church papists', who attended the reformed service merely in order to comply with the law, they should be left in peace in the hope of later reconciliation.

Hooker therefore counselled caution in the face of diversity and variety, and disputed the notion that 'Scripture is the only rule of all things which in this life may be done by men.' The sacred books are the fount of divine law, he wrote, but they need elucidation and interpretation. They cannot be understood by private judgement alone. It is wrong to attribute 'unto Scripture more than it can have', and human reason can be applied to its study and application. The pursuit of certainty in matters that could not be adequately understood in this life is not fruitful; debates on predestination, for example, are unnecessary and harmful. Human learning is contingent, reliant on variable sources and incomplete.

God is, as it were, 'a law unto Himself'. The congregation of worshippers must depend upon prayer, and the sacraments, as the fortifications of their faith. He put his trust in collective worship and the open avowal of sacramental grace.

Hooker also stated that one manifest error lay in the belief that the scriptures should determine the structure of the existing Church. There was no one certain model for the faithful, just as there was no one language to be shared by all. The discipline and practice of the Church were not set in stone, but rather changed with time and circumstance. They must be flexible, provisional and susceptible to change. His was a thoroughly English call for practicality and compromise in ecclesiastical affairs. He was instinctively opposed to the gradations of 'doctors, pastors, lay-elders, elderships'. In addition, sermons, which the reformed prized above all else, 'are not the only preaching which doth save souls'. He was attacking not Calvinism directly itself, because he was also of that persuasion, but only the direction in which it was being taken by certain Continental reformers and their adherents in England. As for the strict Calvinism of Geneva, Hooker remarked that 'no age ever had knowledge of it but only ours; that they which defend it devised it; that neither Christ nor his Apostles at any time taught it, but the contrary.' He was in fact challenging the more precise members of the reformed faith. The whole of the reformed English Church was Calvinist in spirit and tendency, but he believed that it should not be exclusive, or prescriptive, and thereby inclined to separatism.

Hooker himself was a learned supporter of the settlement, and argued that the English Church, as governed by Elizabeth, was justified in maintaining those traditions derived from early practice 'till there grow some urgent cause to ordain the contrary', as well as affirming those more recent principles of reform 'generally fit to set forward godliness'. This was the call for what became known as the *via media*, or middle way, which was to define the practices and principles of the English Church. He wrote that 'the mean which is a virtue seemeth in the eyes of each extreme an extremity.' Yet he did not care to dislodge the central truth that the Church of England was firmly established upon Calvinist theology. It was reformed, as he put it, in the manner and matter of godliness. This was taken as 'settled' even in the Elizabethan Settlement.

Hooker had come to understand the indissoluble link between Church and state that was also to characterize the national faith. After the publication of the fifth book, he was asked to preach at Court, where he came face to face with the monarch whose religious dispensation he admired and strengthened. In his later years he was granted the living of St Mary's, Bishopsbourne, Kent, where he continued his ministry until his death. He left the last three books of his work in an unfinished state, a condition that has led many to question the accuracy of the published versions. He had argued, however, that the Church in England could not be defined purely in opposition to papistry. Much of the polemic against Rome was of 'things indifferent' and, despite its foolish errors, the Church of Rome was a true church established upon faith in Christ. Hooker died in November 1600, his influence uncertain. His vision of continuity and of communal grace was perhaps too fulsome for an age that had attained only a perilous balance, but within two or three generations it had become accepted wisdom. He would not have known or understood 'Anglican' as a term of faith. It was not generally used until the last half of the nineteenth century. He would have described himself as a member of the universal visible Church. But his construction and theological defence of the middle way were deeply satisfying for a nation that wished to avoid doctrinal strife. Hooker did not discover or interpret Anglicanism. He invented it.

✝

THE ELIZABETHAN RELIGIOUS SETTLEMENT, which in truth settled very little, was considered to be a 'midge-madge' of ambiguous elements that did eventually come to be known as Anglicanism. It was as alien to the pure spirit of reform, adumbrated in Zurich or Geneva, as it was to the doctrines and rituals of the old faith. This was the rift that Hooker had tried to heal. England therefore became Protestant by degrees, and by a process of accommodation and subtle adjustment. Neglect and forgetfulness, aided by apathy or indifference, slowly weakened the influence of the Catholic religion beyond repair. The passage of time had accomplished what the will of men could not achieve. Yet all this came at a price. The dissolution of the old faith led to an indifference towards the past among many people. For some the sense of continuity and kinship was broken, while for others the old social bonds of the community were severed. In a society that had been heavily dependent upon custom and tradition, the effects were profound. Many of these were soon to become evident.

There was now a wide range of opinions and beliefs on the nature of Protestantism. At one extreme were those partially converted Catholics who wished to retain some of the practices and principles of the Roman Church; they would come in time to be known as 'high'. At the other were those who followed the principles of John Calvin as well as other European reformers, in promoting a 'purified' Church based on the doctrines of double predestination and justification by faith alone, and on a wholesale rejection of Roman beliefs; they would be known as 'low'. In the most schematic terms, one became Anglican and the other Puritan. These became the twin peaks of the English religious sensibility.

Six

Religion as Opposition

Thomas Cartwright (1535–1603), Robert Browne
(*c.* 1550–1633), Henry Barrow (*c.* 1550–1593)

The Church, as established by Elizabeth and defined by
Hooker, was based on authority and uniformity; that is
why Church and state were deemed to be complementary. But
there was an alternative English tradition, one that derived from
the individual pursuit of salvation through an immediate and personal relation to God. This had been the goal, for example, of the
fourteenth-century mystics. The spiritual life was seen as the bond
between human faith and divine love, which required no external
agency, such as a formal Church, to be acknowledged or justified.
John Wyclif and the Lollards had defied or circumvented authority by a path that followed a native English tradition. Conscience
became free, and the individual soul its own mentor. These are
the origins of English separatism that later became known as
Puritanism. It was doubted whether Christ, as understood in the
scriptures, intended to create a Church at all. If any authority were
needed, it could be found in the Bible. These convictions were, of
course, alien to the Elizabethan Settlement.

On 20 June 1567 a congregation of approximately one hundred
assembled at Plumbers' Hall in Anchor Lane, London, where they
began a service without the obligatory prayer book. Their gathering was interrupted by constables from the Sheriff of London, who
promptly arrested the leading members. They had been supposed
to take part in a wedding celebration, but their reasons for meeting

were quite different. There had been a clandestine group of worshippers since the papist days of Queen Mary, but now it had been restored in defiance of the established Church of England. They were brought before Edmund Grindal, the Bishop of London, who asked them why they were 'severing yourselves from the society of other Christians'. These were the original separatists, then, even though they may not yet have used that name. They replied that the New Testament made no mention of clerical vestments, or ceremonies, or bishops, and that they would be judged only 'by the word of God'.

These cloistered faithful were by no means thwarted by official disapproval, and in 1568 Grindal reported that four or five ministers, and some four hundred worshippers, had left their parish churches to join separated congregations. There is every reason to suppose that they continued to do so in the 1570s.

The burden of broad dissent, however, fell upon two dispensations that soon enough became known as the Congregationalists and the Presbyterians. They did not differ in essential doctrine from the Calvinism of the Elizabethan Settlement, but reserved their hostilities for the governance of the national Church. They did not want to replace it, but rather desired to reform its entire structure. This did not save them from condign punishment at the hands of the Elizabethan authorities. The queen herself made it clear that she would allow neither Puritanism nor papistry to upset her new-found religious balance, that she would neither 'animate Romanists' nor 'tolerate new-fangledness'.

✠

IN THE PREACHINGS and lectures of Thomas Cartwright the substance of 'new-fangledness' was first conveyed, so that his life and work bear testament to the origins of Presbyterianism in England. Cartwright was born in Royston, Hertfordshire, in 1535, and at the age of fifteen was admitted as a scholar to St John's College,

Unknown artist, *Thomas Cartwright*, *c.* 1683, engraving.

Cambridge; he was so assiduous and successful a student that ten years later he was appointed a fellow of the college. In 1562 he moved to Trinity College, where he was engaged in a philosophical disputation before the queen. He was rewarded by his appointment as domestic chaplain to the Archbishop of Armagh, but it seems that in this period he became interested in the newly reformed faith of Geneva; this did not prevent him, however, from being nominated as a preacher at his old university. We may suspect that he practised outward conformity while nourishing a more zealous and puritan faith. It is thought that he travelled to Geneva, though this is not certain, but it did become clear that he admired the discipline and ministerial duties of the Genevan churches, which seemed close to that practised by the Apostles.

Towards the end of 1569 Cartwright became Lady Margaret Professor of Divinity at Cambridge. In a set of lectures delivered the following year, concerning the 'Acts of the Apostles', he was wise or foolish enough to propound a system of Church governance that separated civil and ecclesiastical powers. He claimed that members of a congregation should be allowed to elect their ministers, and that the ministers themselves should be examined to determine whether they were able to fulfil their appointed tasks, such as prayer and preaching. He believed that this was the example of the primitive, or apostolic, Church. In that Church there were no bishops or archbishops. There were no priests separated from the laity by their sacred role, but rather ministers or lay elders, who should properly be called presbyters rather than priests. Only those who preached could administer the sacraments or conduct the divine service. When the implications of his teaching were understood, he was deprived of his lectureship and prevented from preaching within the university. He had effectively denied the precepts of the Elizabethan Settlement. In turn, however, he had gathered around him a cluster of zealous reformers.

Cartwright is next to be found performing his role as an academic and lecturer in Geneva itself, where he had become a doctor of divinity at the Academy. These were more congenial surroundings, in which he found a colleague in Theodore Beza (John Calvin's successor as spiritual leader of the city) and became thoroughly familiar with the Presbyterian system. But he did not stay. In the spring of 1572, after learning that Elizabeth's principal adviser, William Cecil, Lord Burghley, did not object to his residence in England, he returned to his native country. This was the year in which the Puritan or Nonconformist leaders addressed a petition to Parliament, known as the Admonition, urging the acceptance of the Presbyterian system. It declared that 'we in England are so far off from having a church rightly reformed, according to the prescript of God's word, that as yet we are not come to the outward face of the same.' Cartwright himself seems to have played no part in the composition of the petition but, with some minor misgivings, approved it. In a second Admonition, published towards the end of the year, the details of that system were outlined.

This was also the time when the first unofficial Presbytery, otherwise known as a consistory or meeting of elders, was established, in the secluded district of Wandsworth in Surrey. It was made up of those, according to the second Admonition, 'whom the parish shall consent upon and choose, for their good judgement in religion and godliness'. They represented a court that might exclude or excommunicate offenders, select or deprive ministers, and decide on matters of doctrine. In turn they were soon to be governed by Church sessions and by conferences or synods parochial and national. Discipline and mutual edification were the keys. The elders were to press on with the process of reform, which was in danger of being stalled by the national settlement. They were becoming a formalized hierarchy, in other words, which seems to have been the fate of most organized religions.

Their presence was an irritant to those in authority. In January 1565 Elizabeth instructed her Archbishop of Canterbury, Matthew Parker, to enquire closely into 'the varieties, novelties and diversities' that were springing up. Then, in November 1573, she despatched a letter to her bishops ordering them to take action against any Nonconformists they might detect. Cartwright himself, as leader of the Presbyterian and de facto Puritan movement, was now at risk. In order to avoid prosecution he fled to Germany, where he enrolled as a student at the university in Heidelberg, a city that was a centre of Presbyterianism. In 1576 he moved on to Basle and its university, emphasizing the fact that the English Dissenting tradition owed a large debt to Continental reformers. In 1577 he moved again, to Middelburg in what is now the Netherlands, to work with the guild of merchant adventurers there. This, too, was a haven for Dissenters. Already known as the leading light of Presbyterian and Puritan belief, he then continued his ministry among the merchants of Antwerp.

In 1582 Cartwright returned to Middelburg, but the air of the Low Countries did not suit his constitution and his health soon began to fail. It was necessary for him to find a more favourable climate, but on his return to England in the spring of 1585 he was pursued as an agent of sedition. He was arrested and despatched to prison, but only for a short time; Lord Burghley procured his release, and Cartwright's reputation as a faithful man of God preserved him. He was not a separatist, and continued to pledge his allegiance to the national Church. Presbyterianism, for him, was concerned only with matters of reform, not of revolution. Soon enough he was appointed Master of the Lord Leycester Hospital in Warwick.

In the face of manifold threats from Catholicism – from Jesuit missionaries, from Philip II of Spain and from the machinations of Mary Stuart – there was a policy of forbearance if not tolerance towards the Nonconformists. It was also the case that some members of Elizabeth's council, Burghley among them, were themselves inclined towards a stricter Protestantism. This was evident in the case of a close associate of Cartwright, Walter Travers, who has some claim to being the second author of Presbyterianism in England. In 1579 he had become minister of the Presbyterian church for the English merchants in Antwerp, in which post he had been duly ordained. But the following year he returned to England, where he was appointed lecturer at the Temple Church.

This was, of course, the church of which Richard Hooker became Master in 1585, a post that Travers had sought. Travers was now formally Hooker's assistant, but that did not prevent him from expounding his principles of dissent in the face of Hooker's more moderate conclusions. Both men now preached at the Temple, and it was said that 'the pulpit spake pure Canterbury in the morning and Geneva in the afternoon.' The result was public controversy, to the extent that the lawyers themselves relished the debate, and it became evident that early Protestantism in England could mean two different things. It was this dispute that helped to inspire Hooker in the composition of *Ecclesiastical Polity*, which delivered a strong but magisterial rebuttal to Presbyterian claims. The battle of the pulpits, as it became known, was the battle for the English soul. It was not concluded then, and still exists now. Travers was eventually prohibited by the Archbishop of Canterbury, John Whitgift, from preaching in the Temple Church or elsewhere, on the grounds that he had not been properly ordained. But he then spent his time and labour in composing for the Presbyterian faithful a *Book of Discipline*, which was adopted by a general conference in 1586 as the basis of their practice and belief. It was becoming an organization rather than a movement, and Cartwright played the largest part in its direction. He and Travers were the twin engines of Presbyterianism.

As such they became the targets of episcopal wrath, as the orthodox Elizabethan Church became more confident after the execution of Mary Stuart in 1587 and the defeat of the Spanish Armada the following year; it had established itself as the true Church under the aegis of a triumphant queen, and was ready to confront those who opposed its ordinances. Travers himself was protected by his alliance with Burghley, being appointed his chaplain and then tutor to his son. It is evident that the queen's most senior adviser was among the 'hotter' Protestants. With the connivance of Burghley, Travers was then appointed Provost of

Trinity College, Dublin, where he stayed for four years before returning to England and to retirement. He was scarcely noticed again, a circumstance that corresponds with the abrupt decline of Presbyterian fortunes as a result of official sanctions.

In the face of these sanctions Cartwright himself was in fear of arrest and imprisonment, and in October 1590 he was brought before the ecclesiastical Court of High Commission on matters as diverse as unlicensed preaching and the misuse of hospital funds. He was accused of setting up an unlawful church among the merchants of Antwerp. He had been heard to denounce bishops and the Book of Common Prayer. His true offence, however, was to become the most earnest proponent of Puritanism, and the leader of a growing Nonconformist party, in Warwick itself, where he was still Master of the hospital. As a result, he was consigned to the Fleet Prison before being taken for trial to the Star Chamber in the Palace of Westminster the following year.

Cartwright's imprisonment and prosecution dismayed his colleagues and associates, and confirmed the fact that the Presbyterian cause was in jeopardy. When the queen was asked to allow more preachers within the Church, she refused. She disliked the panoply of what were called 'conferences, disputations, reasonings, prayers, singing of psalms, preachings, readings, prophesyings, fastings' that accompanied the Puritan cause, just as much as she detested the attempt to reconstruct the religious hierarchy with the introduction of pastors, elders and deacons elected by a congregation rather than ordained by a bishop.

No formal charges were ever proved or concluded against Cartwright, or against others of the same belief in prison with him, but his deteriorating health under the appalling conditions of the Fleet hastened his release in the early months of 1592. Durance vile had embellished his reputation, however, and his influence was now stronger than ever. Richard Bancroft (later Archbishop of Canterbury) wrote in 1593 that Cartwright's 'authority indeed is very great as being in effect the patriarch of them all. These things that he writeth are almost oracles. Happy is the brother that can come into his company.'

It is likely that on leaving the Fleet Cartwright returned to the Leycester Hospital, but in 1595 he found a haven in Guernsey, where he became the chaplain of Castle Cornet, on a small tidal island off the coast. Guernsey itself was more amenable to Presbyterianism than the mainland, and the island offered the shelter he needed to continue his ministry. The cause in England itself seemed destined to fail, with the unpalatable alternatives of isolation or separation as the only remedy. Cartwright preached his last sermon on Christmas Sunday 1603, and died two days later with all the infirmities of old age and frail health. He was the first prominent Puritan in England, and as such should be acknowledged as part of its spiritual legacy.

✠

THE ENGLISH PRESBYTERIANS, with Cartwright and Travers as their guides, did not wish to leave the Church of England as administered by Elizabeth; they wanted to join it and, by joining, transform it. But there were other Englishmen who wanted to be separated altogether from the established Church, since for them the Book of Common Prayer and the required vestments were the breath and claws of the Antichrist.

In the sixteenth century they can be approached by degrees. Robert Browne came from an affluent family in Rutland that had some familial connection with Lord Burghley; he was accepted into Corpus Christi College, Cambridge, where he is likely to have heard Cartwright's lectures and sermons on the merits of the primitive Church. He also became acquainted with a number of the more Puritan students, as well as 'carefull and zelous' local reformers. After graduation he was appointed schoolmaster in a town, the identity of which has been lost, but it seems he was ejected from the post after denouncing the 'woefull and lamentable state' of the established Church. His old college rescued him, and in 1578 he was appointed to preach at St Benet's Church in the centre of Cambridge, next door to Corpus Christi. He used the pulpit to denounce bishops as 'ravenous and wicked' hirelings, however. He may at this point be deemed a Puritan rather than a separatist, but by 1580 he was advanced to the point at which he considered the true Church to be guided by 'ministers and elders that are chosen out of the congregation to watch over the flock of the godly' or the known brethren. The voice of the chosen was the voice of God.

This did not endear Browne to the authorities, even if he were under the nominal protection of the university. He was filled with an urgent desire to set up his own reformation 'without tarrying for any magistrate' to authorize it, however, and began to preach at conventicles (unlawful gatherings) in Bury St Edmunds and elsewhere, where he attracted some hundred or so followers 'in one covenant and fellowship together'. In 1581 he became an assistant minister at the chapel of St Giles Hospital in Norwich, a city renowned for radical Puritans, and there he wrote that 'God will receive none to communicate and covenant with him, which as yet are one with the wicked.' In Norwich, also, he gathered some faithful followers who joined in a covenant to create a new Church. They chose Browne as their pastor.

These manifest separatists were in turn to be known as 'Brownists'. They may be compared to the gathering surprised and arrested in the Plumbers' Hall some fourteen or fifteen years before. In June 1583 a royal proclamation was issued in England against Browne and his various tracts. He was pursued by the Bishop of Norwich, was twice taken, twice imprisoned and released. It was time to move on. He and his fellow Brownists decided to travel to Middelburg, a haven for reformed and separatist congregations. There he continued to publish tracts and treatises on the subject of his religion, in which he stated that each particular church comprised a group of Christians who had made a covenant with their God, and that every member of the congregation should be 'a king, a priest, and a prophet under Christ'; no civil magistrate could exercise authority over them. He wrote that 'on this condition will the Lord receive us . . . we come out from among the wicked, and separate ourselves.'

But there was trouble in this separatist paradise. Disillusioned by conflict with some members of his congregation, Browne moved on to Presbyterian Scotland, where again he became embroiled in controversy. In 1584 he returned to England, and there, partly under the persuasion of Burghley, he renounced his separatist ambitions and submitted to the orthodox Church. It was inevitable that he would be denounced as a weakling by some and as an apostate by others. He became Master of St Olave's School in Southwark in 1586 and then, five years later, rector of Achurch in Northamptonshire, where he remained for more than forty years. It is not clear, however, that he had lost his old separatist faith. It seems he was suspended from his post in 1617, but in 1626, for no ascertainable reason, he took up his duties once again.

In November 1627 Browne was accused of Nonconformity by certain parishioners, a dispute that was eventually taken to the courts. He seems to have lost none of his zeal or acerbity in pursuing what he considered to be the true faith. When in 1631 he refused to follow the ceremonies outlined in the Book of Common Prayer, he was deprived of his post before being excommunicated. Two years later he struck a village constable and was despatched to Northampton gaol, where he died in his eighties. He has the distinction of being the first English separatist to announce himself as such and to establish what was for him a true Church composed of godly Christians in an independent congregation free from the Church of England. His was the first attempt, also, to provide a coherent or consistent set of beliefs for such a congregation. It became the pattern or paradigm of others.

✚

YET IT IS HENRY BARROW, rather than Robert Browne, who is considered to be the founder of Congregationalism in England. It was Barrow who claimed that the true Church is 'the body of Christ', and that its members

> altogether make one body unto him. All the affairs of the church belong to that body together. All the actions of the church be the actions of them all jointly . . . All the members are jointly bound unto edification and unto all other helps or service they may do unto the whole. All are charged to watch, exhort, admonish, stir up, reprove.

It is as faithful a summary as any.

Barrow himself did not fit the pattern of Nonconformity in his younger days. He was born in about the year 1550, and was a native of Shipdham in Norfolk; nothing is known of him until in 1566 he was enrolled at Clare Hall in Cambridge, from which he graduated three years later. Little is known again until he entered Gray's Inn in 1572, but from later reports it is thought that he spent his time at 'fencing schools' or 'dicing taverns', and in London acquired a reputation as 'licentious and a gamester'. This was standard behaviour for a relatively affluent young man between university and a legal Inn.

But then all was changed. Barrow was walking one day in London with a friend, when he happened to pass a church where the preacher could be heard very clearly. He may have been one of those Dissenting ministers who were invited by sympathizers to mount the pulpit. Barrow, intrigued, asked his friend to enter the church with him 'and hear what this man saith that is thus earnest'. The words were of sin and damnation, of faith and reproof, and were of such conviction that, in the words of Barrow's biographer, they 'touched him to the quick in such things as he was guilty of, so as God set it home to his soul'.

It was a true conversion. Barrow began to engage in conversations with ministers and with the brethren; he left the capital and returned to the country, where he read the scriptures, and prayed, and meditated. It was rumoured that he had turned Puritan, and in fact his now closest friend, John Greenwood, introduced him to the separatist churches hidden in London. It was there that he pursued his arguments for reform. Greenwood himself had been a forceful and earnest preacher among the separatists, but in the autumn of 1586 he was arrested by the officers of the Bishop of London and despatched to the Clink Prison in Southwark.

Barrow came up to the city in order to comfort and perhaps assist his friend, but he was not aware that he himself had already been denounced to Archbishop Whitgift for preaching or promoting sedition. A quarter of an hour after he entered the Clink, he was detained and taken in a wherry to Lambeth Palace, where he was interrogated by Whitgift himself:

> Whitgift: Have you said as reported 'that there is not a true
> Church in England'?
> Barrow: When you produce your witness I will answer.

The dialogue achieved nothing, and Barrow was taken under arrest to the gatehouse of the palace. He spent five months in confinement there, and was examined three times by the ecclesiastical Court of High Commission. In May 1587 he was taken to Newgate sessions, where he was condemned for advancing a 'false ministry and worship'. His judges were no doubt relying on transcripts of his remarks on the necessity for separation from the authorized Church as well as the need for pure Congregationalism. He and his supporters were in no position to threaten the realm, but they were engaged in acts of civic disobedience. Two or three hundred were committed to prison (it is impossible to be more accurate about the number), and some died in confinement.

Barrow was then removed from the gatehouse to the Fleet Prison, which, with its stink and filth, its fetters and sickness, killed as many as the rope or the stake. His fourth examination, in March 1588, was before the Privy Council, where Burghley, believed to be a sympathizer with dissent, described him as a 'fantastical fellow' who has 'a delight to be the author of this new religion'. Barrow himself was not at all abashed. When he was asked to describe the Archbishop of Canterbury, there present, he replied that 'he is a monster, a miserable compound; I know not what to call him. He is neither ecclesiastical nor civil – even the second beast that is spoken of in the Revelation.' It is clear that his separatism had taken him very far.

Barrow was then returned to the Fleet, but even in this close confinement he was able to learn much of what was happening beyond its walls, and was able to issue his writings with the aid of visitors. These liberties would not have been possible without generous donations of money to his gaolers, in a world where coin was the key. His tracts, letters and treatises were smuggled out of prison, published in Dort, and were to be found in Flushing and in Brill; these were ports in the Low Countries from which Nonconformist literature was distributed. There is no doubt that copies were also available for the faithful in England.

The most significant of these writings must rank as the first separatist declaration to be written in English. *A Brief Summe of the Causes of Our Seperation, and of Our Purposes in Practise* was published in 1588, and announced among its principles 'our forsaking and utter abandoning of these disordered assemblies as they generally stand in England', by which is meant the services of the Church of England. They 'worship the true God after a false manner' and 'have a false Antichristian ministerie imposed upon them'; in addition, these churches 'remaine in subjection unto an

Antichristian and ungodly government'. Nothing could be clearer in its rejection of the Elizabethan polity.

In the spring of 1592 preachers were despatched to 'confer' with Barrow and the other religious prisoners, but their real purpose was to uncover or discern more evidence against them; in the year before, Parliament had passed an Act 'for the punishment of persons obstinately refusing to come to Church and persuading others to impugn the Queen's authority in ecclesiastical causes'. This might have been directly aimed at Barrow's Congregational faith. His conditions of confinement were somewhat eased in this period, perhaps at Burghley's urging, but they could in no way incline Barrow towards apostasy. His faith was fresh and ever renewed, his fate already determined. New articles were proved against him and, after another trial for his beliefs in March 1593, he was sentenced to death. The only question lay in the manner of his execution. Would he be hanged, drawn and quartered for treason, or burned at the stake for heresy?

Barrow's beliefs were never in doubt, however, since he professed them freely in conferences with orthodox preachers and with his interrogators. The exact pattern of the true Church is vouchsafed in the New Testament, and scripture is 'the light that shineth in dark places'. In this creed he was at one with other Dissenters. But his belief and practice took a different path. He asserted that the true Church 'is a company of faithful people – separated from the unbelievers and the heathen of the land – gathered in the name of Christ'. That godly congregation, even if it contain only two or three people, is the sole source of faith and discipline, so that 'every particular congregation has the power of our Lord Jesus against all sin and transgression . . . and [to] excommunicate the obstinate offenders.' It is an inspired community. Thus there is no spiritual difference between the people and the ministers. Its service itself must be simple, consisting of prayer, reading and exposition of scripture, followed by exhortation. If there is to be singing, it must be only of the Psalms. It was the duty of the monarch to extirpate all religions other than the true one, to the extent that the church buildings of the ungodly should be destroyed. Barrow himself was taken to the scaffold rather than to the fire, and died as a traitor and not as a heretic. But his witness survived, and became a significant aspect of the English soul.

English school, *Lancelot Andrewes*, *c.* 1660, oil on canvas.

Seven

Religion as Sermon
Lancelot Andrewes (1555–1626),
John Donne (1572–1631)

Lancelot Andrewes was born in 1555 within the London parish of All Hallows, just west of the Tower; in common with Thomas More less than a hundred years before, he was a Londoner whose spirituality blossomed in the crowded streets of the city. He was the eldest of thirteen children, and, according to his first biographer, his parents were 'honest and religious'. His father, Thomas Andrewes, was a 'seafarer' – which might mean merchant, captain or sailor – who became a Master of Trinity House in Deptford. But the call of the sea did not reach his son, and it seems that from his early days Lancelot had a thirst for learning. At the age of seven or eight he attended Cooper's Free School in Ratcliffe, just north of the Thames, before moving on to Merchant Taylors' School under its headmaster, a famous pedagogue, Richard Mulcaster. In later life Andrewes placed a portrait of Mulcaster above the door of his study.

At Merchant Taylors' Andrewes pursued his education in Greek, Latin and Hebrew, the avenues to divinity, and was so eager to learn that he neglected the ordinary pursuits of childhood. Time away from his books was time wasted, and it is reported that he studied late into the night before rising at four to continue. He had what John Donne castigated in himself as a 'hydroptic, immoderate desire of human learning and languages'.

In the autumn of 1571, at the age of sixteen, Andrewes was awarded a scholarship to Pembroke Hall, Cambridge, and he would remain at the university for the next fifteen years. This was a period when the newly established national Church was challenged by the force of Puritan dissent, which had, as one of its centres, Cambridge itself. But Andrewes was not unduly affected by external events. It is said that he did not take direction from his tutors or contemporaries, for example, but learned and studied by and for himself. That is often the way with dedicated scholars. He was described by the antiquary John Aubrey as a 'great long boy', which suggests a certain clumsiness, and his early biographer remarked that 'his ordinary exercise and recreation was walking either alone by himself, or with some other selected companion, with whom he might confer and argue, and recount their studies.'

Those studies were very fruitful, and it is reported that as an adult Andrewes knew at least six ancient languages, among them Chaldean and Syriac, and fifteen modern languages. This may account for his fascination with the protean meaning of words so eloquently evident in his sermons. He was equally successful in academic preferment, attaining a bachelor of arts in 1575 and master of arts three years later. He was ordained a deacon and priest in 1580, the first step in an inevitable ecclesiastical career, and began a course of lectures on the Ten Commandments in the chapel of Pembroke. It was said that the people of the town, as well as the members of the college, crowded into the chapel on Sunday afternoons in order to hear him.

Andrewes's ability had now become so well known to his contemporaries, both in Cambridge and in London, that a large number of students attended his lectures and took down notes upon them. In a preface to an edition of those lectures, published in 1642, the compiler stated that 'he was scarce reputed a pretender to learning and piety then in Cambridge who made not himself a disciple of Mr Andrewes,' whose writings 'have in many hundreds of copies passed from hand to hand, and have been esteemed a very

Library to young Divines, and an Oracle to consult at, to Laureat and grave Divines'. In the small world of sixteenth-century governance, where Church and state were so closely aligned as to be inseparable, such a reputation would have echoes.

Henry Hastings, 3rd Earl of Huntingdon, who had been made President of the Council of the North, set up to improve the administration of justice in northern England, asked Andrewes to be his chaplain and to reach out to the many Catholics in his discontented bailiwick. A man of God was also expected to be a man of government. This was also the period when Andrewes was appointed chaplain to Elizabeth I, as well as to Archbishop Whitgift. Sir Francis Walsingham, the secretary of state with wide powers, also became one of his patrons and granted him official posts at St Paul's Cathedral, the church of St Giles, Cripplegate, and Southwell Minster. The church of Cripplegate was in the heart of London, and ministered to a mixed population of craftsmen, players, merchants and the general throng of the city. St Paul's itself was essentially an extension of city life, its nave filled with hawkers, strollers, petty thieves and casual visitors, whose 'huzzing and buzzing' rose into the unhealthy air. A contemporary satirist described it as 'a kind of still roare or loud whisper . . . It is the great Exchange of all discourse and no businesse whatsoeuer but is here stirring and afoot . . . It is the Theeues sanctuary, which robbe more safely in the Croud, then in a wildernesse.'

Andrewes had made the stark transition from the cloistered world of Cambridge to the wider sphere of London, a process that was accelerated with his appointment in 1601 as Dean of Westminster, where he became busily engaged in the life and work of the scholars in the school attached to the abbey. It was said that he 'never walked to Chiswick without a brace of young fry and in that wayfaring leisure had a singular dexterity to fill those narrow vessels with a funnel'. In other words, he talked and taught as he walked.

In this period too, Andrewes became known as a preacher to the public world. As chaplain to the queen, he delivered at least twelve sermons at Court and continued his ministry with sermons in the cathedral, in St Paul's churchyard, at Spitalfields, and at other traditional places. He was pre-eminent in learning, but so precise and intense is his oratory that he transcends his period. He was admired and copied by his contemporaries, who considered him the greatest preacher of the age. Two notable stylists of prose, Thomas Nashe and John Lyly, would attend his sermons together, but his admirers were not confined to the sixteenth and seventeenth centuries. The twentieth-century poet T. S. Eliot, for example, considered him to be 'the first great preacher of the English Catholic Church', whose sermons 'rank with the finest prose of their time or of any time'.

✚

YET THAT PROSE was long in the making. The English sermon is coeval with the English Church. It was until the seventeenth century a principal form of public entertainment, and one of the few sources of public news. Sermons were delivered on high days, holy days, religious festivals and Sundays. Sunday slowly became a usual day for preaching, and it afforded two opportunities, with a relatively short one for morning Mass and a longer in the afternoon, after dinner. Some people in fact went from church to church, to hear one sermon after another. This was described as 'gadding about', and suggests how much preaching had become both a spectacle and a recreation. There was also the matter of decorum. A preacher would modify his style or language to suit the nature of his audience; in minsters or cathedrals it might be a high style of amplification and persuasion, while in the churchyard, or by the market cross, it would be more direct and immediate.

The pulpit was in fact the place where common or vernacular English was spoken, by monks or clergy, and so it offered an irresistible allure to the majority, who could not read or write. The sermon became the inspiration for verse satire, as well as the source of material for the popular drama of the mystery plays and for early English comedy. It could fairly be said, in fact, to represent the first examples of medieval English literature. Moral instruction in the thirteenth and fourteenth centuries was couched in the form of sermons with stories, homilies, jests, riddles and moral examples that in their variety and profusion rival Chaucer or Langland. The priest might also include verses to flavour his delivery.

And so the doctor, the thief, the cook, the braggart, the prostitute and the scold all crowd into the pulpit. This was the only world the congregation, gathered in the church or field, knew. Stock types and characters were described. The familiar proverbs were repeated. Pride comes before a fall. He who loves me, loves my dog. What others do may I not do so too? The preacher would use the common speech of the time. He might begin with a call to 'good sirs' or 'good friends' or 'worshipful men and women', and continue in the same familiar style. 'Now you may ask me . . . Well, I will tell you . . . you may draw him round about the town with a pudding.' He would sometimes apologize: 'I left two things out last Sunday because the time was short.'

The 'low life' of Elizabethan drama derives from the sermons of the period. In that respect the preacher preceded the dramatist. The open-air preaching, first practised by the friars, also helped to create the appetite for display. The expressions and gestures of the preachers were re-created by the early players. The medieval 'boy bishops', who were used to parody adult bishops, were the forerunners of the child actors at Blackfriars and elsewhere. The inaugural sermon of these little bishops generally concerned the spiritual condition of children. 'Well well!' preached one child with mitre and crozier, 'all is not gold that shynes nor all are not innocents that beare the face of childer.'

Yet the listeners and spectators before the pulpit were asked to reach beyond the literal meaning: 'By the five loaves the holy doctors understand the five Books of Moses which are compared to a barley loaf; for a barley loaf is on its outside rough in part and harsh, yet within it is full of the purest flour.' The incidents and parables of scripture are conveyed in such realistic and immediate detail that they might be happening in an adjacent lane. The people showed a characteristic interest in the quaint or curious personal details of the saints or the Apostles, which they might also find in the wall paintings and colourful statues of the church itself. In some sermons the story of Cinderella is used for homiletic purposes. As Chaucer's Pardoner puts it:

> Than telle I hem ensamples many oon
> Of olde stories, longe tyme agoon:
> For lewed peple loven tales olde;
> Swich thinges can they wel reporte and holde [consider].

Many preachers came from the mendicant friars, particularly from the Dominicans and Franciscans, and it is not at all surprising that they took the side of the poorer and more oppressed laity. They shared a sympathy for the lower ranks, with itinerant or unlicensed preachers and with the Lollard 'poor priests' or 'hedge priests'. They would inveigh against the sins of the rich and the worldly, and freely criticize those in authority, as well as the high-ranking clergy who supported them. They voiced popular protest, and are generally seen to have fomented and even organized peasant unrest. The priest John Ball, whose sermons helped to create the rebellion of 1381, is a case in point. There is only a small gap between the homilies in the pulpit and the songs of the street. The dramatic intensity and depth of feeling often found in the sermon fostered verse satire but, more importantly, provoked social and political dissent. That is not the whole story, of course.

Many preachers supported the established order and condition of the world, extolling humility, patience and acceptance of what was for many a harsh lot. The pulpit could directly affect the life and actions of those who listened.

Some members of the congregation, however, were still immune to its blandishments, and any descriptions of popular piety must take account of human nature: 'Marry, I am going to St Thomas of Acres to the sermon; I could not sleep all this last night and I am going now thither: I never failed of a good nap there.' Many would stand rather than sit, so that they might more easily escape. That is why the best sermons were often considered to be the shortest. On some occasions a church servant would stand at the back of the congregation and signal to the preacher when it became weary or restless. One London Franciscan preached so often on the Decalogue that he became known as 'friar John of the Ten Commandments'; his servant told him that 'every man knows what you will say, as soon as you begin, because they have heard it so often.' Brevity was not the only virtue, however. The handsomeness of the preacher could also be taken into account; if the preacher were in some sense an actor, his appearance mattered to the male as well as female members of the congregation.

By the close of the sixteenth century the sermon had become more learned and more respectable. The clergy were taken largely from the universities, and the congregation had become more accustomed to the 'new learning'. The general form of the sermon had already been adopted. A sentence or two from an episode or parable in the New Testament was paraphrased, then interpreted in a variety of ways. Erasmus ridiculed the more fanciful allegories, but the spiritual meaning was made clear. The four rivers of Paradise, noted in Genesis, represented the cardinal virtues of 'rightwysnes [righteousness], temperaunce, prudence and strengthe, wherewith the hole soule myght be washed and made plesaunt lyke as with so many flodes'. In this way the thirteenth-century teaching of Thomas Aquinas filtered down to the fifteenth-century shopkeeper.

Other preachers would take a text and follow it to its conclusion, with the help of literal and spiritual interpretations. Sermons directed at clergy or Court, characteristically in Latin rather than English, would be based on certain principles, with the theme followed by exordium, prayer, introduction, division and discussion. Even the longest and most complex sermons would have the same or similar structure. It was part of the system of rhetoric taught in the schools and universities.

The sermons of the early reformers, disavowing Catholic belief, tended to be more direct and forceful. A reformed preacher might have a plain style without the Latinate periphrases of his predecessors: 'Yf a man steppe in snowe or sonde: after hys departing remayneth a steppe. So after the acte of creacion remayneth behynde the hond werke of god in the creature.' Just as, if a man steps in snow or in sand, the imprint of his foot remains, so in the act of creation the figure of God remains in the child. Just as rubbing makes rusty iron shine, so tears of penitence clean the soul; just as you will first look at the paintings on a wall rather than the wall itself, so will God first see the sins 'painted' on the soul.

One method of delivery was known as the 'Sermon on the Card', in which the preacher used the analogy of four suits in a pack of cards to make his point. The player must put his trump card, his heart, on the right suit to win his reward. 'Now you have heard what is meant by this first card,' Hugh Latimer said, 'and how you ought to play with it, I purpose again to deal unto you another card, almost of the same suit; for they be of so nigh affinity, that one cannot be well played without the other.'

By the sixteenth century the sermon had become a ritual occasion on holy days or festivals. Those who stood about the pulpit might memorize it as best they could, so that they might repeat it to family or friends. Others would take notes for the same purpose, or would be ready to leave the crowd and return with news of the sermon to their companions. On ordinary occasions and in the small parish church, the preacher of the day might simply transcribe his words from an approved collection of sermons or a sermon handbook. Those who put together extracts from other sermons were sometimes known as 'jumblers'. This was not standard practice, however, and a more usual method was to be found in the 'theatre of memory'; thus theatre was part of the art of memory, whereby the preacher would visualize a house with many rooms or a church with many chapels, in each of which was a mnemonic device to picture a theme. They might be images of virtue or symbols of suffering. The orator would wander through them in his mind and visit each room or chapel in turn.

The seventeenth century, however, was the great age of the sermon, largely because matters of faith were pre-eminent in contemporary politics and controversies. At a time of religious conflict, the sermons might become the equivalent of urgent news denouncing opponents or seeking allies. Paul's Cross was as familiar to citizens as London Stone or Aldgate Pump. It stood in the precincts of the cathedral, and marked a great medieval tradition as the site of the city's most important outdoor pronouncements. It comprised an octagonal structure, made of wood and mounted on a stone base, which was in turn surmounted by an arched roof and a cross. A crowd of people stood beneath it, with galleries on two sides of the churchyard. In certain respects it resembled an Elizabethan playhouse – which, in a society of spectacle, in essence it was. It was a place for proclamations and for the delivery of public news, when the results of the latest battle or the last words of a condemned felon were announced. Heretics were forced to recant upon it. But the sermon became pre-eminent. The first is recorded there in 1330, and the preaching continued for more than three hundred years. The audience or congregation was often very large;

reports of a thousand or more may be an exaggeration, but they do exemplify the central role of the sermon in the daily life of the city. The Sunday morning sermon was always the most popular, and curates were asked to complete their church services before nine o'clock so that they could gather by the Cross with their parishioners.

The assembled people were attentive but often noisy and agitated, with fights breaking out or insults directed at the preacher. On one occasion, 'certain leude and ille disposed made a hollowing and such a cryinge *thou lyest*' that a dagger was aimed at the unfortunate cleric, who was pulled back just in time. On another occasion shots were fired from a house beside the churchyard. Certain preachers were given an armed guard, and at times of disaffection, soldiers were placed among the congregation. One bishop confessed that he spoke 'with much fear and trembling'.

The sermons themselves were long, lasting for two hours, after which, as a sixteenth-century pamphleteer put it, 'after they have tarried there for a while, to here some newes, and the preacher at the prayers, lorde how they vanishe away in clusters, repairing into Paules and either by or sell some bargaine in the body of the churche.' During the period of the Reformation, and the various changes wrought by Edward or by Mary, the Cross became the centre for what might now be called propaganda. At the time of the Elizabethan Settlement it was the principal site for the purveying of news, with the clergy addressing or haranguing the crowd. One of them, attacking 'Romish' or 'papistical' doctrine in 1602, had a 'long browne beard, a hanging looke, a gloting eye, and a tossing learing jeasture'. Paul's Cross was at the centre of national affairs.

✠

WHEN LANCELOT ANDREWES attended the Privy Council, to which
James had appointed him in 1616, he would enquire if any questions were to be asked concerning the affairs of the Church; if
not, he said very little or nothing during the proceedings. He did
not care for the clamour of the world. When he was Bishop of
Chichester, and then of Ely, he was more concerned with scholarship and with his pastoral duties. His influence at Court was, in
essence, a tribute to his central loyalty to the established Church,
to his administrative abilities, and to his moderation in all matters
of dispute. As a supporter of the Elizabethan Settlement he did
not wish to change the administration or the liturgy of the Church.
He sympathized with the orthodox and understood the Puritan.
He declared the controversial subject of predestination too great
a matter to be understood. For all his learning, he was in English
terms a practical man. His counsel could be trusted.

The full extent and nature of Andrewes's gifts were revealed
during the reign of Elizabeth's successor, James I, a king who
believed that he was as skilled in theology as he was in policy. He
was also a great lover of sermons, rivalling his passion for hunting,
and he came very soon to recognize Andrewes's outstanding
ability.

In January 1604 the king summoned Andrewes to the Hampton
Court Conference, which was ostensibly designed to adjudicate
between the rival claims of the orthodox and the puritan in the
Church of England. It did not resolve the problem, but it did
lead to the new translation of the Bible that became known as
the Authorized Version. Andrewes was chosen to preside over
the committee that considered the first eleven books of the Old
Testament, from Genesis to 2 Kings. This was work wholly to his
taste. It was in this period also that he was judged to be first among
preachers, both for his learning and for his oratory.

Andrewes had preached his first known sermon in the open-
air pulpit in the churchyard of the priory of St Mary Spital, at

an annual event known as the 'Spital sermon'. On such public occasions he could be vehement, as in this tirade against certain contemporary preachers:

> every Dunce took upon him to usurp the Pulpit, where talking by the hour glass, and throwing forth headlong their incoherent, misshapen, and evil-smelling crudities . . . they have the luck foresooth to have it called by the name of Preaching . . . the very Church is infested with as many fooleries of discourse as are commonly in the places where they shear sheep.

In his commentaries on scripture and on doctrine, however, Andrewes ascends from the valleys into the heights. He was called a 'witty' preacher, but not in any contemporary sense. His was a grave and learned style in which wit came from suggestive metaphor and from subtle argument. He sought out antithesis and paradox not for their own sake, but to challenge conventional meaning in the presence of the divine. From 1605 to the end of the king's reign in 1625, Andrewes's most important sermons centred on the great festivals of the English Church – Nativity, Crucifixion, Resurrection, Pentecost – and upon the mysteries of faith that they celebrate, as at the Incarnation:

> Signs are taken for wonders. 'Master, we would fain see a sign,' that is a miracle. And in this sense it is a sign to wonder at. Indeed every word here is a wonder . . . The Word without a word; the eternal Word not able to speak a word . . . But yet, all is well; all children are so . . . At His birth; a cratch [a frame for hay] for the Child, a star for the Son; a company of shepherds viewing the Child, a choir of Angels celebrating the Son. In His life; hungry Himself, to shew the nature of the Child; yet 'feeding five thousand',

to show the power of the Son. At His death; dying on the cross, as the 'Son of Adam'; at the same time disposing of Paradise, as the 'Son of God' . . . that He might be liable He was a Child, that he might be able He was the Son; that He might be both, He was both.

Andrewes introduces a text to correspond to the season or festival, then elucidates it in the fullest manner. He divides and commonly subdivides it, while continuing his theme with similes, metaphors and other figures of speech. In this, he follows the Renaissance and even the medieval form of preaching. After his Christmas sermon of 1609, a courtier wrote that he had preached 'with great applause, being not only *sui similis* [like himself] but more than himself by the report of the King and all his auditors'. The king, in fact, placed a copy of that sermon under his pillow.

Short sentences – sometimes merely a phrase – move forwards in order of meaning and further meaning with the use of parallels and paradoxes, oppositions and analogies. Andrewes finds truth, or the Word, within a word or in the syntax of a sentence. It might be described as the grammar of God. The use of contrast or parallel may reveal two orders of reality, so that the objective reality is grasped by faith as well as by intellect. He goes to the very edge of reasoned or consecutive discourse. He would take up a word and speculate upon it, enlarge upon it, divine and define it. He employs repetition and recapitulation, definition and redefinition, to press the meaning upon his auditors. He delays and lingers on a word:

And now, to look into the name. It is compounded, and to be taken in pieces. First, into *Immanu* and *El*; of which, *El* the latter is the more principal by far, for *El* is God . . . for as in *El* is might, so in *Immanu* is our right to His might.

It has been said that he picked a word to the bone. T. S. Eliot employed another metaphor when he wrote in an essay on Andrewes that he takes each word 'and derives the world from it; squeezing and squeezing the word until it yields a full juice of meaning which we should never have supposed any word to possess'.

There were less fulsome remarks. One lord told the king that Andrewes 'did play with his text as a jackanapes does, who takes up a thing and rises and plays with it, and then takes up another and plays a little with it. Here's a pretty thing and there's a pretty thing.' For Andrewes, divinity became a form of poetry, nourishing each word and syllable in a line of beauty; what had been rhetoric, in the manuals of instruction, became poetry:

> A cold comming they had of it, at this time of the yeare; just, the worst time of the yeare, to take a journey, and specially a long journey, in. The waies deep, the weather sharp, the daies short, the sunn farthest off in *solstitio brumali*, the very dead of *Winter*.

It was a method of intense concentration, divining the full meaning of a word or phrase from its sound, its syllables and its associations. He even considered syntax as a guide to interpretation. Texts are placed together as if in a mosaic. It could be described as a lapidary exercise, stone upon stone, with the mortar of rhetoric:

> Of which words there is not any one waste or to spare. Every one of them is *verbum vigilans*, as St Augustine speaks, 'awake all'; never an one asleep among them. Each hath his weight. Nor never an one out of his place, but, as Solomon speaks, 'upon his right wheel', standing just where it should.

This may imply that his oratory is fitful or abrupt, but in fact it is part of a flowing forwards movement. Andrewes was concerned with theological speculation not for its own sake, but for the profound revelation that exists within it. In English fashion he renders it concrete. He plays upon words in a simpler way: 'Compassion is but passion at rebound'; 'This adoption is the fulness of our option'; 'If it be hard to endure, it must be more hard to endure hard things; and of all things hard to be endured, the hardest is death.'

It seems that Andrewes wrote down and revised his text before its delivery. He might have memorized certain passages, then delivered them as if extempore, with appropriate gestures and expressions. He would have mastered the art of public speaking, perhaps from the example of players or more likely from other preachers. One contemporary noted that 'he never heard man speak with such a spirit.' He often used vivid or colloquial images that would have invited dramatic interpretation. Ever since his days at school and university, he was known for his ability to summon up texts and examples, and he was blessed with an excellent memory. In the full flood of his speech, allegory and prophecy, theology and liturgy come together, as in this passage concerning Mary Magdalene:

> And now lo Christ is found alive. That was sought dead. A cloud may be so thick that we shall not see the sun through it. The sun must scatter that cloud, and then we may. Here is an example of it. It is strange a thick cloud of heaviness had so covered her, as see him she could not through it; this one word, these two syllables, *Mary*, from His mouth scatters it all. No sooner had His voice sounded in her ears but it drives away all the mist, dries up her tears, lightens her eyes, that she knew Him straight.

In the spring of 1625, after the death of King James, Andrewes was confined to his bed with 'a sore fit of the stone [gallstones] and gowte'. In the last two years of his life he was fully aware of his impending death and, according to the Bishop of Rochester, was engaged in continual prayer. He died in the early morning of 25 September 1626. His body was taken from Winchester House and interred in St Saviour's, in the same parish of Southwark. William Laud declared that 'the greatest light of the Christian world has been extinguished.' Andrewes's style and manner of preaching, however, did not long survive his passing. In 1683 John Evelyn noted in his diary that

> a stranger, an old man, preached much after Bp [Bishop] Andrews's [*sic*] method, full of logical divisions, in short and broken periods, and Latine sentences, now quite out of fashion in the pulpit, which is grown into a far more profitable way of plaine and practical discourses.

The preacher had come down from the pulpit in an explicit sense.

AMONG THE GREATEST of English poets, John Donne was also mighty among the preachers in the great age of preaching. He was born in Bread Street, at the centre of the City of London, at some point in 1572; the month and week of his birth are unknown. His father, also christened John, was a successful ironmonger who died when the young John was scarcely four years old. The father was given a lavish funeral in his parish of St Mary Olave's, but it is likely that he was what was known as a 'church papist', who disguised his Roman Catholic faith by outward conformity to the Church of England. He married Elizabeth Heywood, who had come from a family of strong and loyal Catholics; one of her immediate ancestors was Thomas More, who had lived in Milk Street, just a short distance from Bread Street. The ties of family and faith were often close in seventeenth-century London. Donne wrote,

> as I am a Christian, I have ever beene kept awake in a meditation of Martyrdome, by being derived from such a stocke and race, as, I beleeve, no family (which is not of farre larger extent and greater branches) hath endured and suffered more in their persons and fortunes, for obeying the Teachers of Romane Doctrine, then it hath done.

The course of his early life was directed, if not determined, by his religious faith, where the watchwords were secrecy and caution.

Donne was brought up at home and given a private education, through which he gained proficiency in French and Latin; he was admitted to Hart Hall, Oxford, at the age of eleven, and remained there for three years. It was a young age to enter university, but it was not unusual at the time. His early biographer, Izaak Walton, suggests that he was considered by his tutors to be 'one who was rather born, than made wise by study'. He did not graduate, however, since that would mean affirming the Oath of Supremacy, which made Elizabeth I head of the Church, and subscribing to the Thirty-Nine Articles. For the young Catholic, that would be impossible.

From Oxford Donne proceeded by a familiar path to the Inns of Court, the legal quarters of London where a university education was polished and refined by disputation and drink as the first steps in making a London career. He was in all matters an Elizabethan gentleman, and proceeded to Lincoln's Inn as a matter of course. It seems that he acquired a private tutor in mathematics while there, but his principal study lay elsewhere. In later life he revealed that he could not be content 'till I had, to the measure of my poore wit, and iudgement, suruayed and digested the whole body of Diuinity', in which he included the doctrines of both

Rome and Geneva. This was a high ambition, but it is also a measure of his native spirituality. His Catholicism was not simply a set of principles, but an attitude towards the world.

But theology may also have a sharp edge. In this period Donne's younger brother, Henry, was arrested and imprisoned for concealing a Jesuit priest in his lodgings. It was a heinous offence. The priest suffered death, while Henry was consigned to the Clink before being taken to Newgate Prison, where he died of sickness and general neglect. There is no record of John's reaction, but perhaps as a result he decided to leave England and to enlist in the armada of Essex against Spain and the Spanish colony of the Azores. On his return he found employment as the secretary to Sir Thomas Egerton, Lord Keeper of the Seal, in which post he remained for three or four years. But this was the prelude to a time of trouble. These pages are devoted to his preaching rather than to his poetry, but the centre and the substance of his life lay in the poems he wrote down on stray squares of paper and which circulated among friends and acquaintance. The later poet Samuel Taylor Coleridge remarked on Donne's 'wonder-exciting vigour, intenseness and peculiarity of thought', and that thought had a fierceness and sharpness that burned and still burn in his words.

Donne served Egerton as secretary both at Whitehall and at his residence of York House along the Strand. He was still a 'man of the town', but his single life came to an end towards the close of 1601. He had met Anne More, Egerton's niece, who had come to London, and it seems that they were soon in a close bond. Letters were exchanged and clandestine meetings arranged, until they could no longer contain or deny their passion for each other, and were secretly married. Her uncle and her father were both furious in their opposition and, since the marriage was at first thought to be invalid, Donne was confined in the Fleet Prison. After his release, and after the union was judged to be lawful, the strife began to fade. The couple moved to a house in Surrey, lent to them by a cousin of Anne, and Donne settled down to married life. Children emerged at regular intervals, and he did his utmost to keep up the spirits of both himself and his wife, but these middle years were generally ones of disappointment. He could not find employment at Court, however hard he attempted to do so, and he seemed destined to live quietly in the country for the remainder of his life. He took up once more the study of divinity and canon law, with no possible hope of its practical application, and pursued the friendship of several influential women. He visited the city from time to time in order to enjoy the company of various wits, courtiers and poets. Out of his weariness and melancholy he composed a treatise on suicide, *Biathanatos*, which in part reflects his preoccupation with death and dissolution.

Donne had been urged by friends and acquaintances to take up some position in the established Church as a suitable home for his gifts and interests. It is not clear whether he retained any of his youthful Catholicism, but he had certainly made his peace with the English state; his service with Essex and his employment with Egerton confirm that. He had also become weary of endless religious controversy.

Yet Donne was at first reluctant to enter the Church, there having been, as he put it, too many 'irregularities of my life'. But on the urgent advice and insistent persuasion of the Dean of Gloucester, an old friend, he began to consider the possibilities. He was being offered an income and a position, both of which he had lacked for many years. He had always been half in love with divinity, or theology, as a discipline, but now that might come to fruition. He possessed the gifts of erudition and expression, which could be put to private and public use.

And so Donne was ordained on 23 January 1615 by the Bishop of London; in the following month the king conferred upon him a doctorate of divinity and also appointed him to be one of the 48 royal chaplains. He had come, perhaps, into his true inheritance.

Donne's first surviving sermon was preached at Greenwich on 30 April that year. In the autumn of the following year he was appointed Reader, or preacher, in divinity at Lincoln's Inn. He was expected to give sermons on the forenoon and afternoon of each Sunday of term, which amounted to fifty sermons a year. He also preached at Paul's Cross, that popular resort of citizens, and at St Mary Spital, where one of his sermons to the assembled people lasted for two and a half hours. He preached in the Chapel Royal before a king who considered himself a connoisseur of sermons. From the beginning of his new calling, Donne trained himself to speak easily, and learned how to adopt the right posture and the correct manner. It is said that with a friend he visited certain churches where he was allowed to test himself in the pulpit. He studied with success, and Walton wrote that he spoke 'with a most particular grace and an unexpressible addition of comeliness'. He was now in his early forties, but he had retained his bright eye and keenness of expression. He was always well dressed, in the fashion of the time, and seemed also to be preternaturally sharp and alert.

But Anne's death at the age of 33, in the summer of 1617, changed everything. She had borne twelve children in sixteen years of marriage, and no doubt the strain of continual childbirth hastened her death. It was a devastating loss, and may have deepened Donne's commitment to the life of the Church. The first sermon he delivered after her death, at St Clement Danes, where she had been interred, was on the text of Jeremy: 'Lo, I am the man that have seen affliction.'

Despite his grief Donne could not remain in a cloistered state, but had to resume his duties. In one sermon he declared that 'every man hath a Politick life, as well as a natural life; and he may no more take himself away from the world, then he may make himself away out of the world.' And so it proved. In 1621 he was appointed Dean of St Paul's Cathedral, one of the most senior clerics of the greatest church in the land. It was there that he delivered his most important sermons. His fame as a preacher rose, and his oratory in the pulpit drew crowds into the cathedral. He was a Londoner speaking to Londoners. Some of his congregation would write down notes of his sermons, for further reflection, or commit them to memory.

During Donne's ministry at the cathedral he was engaged continually in business, both clerical and secular. He rose each morning at four, and Walton wrote that

> the latter part of his life may be said to be a continued study; for as he usually preached once a week, if not oftener, so after his Sermon he never gave his eyes rest, till he had chosen out a new Text, and that he might cast his Sermon into a form, and his Text into divisions, and the next day betook himself to consult the Fathers, and so commit his meditations to his memory, which was excellent.

He did not read his sermons, in other words, but learned them. With his notes in front of him, he could begin. Even though the sermons varied in length from one to two hours, this was not a remarkable feat in this period.

✛

ONE HUNDRED AND SIXTY sermons by Donne (or, as he was at this time called, Doctor Donne) survive from a period of fifteen years. He began with the careful preparation of texts and notes, which were then given shape with the conventional structure of parts and divisions that had not changed much since the fourteenth and fifteenth centuries. But even though the form may have been similar, the manner had changed.

Donne's sermons are as original and as distinctive as his poetry, wholly part of their age but inspired by the nervous intensity and emotional rhetoric of the man himself. A sermon before the king at Whitehall, for example, is built up with contrasts and oppositions, with the continual drawing out of conclusions, with questions and speculations. The passion and the intellect are combined:

> but then lame and decrepit soul, gray and inveterate sinner, behold the full ears of corn blasted with a mildew, behold this long day shutting up in such a night, as shall never see light more, the night of death; in which the deadliest pang of the Death will be thine Immortality: In this especially shalt thou die, that thou canst not die, when thou are dead; but must live dead for ever.

Donne conveys his meaning with repetition and close variation, as when he speaks of 'a plague that shall not onely be uncureable, uncontrollable, unexorable, but undisputable, unexaminable, unquestionable', and that at the Judgement 'many, and many, and very many, infinite and infinitely infinite, are the terrours of that day.'

There is a constant movement forwards, a rhythm of feeling, that drives on the meditation. As an instinctive poet even within the pulpit, Donne is acutely aware of the shape and sound of his words, of feeling finding form. The organ swells. The wave rises and breaks upon the shore. His style has sometimes the brightness and quickness of a lightning flash with a number of relatively short sentences that have a cumulative power. He draws out the syllables for their cadence and in their combination he creates melody: 'We die in the light, in the light of God's presence, and we rise in the light, in the sight of his very Essence.'

As a poet and as a preacher, Donne was drawn to extravagance. Lancelot Andrewes delighted in short sentences, but Donne luxuriates in long sentences composed of short and supple phrases. His writing is eminently theatrical and wholly rhetorical.

The most vivid allusions and the most recondite learning are harnessed together to provoke surprise. As a consequence the sermons possess an urgency and an immediacy that are instantly recognizable as his own:

> I throw my selfe downe in my Chamber, and I call in, and invite God and his Angels, thither, and when they are there, I neglect God and his Angels, for the noise of a Flie, for the ratling of a Coach, for the whining of a doore . . . A memory of yesterdays pleasures, a feare of tomorrows dangers, a straw under my knee, a noise in mine eare, a light in mine eye, an any thing, a nothing, a fancy, a Chimera in my braine, troubles me in my prayer.

He was an earnest and powerful preacher, inciting the people to prayer and penitence, sometimes weeping with them, always exhorting them, and often guiding them, according to Walton, 'like an Angel from a cloud'. He was an actor and a performer in what was in part a dramatic monologue, and one diarist noticed his control of 'gestur and Rhetoriquall expression':

> One humour of our dead body produces worms, and those worms suck and exhaust all other humour, and then all dies, and all dries, and molders into dust, and that dust is blowen into the river, and that puddled water tumbled into the sea. And that ebbs and flows in infinite revolutions.

Donne's style nevertheless possesses a directness and simplicity that were needed in the pulpit and before a congregation. It is not colloquial, but it is plain: 'I consider too, that with this streame of fire, from him, there shall bee a streame, a deluge, a floud of teares from us; and all that floud, and deluge of teares, shall not put out one coale, nor quench one sparke of that fire.' He had humour as well as learning, wit as well as rhetoric, in a cascade of metaphors and images, speculations and paradoxes, short colloquial asides and lengthy expositions. He seems to have been born for the pulpit, leaning forwards to persuade or to cajole, to console or to terrify. He speaks often of death and of hell:

> to fall out of the hands of the living God, is a horror beyond our expression, beyond our imagination . . . That that God should frustrate all his owne purposes and practices upon me, and leave me, and cast me away, as though I had cost him nothing, that this God at last, should let this soule go away, as a smoake, as a vapour, as a bubble, and that then this soul cannot be a smoke, a vapour, nor a bubble, but must lie in darknesse, as long as the Lord of light is light itselfe, and never a sparke of that light reach to my soule; what Tophet is not Paradise, what Brimstone is not Amber, what gnashing is not a comfort, what gnawinge of the worm is not a tickling, what torment is not a marriage bed to this damnation, to be secluded eternally, eternally, eternally from the sight of God?

It is possible to sense his invention and his delight in words almost overwhelming his original perception. The triple repetition of 'eternally', perhaps in a softer and softer voice or in a louder and louder, is a device for the pulpit, where his tone and emphasis might master the congregation. He is possessed of a sensibility that finds meaning in paradox and opposition. Where Andrewes stopped and considered a word in all its complexity, Donne stops and considers himself: 'I sinn'd, not for the pleasure I had in the sin, but for the pride that I had to write feelingly of it.'

DONNE WOULD SERVE for ten years in the cathedral, but age and infirmity were creeping upon him. He considered himself 'a dry cynder . . . a Spunge, a bottle of overflowing Rheumes . . . an aged childe, a gray-headed Infant, and but the ghost of mine own youth'. In the summer of 1628 he suffered from a fever that visited him at regular intervals, with what he called 'damps and flashes', and over the next two years he was afflicted by the wasting disease then known as consumption. He had often envisaged his death, in prose and poetry, and now expressed a desire to die in the pulpit. He gave his last sermon at Court in February 1631, when he was so worn and wizened that he might have been an emblem of death itself.

In the middle of the following month, Donne contrived a spectacle or memento mori. A carpenter made a wooden platform with a model of a funeral urn at its front. Donne then brought in a winding sheet with knots at his head and feet, in the fashion of a shroud to cover a corpse. He wrapped himself in the shroud, stood upon the urn with his pale, emaciated face turned towards the east in honour of Christ's coming. An artist painted the memorable scene on a wooden plank, and Donne was so pleased with the result that he placed it by the side of his bed. It was now a deathbed in the vivid and theatrical style of his sermons. He was talking to those around his bed until the last minutes of his life; when the final moment came, he lapsed into silence and arranged his hands and body in the solemn posture of the dead. It was the final bravura performance.

John de Critz the Elder (attrib.), *James I*, n.d., oil on panel.

Eight

Religion as Scripture
The Authorized Version (1611)

The accession in 1603 of James VI of Scotland to the throne of England, as James I, may have offered some relief to the Presbyterians and other Nonconformists, who had been all but suppressed in the later years of Elizabeth's reign. James had been raised in a country that was directed by Presbyterian rule, and it might be expected that he would look with a clear, if not necessarily benevolent, eye upon Dissenters elsewhere. He was considered to be in favour of reformed Protestantism and was well known for his love of sermons and his delight in theological debate. This was promising. It was not recalled, or was deliberately forgotten, that he had expressed boredom or dismay with the sectarian arguments of the Scottish elders.

On his long journey into England, the new monarch was presented with what was called a Millenary Petition by virtue of the fact that it had been signed by a thousand ministers. It was of Puritan or Nonconformist persuasion, objecting to certain portions of the Book of Common Prayer, to ministers who did not preach, and to pluralism. In moderate terms it suggested that the sign of the cross should be removed from the baptismal ceremony, and that the marriage ring was unnecessary. The words 'priest' and 'absolution' should be 'corrected' and the rite of confirmation be abolished. The cap and surplice, believed to be the vestments of conformity, were not to be 'urged'. Their requests were mild enough, no doubt in the belief that it was better to emphasize the earnestness and the strength of their demands than to alienate the king with too much enthusiasm for radical change.

James did not address the petition directly, but one of his first significant acts after his coronation was to call a general conference of religion at his palace of Hampton Court in order to debate the issues raised by the document. Five distinguished and learned Puritan ministers were matched against the leading ecclesiastics of the realm, monitored by the king himself, who liked nothing so much as doctrinal debate. It was reported later that he had 'so tempered' Puritan demands there that 'harmony hath been the better ever since.' This was not entirely accurate. The proceedings of the first day, 14 January 1604, were confined to the king and his bishops in discussion over the details of the petition. On the second day the Puritan ministers were invited to attend. John Rainolds, the most prominent of them, was the first to be called; in his testimony he argued that the English Church should fully embrace Calvinism. James was not inclined to accept this, but he was willing to concede certain matters to the Nonconformists in the evident belief that a middle way would encourage unity within the Church. He was quite willing to embrace what he called 'moderate Puritans'.

All seemed to be proceeding without much incident until Rainolds recommended that the bishops of the realm should consult with the 'presbyters'. At this the king bridled. He knew enough of presbyters from his years in Scotland, where they did not treat him with appropriate respect. He had been called by one of them 'God's silly vassal', and he did not wish to repeat the experience. He told Rainolds and his colleagues that they seemed to be aiming 'at a Scottish Presbytery which agreeth with monarchy as well as God and the devil'. He added, 'until you find that I grow lazy, leave it alone.' This was the occasion when he is supposed to have exclaimed 'no bishop, no king', by which he meant that the divine right of kingship was upheld by the ecclesiastical hierarchy; if one step in order is displaced, all may fall. This was a direct hit against Presbyterianism, Congregationalism and a number of associated sects. It was now evident that there was not one national Church, but at least two Churches with different meanings and purposes. This was, in broad terms, the future of English Protestantism.

James had made one concession, however, which had significant consequences. Rainolds had asked him to decree that 'one only translation of the Bible . . . [be] declared authentical, and read in the church'. This was considered acceptable and even necessary by the king, who wished to bring a form of unity to the established Church. The task of translation was begun at the end of 1604, the year of the Hampton Court conference, and was undertaken by 47 scholars chosen from among Puritan divines as well as from more orthodox churchmen. All of them, however, belonged to the Church of England. It is an indication of the unsettled state of religious belief that schismatics and Dissenters were disqualified from the work. Sections of the Bible were given to six committees derived from Oxford, Cambridge and Westminster. They had all completed their work by the end of 1608, and in the following year their texts were sent to Stationers' Hall for review.

THE VERNACULAR BIBLE had always been the long-wished-for and long-promised sanctuary for the English soul. It has been remarked that, by the late sixteenth and early seventeenth centuries, 'the English became the people of a book, and that book the Bible.' Historians of later periods have confirmed that the Bible is central to any understanding of the English sensibility. It has never been the property of Dissenters or evangelical Christians, despite their fervent attachment to it. It has belonged to the cottage, the manor and the parish church.

The earliest translation of Genesis is to be found in the Old English of the late seventh or early eighth centuries, and appears again in Middle English, in metrical paraphrases of the fourteenth century; the book itself is invoked by Chaucer and by Langland, who in *Piers the Plowman* refers to 'Genesis the gyaunt, the engendrour [begetter] of vs alle'. The Bible was part of the warp and woof of English spirituality.

John Wyclif's Bible of 1395, better known as the Lollard Bible, marks the first defiantly English translation of the sacred scriptures in the face of official condemnation. Wyclif's English, or that of those who undertook this translation, is simple and direct, with a brevity and clarity that made it part of the language; it was the mark of the native inclination towards the practical and the pragmatic, and thus aligned with English identity and the line of English religious history.

The natural successor of Wyclif was William Tyndale, whose triumphs and travails have been documented in an earlier chapter. He declared that his translation was designed to 'sucke out the pithe of the scripture' so that the simple ploughman might understand it. After it was published in Worms in 1526, copies were smuggled into England in larger and larger quantities so that in a true sense Tyndale became one of the fathers of English Protestantism.

The appetite for the English Bible, once awakened, became immense. Five major translations appeared over the succeeding thirty years, all to a large extent based on Tyndale's original. The first complete Bible, published in 1535, was the work of Miles Coverdale. He was concerned to resolve differences between translations, and to smooth out complexities; as a result, his translation is characterized by its ease and naturalness. It has been said that he possessed 'a real gift in melodious expression' that anticipates the music of the Authorized Version. The language itself may spring out of moderation and conciliation.

Two years after the Coverdale Bible was published another English work, known as Matthew's Bible, was printed; it was named after the pseudonymous translator, rather than the Apostle, but it was essentially a conflation of Tyndale and Coverdale, with certain marginal notes appended. Coverdale then in turn supervised the revision of Matthew's Bible in order to create in 1539 what became known as the Great Bible. This had on its frontispiece an engraving of Henry VIII handing the volume in question to a grateful Archbishop of Canterbury and assorted members of the clergy. John Strype, a clergyman and historian, recorded that 'everybody that could bought the book, or busily read it, or got others to read it to them.' The English Bible had at last become a central token of the national culture.

Another version, Taverner's Bible, was disseminated in 1539. It was no more than a revision of Matthew's Bible, despite the better Greek scholarship of its translator, and it had little effect. The Bishops' Bible of 1568, an orthodox version revised under the aegis of the Archbishop of Canterbury, was hardly more successful.

Of incomparably greater influence was the Geneva Bible of 1560. Sixty editions appeared during the reign of Elizabeth, complete with footnotes, verse numbers and marginal commentaries of a Calvinist turn. By the middle of the seventeenth century some 140 editions had been published. It has the distinction of being the first English Bible to be printed by mechanical means, and was produced in compact quarto size, rather than the more cumbersome folio. This may account for some of its popularity, but the radical tone of its annotations provides the true explanation. These were in large part composed by a group of Protestant exiles who had migrated to Geneva, the city of Calvin, in the wake of the Marian persecutions.

But if it was the work of several hands, it relied upon its precursors to the extent that it continued the tradition of what might be called English spiritual music. Its first line, 'In the beginning

God created ye heaven and ye earth,' has sounded ever since. It was used by both Shakespeare and Marlowe, a circumstance that emphasizes its significant role in the national consciousness. (The fact that Shakespeare knew this version thoroughly suggests that he was not a covert Roman Catholic.) It was not admired, however, by James I, who considered that its Calvinistic annotations were 'very partial, untrue, seditious, and savouring too much of dangerous and traitorous conceits'. That is why he embraced with enthusiasm the notion of a new translation at the Hampton Court conference.

The Authorized Version that duly emerged has been described as 'the most influential version of the most influential book in the world', and 'the most important book in English religion and culture'. It is impossible to use the English language without being influenced by its cadence and vocabulary, which are in large part taken from Tyndale, whose own translation had been published almost a hundred years before. It is significant, too, that this authoritative work should have been produced out of compromise and conciliation. All previous English versions of the scriptures are echoed within its text. It might even act as a mirror of Englishness itself, and by extension of the English soul.

The preface to this version, commonly known as the King James Bible, is itself an epitome of the English religious genius for assimilation and adaptation. It asserts that the act of translation from the Greek and Hebrew is one 'that openeth the window, to let in the light; that breaketh the shell, that we may eat the kernel . . . that removeth the cover of the well, that we may come by the water'. This was the text that helped to form the English imagination and transform the language into the medium for conveying powerful spiritual truths. The nineteenth-century poet Matthew Arnold asserted that there is 'an English book and one only . . . where perfect plainness of speech is allied with perfect nobleness'. We can trace it in the work of Milton and of Bunyan, of Tennyson and of Byron, of Johnson and of Gibbon, none of whom, according to Arthur Quiller-Couch, could resist 'the rhythms of our Bible . . . it is everything we see, hear, feel because it is in us, in our blood.' The connection between the English imagination and English spirituality is a continuous and permanent one.

Robert White, *George Herbert*, c. 1670, drawing.

Nine

Religion as Poetry

George Herbert (1593–1633)

G eorge Herbert was born in the town of Montgomery, by the border between Wales and Shropshire. This area, once commonly known as the Welsh Marches, has been fruitful of visionaries and poets. At the time of his birth he was one of six children who lived with their parents, Richard and Magdalen Herbert, in the commodious mansion of Blackhall. Their comfortable situation was brought about by their eminence. The Herberts were the most prominent family of the Marches, and their leading ancestor had been created Earl of Pembroke in the twelfth century. On the death of her husband, in 1596, Magdalen moved with her children to Eyton, southeast of Shrewsbury, before moving on again to the more noble surroundings of Oxford, where she might supervise the education of her eldest son, Edward. Her pains were successful because, as Lord Herbert of Cherbury, he became known as a philosopher and theologian who earned the title of 'the father of Deism', a religion of nature and reason quite different from that of his younger brother.

In 1601 Magdalen moved again, this time to a more permanent address by the Charing Cross in London. Hers was a large household, comprising some fourteen servants. In these prosperous surroundings, the young George Herbert took his bearings. At the age of twelve he was enrolled at Westminster School, where he experienced the rigours of a Renaissance classical training in which he was well versed in Latin and Greek together with classical history, prosody and theology.

But George's education took place beyond the bounds of the schoolroom. His mother was a woman of wide learning and even wider acquaintance, who invited to her table various luminaries of the London world, among them John Donne, Lancelot Andrewes and the composer William Byrd. This was the life of music and poetry to which Herbert was introduced. He wrote poetry of his own, in Latin and in English, but in his youth he was also adept at playing the lute and the viol. From Westminster School he proceeded to Trinity College, Cambridge, in the autumn of 1609. This was also the year in which Magdalen Herbert married Sir John Danvers, a young man (scarcely eight years older than George himself) who had travelled to Italy and France, and who took an especial interest in architecture and in the Italian garden. But he was by no means a well-bred amateur. He took a keen interest in George's progress, and welcomed him to his orderly house and garden in Chelsea.

At Trinity College, Herbert climbed the ladder of academic preferment from bachelor to master of arts, and from minor to major fellow of his college. He was an aristocrat, and in his youth behaved as such; he dressed well, and kept a certain distance from his supposed inferiors. This awareness of his position never left him, as a poet or as a priest. In the early summer of 1518 he was given his first university office as praelector or reader in rhetoric, for which he was obliged to lecture four or five mornings each week.

Soon enough Herbert was acting as assistant to the University Orator, a post to which he himself aspired. He wrote to Danvers in the autumn of 1519 that

> the Orators place (that you may understand what it is) is the finest place in the University . . . for the Orator writes all the University Letters, makes all the Orations, be it to

King, Prince, or whatever comes to the University . . . and
such like Gaynesses, which will please a young man well.

It must also have occurred to him that he might advance to high
offices of state, as his predecessors in the oratorical role had done.

It may seem paradoxical that a great religious poet should once
have entertained public ambitions, but it is not so incongruous.
The role and nature of rhetoric were central to Herbert's understanding and thus to his poetry. Cicero's principles in the art of
oratory had been *docere*, *delectare*, *movere*: to teach, to delight and
to persuade. This is precisely what he attempted in his verse as
well as in his public life.

In another letter to Danvers, whom he treated now as a friend
and confidant, Herbert remarked, 'you know, sir, how I am now
setting foot into Divinity, to lay the platform of my future life.' He
was considering his ordination as the natural conclusion of his university career, a step that his mother was urging him to take. The
established Church was his patrimony, his 'portion', the fruit of his
family alliances and university connections. In this period he also
mentioned that he was beset by 'sickness' and had not yet recovered. He was always prone to poor health, and Izaac Walton, his
first biographer, noted that 'he had a body apt to a *Consumption*,
and to *Fevers*, and other infirmities which he judg'd were increas'd
by his Studies.' These 'Studies' were also concerned with the new
science, since Herbert translated into Latin a good part of Francis
Bacon's *The Advancement of Learning*.

At the beginning of 1620 Herbert succeeded in his ambition
and was appointed University Orator, a post that involved a world
of business. Two roads diverged in the dark wood of this world,
the pursuit of divinity and the ambition for public service, and
he may have been uncertain of his choice. There was in fact no
necessary disparity between a life of piety and a life of service, as
Thomas More had proved, but Herbert seems to have been prone

to self-doubt. The notion of ambivalence, or of self-questioning, often enters his poetry. It was a rhetorical stratagem, but it may have been a reflection of his own experience. He consulted one of his mentors, Lancelot Andrewes, now Bishop of Winchester, but no doubt he took the advice that best suited him.

In the spring of 1623 Herbert addressed a 'farewell oration' to James I, who had briefly visited the university. The king was pleased by the sermon, and asked for a copy. In the autumn of that year, Herbert was to give an oration at the University Church on a more difficult occasion. The king's son Charles had just returned from a mission to Spain to obtain the hand in marriage of the Spanish king's daughter. It was not a success, and Charles was incensed by the behaviour of the Spanish authorities. Now he was all for war, while James was all for peace. This was the moment when Herbert delivered his oration to the assembled members and authorities of the university. In it, he walked a fine line with a flourish, delicately praising peace but also congratulating Charles on his ardour and constancy. It was a well-judged performance and could only have increased his reputation in the concentric circles of Court and university.

But that was no longer his purpose. Herbert seems to have lost the appetite for oratory. He delegated some of his work to the Deputy Orator, and in June 1624 he was granted leave of absence 'on account of many businesses away'. Among these 'businesses' was his entry into Parliament for the borough of Montgomery; this was a familial duty rather than a declaration of intent, and he did not remain in that assembly for more than four or five months.

This seems to have been for Herbert a period of reflection and restlessness, of prayer and uncertainty. He hovered for a while between piety and preferment, but at some point, according to Walton, he declared 'his resolution to enter into *Sacred Orders*'. He had been ordained as deacon at the close of 1624; it was the necessary step before priesthood, and barred him from taking any further public employment. The road had been taken. In 1626 he was appointed a canon of Lincoln Cathedral and prebend in the small parish of Leighton Bromswold, Huntingdonshire. These posts involved minimal clerical duties and provided a steady if small income. More significantly, Leighton Bromswold was close to a small community, at Little Gidding, which had been set up by Nicholas Ferrar, a friend and fellow communicant. Little Gidding became, for Herbert, a vision of spirituality in the world. It became a corner of the English soul.

✠

FERRAR AND HERBERT had known each other from the days of university, with Herbert at Trinity and Ferrar at Clare Hall, and resumed their friendship – if it had ever been broken – at the Parliament of 1624, where Ferrar was member for Lymington and Herbert for Monmouth. They had many social and familial ties, but they were more securely bound by their shared piety. Ferrar had removed from London in 1625 as a result of the plague, and had retired with a small group of family and friends to Huntingdonshire. He was ordained the following year but, with an income and a parcel of land, he did not aspire to the priesthood. Instead he established a form of communal living based on the doctrines of the Church of England.

In the ancient manor or estate of Little Gidding, some 12 miles from Huntingdon, was a small church used as a barn for hay, a shepherd's cottage, and a manor house in ruinous condition. Ferrar determined to restore the church and renovate the manor house, so that it might become a common dwelling for those who had travelled with him. The church became an oratory, where the community recited the Litany each day, and Ferrar devised a scheme whereby the rules of a conventional religious house were combined with the exigencies of daily living.

The men and boys (together with three schoolmasters) were at one end of the house and the women at the other; it also contained a school, a medical surgery for the people of the district, and a form of miniature almshouse for poor widows. The household rose at five in winter, and four in summer, so that they might pray, or sing, or read, at the appointed times. Herbert was a constant visitor, and it was he who suggested that Ferrar might institute a 'night watch' or vigil of prayer and meditation in the early hours of the morning. One of the principal tasks of the women lay in the making of 'Harmonies' or 'Concordances', in which parallel passages of sacred books were stitched up or sewn together. And so, as one chronicler of Little Gidding has put it, 'the weeks passed in a grave and cheerful monotony, marked only by recurring Sundays.'

✠

SINCE HERBERT HAD no particular duties in Lincoln or in Leighton Bromswold and, since he was suffering once more from what Walton described as '*Quotidian Ague*', he returned to the house of his mother and stepfather in Chelsea, and to the various houses of his numerous relatives. In these family circumstances, in March 1629, he met and married Danvers's cousin Jane Danvers, who was described by John Aubrey, her relation, as 'a handsome *bona roba* and ingeniose', which may be translated as well rounded with a quick wit. This Chaucerian figure may have been the perfect partner.

In the year after their marriage, Herbert was offered the parish of Bemerton, just west of Salisbury. He was 37 years old when he took this post, and was described by Walton as 'of a stature inclining towards Tallness; his Body was very strait, and so far from being cumbred with too much flesh, that he was lean to an extremity.' Spells of illness and of anxious thought had left their mark, therefore, but he welcomed his future life as a priest.

Walton records that on the day of ordination Herbert

> was shut into Bemerton Church, being left there alone to
> Toll the Bell . . . he staid so much longer than an ordin-
> ary time, before he returned to those Friends that stayed
> expecting him at the Church door, that his Friend Mr
> Woodnot looked in at the Church window, and saw him
> lie prostrate on the ground before the Altar; at which time
> and place (as he after told Dr Woodnot) he set some Rules
> to himself, for the future manage of his life; and then and
> there made a vow, to labour to keep them.

It was a Catholic gesture, but a Protestant resolution.

Walton also made the significant observation that 'there would
be no need for this age to look back into times past for examples
of primitive piety; for they might be all found in the life of George
Herbert.' For Walton, Herbert was the proof that Protestantism
was the true heir of the ancient English Church. It was also the
key to Herbert's own faith.

He had anticipated the priestly role in a small prose treatise,
The Country Parson (1632), in which he sets up the model of the
priest as 'in God's stead [place] to his Parish'. He must 'not only
be a Pastor, but a Lawyer also, and a Physician'. He should be an
orator as well, in the true rhetorical tradition, whose expositions,
exhortations and sermons were intended to draw his congregation
towards the Christian life. After the Elizabethan Settlement the
priest took on a pastoral as well as a spiritual role, if the two can
be distinguished, and was the true leader of the community with
which he had been joined. As a faithful servant of the Church,
Herbert no doubt fulfilled these obligations. He may have taken
on this relatively lowly role in a minor parish as a form of mortification; but, as an aristocrat, he may have been drawn to a life
of service both patrician and paternalistic. Certainly, according

to Walton, he acquired a reputation for saintliness among his parishioners.

The external events of Herbert's last three years at Bemerton were few. He began to restore the parish church, and varied his parochial routine with visits, twice a week, to Salisbury Cathedral, where he attended the choral services. While at Salisbury, according to Walton, 'he would usually sing and play his part at an appointed private Music-meeting.' For him, the metaphor of music ran deep. Man is God's lute.

A story is attached. When Herbert once arrived at music practice it was noted, in no friendly spirit, that he was somewhat dishevelled. He had been helping a poor man with his horse and had given this man some money, as he so often did to the needy. He said, mildly enough, that 'the thought of what he had done would prove music to him at midnight and that the omission of it would have upbraided and made discord in his conscience,' concluding, 'and now let's tune our instruments.'

Herbert's was a life of music and piety, but it was a short one. The constant burden of ill health, with accompanied agues and consumptions, wore him down. Yet he almost embraced sickness, if only because he believed that sickness was the consequence of sin. His poetry recognizes that affliction itself is tutor and pupil, punishment and blessing, cloud and sun. Here is the prayer he offered in response to it: 'Lord, abate my great affliction, or increase my patience: but Lord, I repine not, I am dumb, Lord, before thee, because thou doest it.' This heroic passivity is to be seen in almost all his greatest poems.

✚

THE DATING OF Herbert's poems is not clear, but it is supposed that the majority were composed in the period between diaconate and priesthood. They survive in manuscript copy, but they were not published in his lifetime, and contemporary references suggest that they were circulated within a small group. They may have been collected over a period of some six or seven years, in a process of revision and rearrangement, while the general shape of the proposed volume may already have been clear. A poem of 77 stanzas, 'The Church-Porch', serves as an introduction to the 164 shorter poems of 'The Church', which is in turn followed by a longer poem entitled 'The Church Militant', so that its arrangement is in part determined by the life and worship of the English Church.

The poems might not have been published at all without the work of Ferrar on Herbert's behalf. As Herbert lay close to death, he asked a friend to convey a sheaf of manuscripts to Ferrar, saying that

> he shall find in it a picture of the many spiritual conflicts that have passed betwixt God and my Soul, before I could subject mine to the will of Jesus my Master: in whose service I have now found perfect freedom; and then, if he think it may turn to the advantage of any dejected poor Soul, let it be made publick: if not, let him burn it.

Ferrar did not burn the poetry, but instead gave it due place in a volume that he entitled *The Temple*, a name that might allude to the architecture as well as the tone of the volume.

On first reading, many of Herbert's poems seem distinguished by their clarity and simplicity, but if they are simple in form and manner, they are not simple in meaning:

> O all ye who passe by, behold and see;
> Man stole the fruit, but I must climbe the tree;
> The tree of life to all, but onely me:
>   Was ever grief like mine?

The sorrows of Adam's Fall and Christ's Crucifixion are here commingled in a miracle of association. The same refrain of grief is repeated in 64 stanzas of 'The Sacrifice':

Behold, they spit on me in scornfull wise,
Who by my spittle gave the blind man eies,
Leaving his blindnesse to mine enemies:
                    Was ever grief like mine?

The notion of blindness is transposed from meaning to meaning, from miracle to metaphor, while being sustained by the insistent rhyme. In many poems there is the same pulse of devotion, the same ultimate surge of grace and meaning:

             Teach me thy love to know;
That this new light, which now I see,
             May both the work and workman show:
Then by a sunne-beam I will climbe to thee.

The tone sometimes seems conversational:

Love bade me welcome: yet my soul drew back,
             Guiltie of dust and sinne.
But quick-ey'd Love, observing me grow slack
             From my first entrance in,
Drew nearer to me, sweetly questioning,
             If I lack'd any thing.

A guest, I answer'd, worthy to be here:
             Love said, You shall be he.
I, the unkinde, ungratefull? Ah, my deare,
             I cannot look on thee.

Love took my hand and smiling did reply,
 Who made the eyes but I?

Truth, Lord, but I have marr'd them: let my shame
 Go where it doth deserve.
And know you not, sayes Love, who bore the blame?
 My deare, then I will serve.
You must sit down, sayes Love, and taste my meat:
 So I did sit and eat.

But this is speech raised into music, like the prayers of the faithful. The short and simple words are combined in melody, on the understanding that for Herbert music offered a glimpse into the spiritual world. Love, in the poem, is all-encompassing. It may signify God, or Christ, or the Church itself as the embodiment of Christ on Earth.

This is one of the keys to Herbert's faith, known by the nineteenth century as Anglicanism. The Church of England, as established by the Elizabethan Religious Settlement, was for him the proper arena for the pursuit of the Christian life. It is the setting for his poetry, just as it became the protector of his life. He was eager to restore his own parish church at Bemerton just as, in his poetry, he created an image of the spiritual Church rising above the fallen Earth. *The Temple* reflects 'the spiritual temple'. The most apparently private and intimate of Herbert's confessional poems also have a sure foundation:

Thou art both *Judge* and *Saviour*, *feast* and *rod*,
Cordiall and *Corrosive*: put not thy hand
Into the bitter box; but O my God,
 My God, relieve me!

In this poem, 'Sighs and Grones', the expression of private agony is amplified with reference to Exodus and Psalms from the Old Testament, and to Revelation from the New. The hand that strikes is also the hand that soothes. Throughout Herbert's poetry, the melody of self-examination is mingled with phrases and images from the Bible or the Book of Common Prayer; private meditation is therefore at one with the devotional texts and the traditional expression of the Church. As at a service, the music is in the air, but you cannot tell from what soul it comes. This is in fact the music of Herbert's being. For him, the Church itself – in its rituals and sacraments, in its congregations, even in its architecture – is the paradigm of holy living and holy dying. That is why the order of the poems is in part determined by the sequence of liturgical seasons and festivals, as well as by the daily rhythm of common prayer.

The Temple contains a poem in the shape of wings, and one in the shape of an altar so that, as in church ritual, the form conveys the meaning. There are many poems that are short, melodic and compact, with titles such as 'The Windows':

> Lord, how can man preach thy eternall word?
> He is a brittle, crazie glass:
> Yet in thy temple thou dost him afford
> This glorious and transcendent place,
> To be a window, through thy grace.

and 'Vertue':

> Sweet day, so cool, so calm, so bright,
> The bridall of the earth and skie:
> The dew shall weep thy fall to night
> For thou must die.

and 'Death':

> Death, thou wast once an uncouth hideous thing
> Nothing but bones,
> The sad effect of sadder grones:
> Thy mouth was open, but thou couldst not sing.

The measure of the music, in which poetry and piety combine, is also the measure of the man. The double legacy has recommended Herbert to subsequent generations, and was highly influential among the religious poets of the late seventeenth and eighteenth centuries. He was taken up and imitated by Richard Crashaw and Henry Vaughan. He was read by Charles II during that king's confinement in the 1650s. He was admired and copied by Wesley, celebrated by Coleridge and praised by T. S. Eliot. He inspired Simone Weil and Ralph Vaughan Williams. He has now joined what is sometimes known as the 'canon' of English literature.

✠

IN THE EARLY SPRING of 1633 Herbert's wife and family gathered around his deathbed at the rectory in Bemerton. He was a month short of his fortieth birthday. In this last illness, he asked others to pray with him, using only the prayers of the Church of England, since 'no other prayers are equal to them.'

John Aubrey, whose uncle attended Herbert's funeral on 3 March, recorded that 'he was buryed (according to his own desire) with the singing service for the buriall of the dead, by the singing men of Sarum [Salisbury].' Herbert was laid in an unmarked grave beside the altar of his parish church.

Anthony van Dyck, *William Laud*, *c.* 1638, oil on canvas.

Ten

Religion as Order

William Laud (1573–1645)

King James counselled moderation in religious affairs, as in all aspects of his rule, but he could never have persuaded his son to exercise the same restraint. Charles I, who succeeded to the throne in March 1625, was of a different temper. He was formal and punctilious, as devoted to the ritual of Court as to the ceremonial of religious observance. He remarked that his purpose was 'to establish government and order in our court which from thence may spread with more order through all parts of our kingdom'. He was animated by the belief that the divine right of kings united Church and state in an indissoluble bond of grace and obedience. We can infer with some certainty, then, that he did not look on Puritanism or sectarianism with any favour. His distaste for Nonconformity may be confirmed by the appointment of Richard Montagu, who became the king's favourite chaplain after he issued a tract denouncing the Calvinist doctrine of predestination.

In the year of the king's coronation, 1626, matters of religion were prominent in the affairs of state. The bishops, meeting in convocation, debated the separation between the broadly Puritan members of the Church of England, who followed Calvinist principles, and the group who were already known as 'Arminians'. This was a name unknown in England before 1615, although its tendency was sufficiently understood. It was of Dutch origin, based on the theological writings of Jacobus Arminius, and described those who were opposed to the tenets of Calvinism. The Calvinist doctrine declared that salvation could not be gained by human striving, since the elect and the damned are preordained. God has saved some, and rejected others, for eternity. The Arminians, however, believed that sacramental grace and good works could assist in the cause of redemption. Arminius had written that 'God truly wills the salvation of all men on the condition that they believe.' Salvation was possible for all, not simply for the elect. Divine sovereignty is not incompatible with free will.

There were, of course, various divisions and discriminations within the theological debates, made infinitely more complex by the general air of religious controversy in this period. Arminianism, because of its opposition to Calvinism, was for example sometimes conflated with Roman Catholicism. The argument was reflected by the devils in Milton's *Paradise Lost* who

> reasoned high
> Of Providence, Foreknowledge, Will, and Fate;
> Fixed fate, free will, foreknowledge absolute;
> And found no end, in wandering mazes lost.

The Arminians had been in an ambiguous position during the reign of James I, as a result of that monarch's residual Calvinism. But his son was of a more determined nature. He had a deep aversion to puritanism in all its forms, which he associated with schism and disobedience. The Arminian notion of grace, with all the ceremony and formality its reception implied, was more congenial to him. That was also the nature of his court and part of his understanding of divine kingship. Above all else Charles I desired a well-ordered and disciplined Church, with undeviating principles as well as uniform customs. In this, his purpose was shaped and established by one man who profoundly changed the religious sensibility of England.

✝

WILLIAM LAUD WAS BORN in 1573 at Reading, then the largest town of Berkshire, where the ruins of its great abbey still stand. He was notably disciplined and eager for learning. At the age of sixteen he was enrolled at St John's College, Oxford, which he later described as the place 'where I was bred up'; he became a fellow in 1593, a bachelor of arts in 1594 and a master of arts in 1598. These were the first and familiar steps of a successful scholar. He was later elected a senior fellow of the college and a proctor of the university itself.

The inclination of Laud's career was already evident in the composition of his thesis for the award of his doctorate of divinity, in which he argued that only a bishop could ordain aspiring ministers and that bishops themselves are, by divine right, of a higher order among the clergy. He was by temperament and vocation an exponent of the orthodox Church of England, and in a controversial sermon on Shrove Sunday, 1615, he denounced the Presbyterians for being as divisive as papists. Soon enough he was taken up by the royal court as a loyal and articulate supporter. He was appointed Dean of Gloucester in 1616 and Bishop of St David's five years later.

On the accession of Charles I in 1625 Laud advanced further into the warmth of royal approval, particularly in his close association with the new king's 'favourite', the Duke of Buckingham. Only a week after James's death, Laud presented to the duke a list of prominent churchmen marked either with an 'O' or a 'P' to signify 'orthodox' or 'puritan'. Thus could the established Church be divided.

In 1626 Laud was appointed to be Dean of the Chapel Royal, and in the summer of that year he delivered a sermon asserting that the king's person was sacred and his office guarded by God. The new king himself participated in the religious debate. When a Calvinist minister preached a sermon in defence of predestination, the king told him to leave the matter alone 'because it was too high for the people's understanding'. After 1628 no Calvinist was allowed to preach at Paul's Cross. A joke circulated on the nature of Arminian beliefs. Question: 'What do the Arminians hold?' Answer: 'All the best livings in England'.

Laud was appointed Bishop of Bath and Wells before being translated to London in 1628; he reached the summit of preferment in August 1633, when he became Archbishop of Canterbury. He could now pursue with vigour his policy of imposing conformity and uniformity on the churches of the realm. He was intent on formal prayer and adoration, with the full panoply of ceremony and ritual as the setting for worship. He said later that these were 'the hedge that fence the substance of religion from all the indignities which profaneness and sacrilege too commonly put upon it'.

This became known as 'Laudianism', a better term than Arminianism since it encompassed what Laud described as 'the beauty of holiness', a phrase that might also have been applied to certain forms of Anglicanism in later centuries and reached its apogee in the Tractarianism of the nineteenth century. The English soul has room enough for those who delight in formal ritual, public ceremony and sacred spaces. Candles and incense, ordained speech and gesture, stained glass and embroidered vestments were for Laud almost the prerequisites to prayer and worship. The emphasis on grace as a means of salvation entailed an emphasis on the sacraments, and so on the formal rituals that surrounded them. The communion table, for example, was better conceived as an altar. The focus was on communal ritual rather than the individual conscience.

In the troubled and divisive days of the late 1620s and 1630s this appetite for Laudianism was certain to provoke dissent and abuse. There were more than enough Calvinists in the Church of England, and elsewhere, to rail against this new uniformity. In the

Parliament of 1629 its members resolved that the 'true religion' was that established by Elizabeth and that 'we do reject the sense of the Jesuits and the Arminians'; the connection was being made between Laud and incipient Catholicism. A decree was passed that anyone who tried to introduce popery or Arminianism into the kingdom would be considered a capital enemy and would pay the price of treason. Yet in truth Laudianism was not popery. Laud was no Catholic, covert or otherwise. He had told the king that 'the papists were the most dangerous subjects in the kingdom.' He was as intolerant of Mariolatry, and what he considered to be the superstitions of the Roman Catholics, as he was of the zealotry and intolerance of the Puritans. Yet, whatever Laud himself believed, his teachings resulted in what must have seemed to many a full-blown return to 'Papist' practice.

Laud was also aware of the doctrine of apostolic succession. He wrote that 'the Roman Church and the Church of England are but two distinct members of that Catholic Church which is spread over the face of the earth'; this came to be one of the key principles of the established Church. He wanted only to restore the worship of the ancient English Church, and '*stare super antiquas vias*', 'stand on the old paths', so that the true Church could be recovered and the ages of English devotion bound together with natural piety. But this was not a period for subtle theology or fine judgement. The political antagonism between king and Parliament was rising to a fever, and on 10 March 1629 Charles abruptly announced the dissolution of the Commons. It would not meet again for eleven years.

In its absence Charles began to set up the machinery of personal government or autocratic rule in which he would be guided partly by the help and advice of Archbishop Laud. At the end of 1629 Laud composed 'A Declaration on the Articles of Religion', in which it was ordained that all clerics must wholly subscribe to the Thirty-Nine Articles, which would in effect prohibit any discussion by ministers, Calvinist or otherwise, on such matters as predestination. He had said of the subject that it was 'unmasterable in this life'. He had now aroused much hatred, and a paper was issued in the London streets declaring, 'Laud, look to thyself, be assured thy life is sought. As thou art the fountain of all wickedness, repent thee of thy monstrous sins before thou be taken out of the earth.'

It might be noted here that Laud was of small stature, a fact that may have endeared him to the king, who stood at five feet tall; he was of a red complexion, inclined to irritability and impatient of contradiction. He was known by some of the puritanically inclined as 'the shrimp', 'the little urchin' and 'the little meddling hocus-pocus'. He continually feared conspiracies against his life or career – not without cause – and was highly superstitious. He brooded over his dreams. Yet these may have been the defects of a character who was diligent and perhaps over-cautious; certainly no one could question his sincerity or his personal honesty.

In October 1633 Laud and the king caused to be republished James I's *Declaration of Sports,* first pronounced fifteen years earlier, which had permitted entertainment and recreation on the Sabbath. May games and maypoles, Whit ales and Morris dances, vaulting and archery were still to be allowed, in defiance of the godly protests about the profanation of the sacred day. For the Calvinists and the stricter sorts of Protestant, the *Declaration* was a poisoned text set to destroy true religion and bring disaster upon the nation. In the same period Laud ordained that the plain communion table of wood be replaced by a stone altar and positioned at the eastern end of the church, where it was to be railed off from the worshippers. It had been returned to its former place as the site of sacramental prayer, in a clear rebuttal of Puritan scruples. In similar fashion it was decreed that fonts be placed at the southwest door of the church. The beauty of holiness was contingent upon the beauty of ritual. Laud appointed only anti-Calvinist bishops, and initiated a series of 'visitations' to various churches for the discovery of clerical disobedience or Nonconformity. In his visitation of the Lincoln diocese, for example, Laud determined that ministers should wear the surplice during the service and make the sign of the cross at baptism, that the people should bow at the name of Jesus and receive communion while kneeling.

The reaction to these measures was no less strong. They strengthened the resistance of those who believed that ceremonial was ungodly, so that many orthodox Calvinists were pressed into stricter Puritanism or even sectarianism. Oliver Cromwell, towards the end of his life, recalled that Laud and his allies had wished 'to innovate upon us in matters of religion, and so to innovate as to eat out the core and power and heart and life of all religion'. It had to be resisted. A secret network of conventicles and discussion groups had been established in London and elsewhere; they communicated with one another by means of manuscript tracts and sermon notes, as well as by conferences and 'conversations' behind closed doors. It was a world of fasts, prayer meetings and scriptural discussions 'waiting for the day'.

That day would soon come. The king's waning fortunes, with his disastrous imposition of a new Book of Common Prayer upon the Scots without the approval of the Kirk, as well as his ill-considered defiance of Parliament, brought down Laud with him. On 18 December 1640 the archbishop was impeached for high treason by the Commons, in a debate in which he was described as 'the roote and ground of all our miseries and calamities . . . the sty of all pestilential filth that hath infected the State and Government'. He was accused of subverting the laws of the nation and of attempting to bring in arbitrary government; he was charged with trying to destroy the established religion and to enter the embrace of the Pope in Rome. He had attempted to extirpate the true and reformed Churches, and fostered a war with Scotland. There was also the charge that, by his machinations, he had separated the king from his people.

Laud was impeached for high treason in December 1640, and consigned to the Tower in the following March. The ultimate verdict was not in doubt, although the sentence was long in coming. He remained in confinement for almost four years, broken and alone, and was not brought to trial until March 1644. That lasted for seven months, but could not come to a conclusion; Laud was quick in his defence, and the prosecution weak or inconsistent. It was clear that the charges against him would not provide enough evidence to prove treason. Instead the archbishop was convicted by an act of attainder, in which Parliament takes on the power of a court of law so that punishment can be given without trial, and he was taken to Tower Hill, where he was beheaded on 10 January 1645.

Laud's execution and subsequently that of his royal master were significant occasions when the two versions of Protestant belief in England came into open confrontation. There were two separate paths, one leading towards Puritanism and Nonconformity and the other towards conformity and orthodoxy. It can be said with some certainty that the imminent Civil War was a war of religions.

Eleven

Religion as Sect

Thomas Helwys (1575–1616) and the Baptists,
John Lilburne (1615–1657) and the Levellers,
Gerrard Winstanley (1609–1676) and the Diggers,
Abiezer Coppe (1619–1672?) and the Ranters, Lodowicke
Muggleton (1609–1698) and the Muggletonians

As early as the 1630s it had become clear that Calvinism could no longer claim to be as central to the English Church as it had been; the rise of Arminianism, and the attempt by Charles I at religious absolutism, had proved that. But what might appear in its place? The Church in England seemed to harbour two types of Protestantism vying for supremacy and, in the time of civil war, this took on a political and military aspect.

The period immediately before open warfare between king and Parliament was one in which antagonisms became more bitter, differences more pronounced, and debate more serious. The argument took some of its heat from different attitudes towards religion. Ought the state to impose one form of religion, or should the free will of the individual be supreme? In matters touching the Presbyterian and the separated Churches, a related question was posed. What was the role of the individual congregation in any presumed national regime of faith? Was each one free to follow its own path?

The appetite for news was fed by pamphlets and tracts passed eagerly from hand to hand, most of them predicting great changes in Church and state, and they were joined by what were described in one satirical pamphlet as 'upstart booksellers, trotting mercuries and bawling hawkers'. Wandering stationers and ballad-mongers would call out 'come buy a new book, a new book, newly come forth!' This mixture of information and opinion was compounded by plays, processions, ballads, playing cards, graffiti, petitions and prints.

Tracts with such titles as 'A Dream, or News from Hell' and 'The Schismatic Stigmatised' were sold for a penny or twopence. The latter pamphlet attacked the dissenting ministers, of whatever persuasion, who crowded in Westminster and elsewhere:

> And instead of orthodox divines, they set up all kinds of mechanics, as shoe-makers, cobblers, tailors and glovers . . . these predicant mendicants and lawless lads do affect an odd kind of gesture in their pulpits, vapouring and throwing heads, hands and shoulders this way, and that way, puffing and blowing, grinning and gurning.

It used to be said the English were always disposed to assert their right to their own opinions, and this was nowhere more true than in the assertion of Nonconformity and separatism. The parishes of London, in particular, were now filled with Dissenters and sectarians. The conventional clergy were often derided or abused in the streets with 'there goes a Jesuit, a Baal-priest, an abbey-lubber, one of Canterbury's whelps!'

The separatists, otherwise known as schismatics or sectarians, had first come to public attention in the middle of the sixteenth century, but by the early 1640s they had become a force to be noticed. One pamphlet described them as once a few who 'crept in corners', but who were now like 'the Egyptian locust covering the land'. They were in fact the culmination of an English spiritual tradition. A bishop told the House of Lords in December 1641 that in London there were some eighty conventicles 'of several sectaries, instructed by guides fit for them, cobblers, tailors, felt-makers and such like trash'. In the same year, it was said that religious matters had 'become the common discourse and table-talk in every tavern and ale-house'. At a time when king and Parliament were in open and bitter division, sectarian preachers and their congregations were considered by many to be a sign of moral chaos that might lead to the end of days. Censorship and central administration had broken down; anything and everything could be said with impunity. Anti-clericalism and scepticism were in the air. For those with an appetite for novelty and reform, this was a period of freedom, while those who felt threatened by change and dissolution retreated further into orthodoxy.

In the early 1640s a diversity of sects and faiths emerged in the generally unsettled state of the nation, from the relatively unknown Divorcers and Soul-Sleepers to the Ranters, Muggletonians, Fifth Monarchy Men, Grindletonians, Familists, Diggers, Levellers, Socinians, Philadelphians, Seekers and Sweet Singers of Israel, all of whom could in turn be confused or conflated with the Quakers, Particular Baptists, General Baptists, Congregationalists, Independents and non-specific Dissenters. However, beneath this turbid flow the majority of the English followed the same beaten path of belief or unbelief as their forebears.

Oliver Cromwell himself set the tone for religious pluralism. A reference should therefore be made to the Independents, the group to which Cromwell belonged. In spirit and in freedom from organization, they were closest to the Congregationalists. They did not avow any particular or formal creed, beyond the broadly based Puritanism of individual congregations or 'gathered churches', and preached toleration of all independent sects in the hope that they might exist in concord. The authority of private conscience and liberty of religion were, in theory, the fundamental attributes of a Christian polity.

From Cromwell's public speeches and private letters it is clear that he believed implicitly in the power of divine will to guide the actions of men. He waited on what he called 'Providence'. He prayed for a sign to show him the way in any great endeavour. He wrote that 'we follow the Lord that goeth before,' and sought for the divine meaning in the events occurring around him. His victories on the field were the blessings of God. Since he had a private sense of what he called 'true knowledge' or 'life eternal', he was impatient of religious debate and doctrinal niceties. What did they matter before the overwhelming power and presence of God? He once said, 'I had rather that Mahometanism were admitted among us than that one of God's children should be persecuted.' This toleration of Nonconformity would soon create a permanent division between Independents and Presbyterians, and was the setting for the rise of manifold sects. Yet the instincts of Cromwell himself would become more rigid as opposition to his rule mounted. Asked to explain why he had ordered the execution of a female Ranter, he said merely, 'I thought her so vile a creature as to be unworthy to live.'

✠

THE EMERGENCE OF the Brownists and the Congregationalists, in the 1580s, is generally considered to mark the advent of the separated or 'gathered' churches in England. But one of the most significant of these new-found or rediscovered faiths was that of the Baptists. The first Baptist church in England was established in Spitalfields, just beyond the eastern limits of the City of London, in 1612, under the guidance of Thomas Helwys. Of Helwys himself little is known. He was born in 1575, at Broxtowe Hall near Retford in Nottinghamshire, and in 1593 he was admitted to Gray's Inn, one of the legal Inns of Court in London. That was the year in which Henry Barrow, one of the first Puritan separatists, was executed, and since the young Helwys was reported to have been associated with a group of Dissenters, the death no doubt confirmed his dissatisfaction with the established Church.

Helwys married Joan Ashmore in December 1595, and together they raised seven children, but they were by no means an orthodox family. In 1606 they were cited for not receiving communion in their parish church, and a few months later they were accused of non-attendance. In the following year Helwys arranged for a group of separatists – among them another leader of the emergent Baptists, John Smyth – to make their way to the freer settings of Amsterdam and Leiden. It was said that he 'above all, either guides or others, furthered this passage into strange countries; and if any brought oars he brought sails'. He then purchased an empty bakehouse and courtyard beside the River Amsel, in northern Holland, where over the next two years he settled other small Baptist families or communities. It was there that the most potent of all Baptist ceremonies took place, when Smyth baptized himself and then baptized Helwys. It was the beginning of a new congregation and a new faith.

Some separatists and reformed Puritans had followed Smyth to Amsterdam in the summer and autumn of 1608, but, as so often happened in small sects, divisions arose between Helwys and Smyth over the organization and practice of their mutual faith. Helwys and some followers returned to England in the winter of 1612–13 to bring the new faith home, and a small congregation was established in Spitalfields, London; Helwys believed that the simplest member of his church was as well versed in spiritual matters as the most learned, and so inaugurated the full democracy of Baptist assemblies. He was arrested, however, soon after he had informed King James in writing that the monarch 'hath no power over ye immortal souls of his subjects to make lawes and ordinances for them and to set spiritual lawes over them'. This might be considered blasphemy, or sedition, or both. Little else is known of Helwys, except that he died in 1616, but he is worthy of notice as the first organizer of the Baptist faith in England.

He was also the first proponent of adult or believer's baptism as a sure token of faith. Like many separatists he was strictly following the precepts of the New Testament, where it was taken as a sacred example that baptism followed an avowal of true faith and the full confession of sins; this was the way of the Apostles, and it could not be changed to become a bauble or even blessing for newborn infants. Only adult baptism could distinguish a true servant of Christ, and only the rebaptized could be the foundation of a lawful Church. If the Church of England was a false Church, as the Baptists believed, then its baptism was also false. Smyth had said in his personal confession of faith, dated provisionally to 1610, 'baptism is the external sign of the remission of sins, of dying and of being made alive again, and therefore does not belong to infants.'

The Baptists were first known, maliciously or mistakenly, as Anabaptists; this was the name of a Dutch sect that, like the Lollards of a previous century, had acquired a reputation for religious subversion. Their control of the German city of Münster for a brief period had led to claims that they encouraged polygamy and wished to ban the private ownership of money. This may have been true of their more fanatical adherents, but in general the Anabaptists pursued a less antagonistic faith. They did believe, however, that they should remain apart from the world, and rejected the idea of civic government and a state Church. There is no doubt that certain elements of the Anabaptist faith did enter Baptist practice, even though the English Baptists forcefully denied any such connection. What happened was in fact indicative of English spirituality and indeed of English culture in general. Certain principles or elements of European origin were borrowed before being adapted to English methods and manners. It was a process of slow assimilation.

This was certainly true of the first English Baptists, who owed as much to Continental tradition as to the segregated national churches of Puritan persuasion. Their congregations were gathered in the spirit of communal belief, animated and inspired by preaching, prophesying and prayer. In this they did not differ markedly from other sectarian assemblies except, perhaps, in their successful growth. There is an early reference in a book of 1608: 'I know some of them Teachers, and specially him that is said to have baptised one of their children in a Barn.' By 1620 the new Baptists were to be found in 'divers counties', and in 1654 a general assembly met in London to coordinate as many as 250 churches and congregations that now flourished in the Midlands, the southeast and London. They generally comprised what might be called the 'middling sort': craftsmen and tradesmen, among them weavers and tailors, bakers and glovers, cobblers and ironmongers. These were independent artisans who were accustomed to follow their own judgement and opinions without the meddling of any parson or magistrate.

But, as in all religious societies, there emerged fundamentally different principles of faith. By the 1640s a division existed between 'General Baptists', who believed in general redemption on the understanding that Christ died for all humankind, and 'Particular Baptists', who upheld the Calvinist doctrine that he had died for the elect. Disagreement on such a fundamental proposition led to dissension, and dissension led to division. There were now two kinds of Baptist. Further argument occurred between those who favoured total immersion in the water of baptism and those who preferred partial dipping or 'washing with water' in the familiar manner. Immersion proved to be the most sacred choice, but as a result certain Baptists were beset by scandals and rumours that they conducted their ceremonies in rivers in the dead of night and that human contact in water promoted immorality. Nevertheless, the Baptist movement survived by sheer force of principle and clear doctrine, and is one of the few sectarian faiths to remain in the twenty-first century.

✛

FROM THE WIDE CONSTITUENCY of the General Baptists emerged another group who became known, at first maliciously, as the Levellers. They have been described as representing the political dimension of the Baptist movement, but in this period politics and religion cannot be separated; both are part of the ebb and flow of belief in a time of confusion. Religious liberty and civil liberty were in fact aligned. As John Owen, a Congregationalist theologian and later confidant of Cromwell, put it in a sermon,

> the peculiar light of this generation is that discovery which the Lord hath made to his people, of the mystery of Civil and Ecclesiastical Tyranny. The opening, unravelling and revealing the Antichristian interest, interwoven and coupled together, in civil and spiritual things . . . is the great discovery of these days.

One of the principal adherents to the Baptists and to the Leveller cause, for example, was John Lilburne, who wrote from a cell in the Tower of London that the divine power 'gave no lordship, nor sovereignty, to any of Adam's posterity, by will and prerogative, to rule over his brethren-men'. This was the language of an eminent Dissenter and Nonconformist.

Lilburne was born in the northeast of England in 1615, and seems to have been first educated at the Royal Free Grammar School in Newcastle, but he was not destined for a genteel or scholarly life. In 1630 he was apprenticed to a clothmaker in Candlewick Street, London, an area that had already become a centre of sectarian religious dissent. From the beginning, his allegiances become clear. He studied the Bible and John Foxe's *Book of Martyrs*, and attended a separatist congregation in the vicinity of his daily work. At the end of his apprenticeship, in 1636, he experienced what he considered to be a spiritual awakening, and from that time forward he became fully engaged in the sectarian cause.

Soon enough Lilburne became acquainted with the leading members of the conventicles, and in 1636 or 1637 he sailed to Holland in order to publish sectarian texts that were considered in England to be heretical or blasphemous. On his return to England he was arrested and arraigned before the Star Chamber, but refused the conventional oath to give true testimony. He was then sentenced to be whipped and placed in the pillory before being consigned to the Fleet Prison, an ordeal he survived in the belief that 'my God in whom I did trust was higher and stronger than my selfe.' He was confined for two years, during which period he was able to write sectarian tracts that condemned the bishops and institutions of a national Church in favour of separate and segregated companies of the elect few. With the aid of Cromwell's first speech in Parliament, he was released from confinement in November 1640, whereupon he married and became a brewer, even as he continued his sectarian polemic and agitation.

In the climate of crisis, when king and Parliament recruited their opposing forces, it is not surprising that Lilburne followed his religious principles with active engagement. In 1642 he became a captain of foot in the Parliamentarian army, with which he fought at Edgehill and Marston Moor. His military career came to an end in 1645, however, when he refused to subscribe to the 'solemn league and covenant' demanded by the Presbyterians of the New Model Army. For Lilburne a national Presbyterian Church was no better than the orthodoxy that had preceded it. To him, a convinced separatist, it was anathema. Such a national dispensation could be acknowledged only if 'they leave my Conscience free to the Law and Will of my Lord and King'. This commitment to Christ alone was out of the question, so he left the army and returned to his wife in London.

This was the beginning of Lilburne's fierce conflict with the Presbyterians and his close association with the Baptists, Independents and other congregations. He became what one opponent called 'the darling of the sectaries', and in this period he formulated the demands that were to become the social and political platform of the Levellers. He became embroiled in a series of struggles with the established powers of the House of Lords, the purged House of Commons and even certain officers of the New Model Army, and was confined for long periods in Newgate Prison and in the Tower of London. His cause was championed by many thousands of London citizens, and by the sectaries he defended, so that the principles of the Levellers had begun to circulate among the people. It was also evident that the Leveller philosophy of equality and religious toleration had already infused the army itself, and in the summer of 1646 a pamphlet entitled 'A Remonstrance of Many Thousand Citizens' pursued the cause of religious reform and social freedom. This comes close to the central principles of radical sectarianism and religious reform, and it is not at all surprising that the most prominent of the Levellers were educated in the belief that the orthodox Church was an obstruction to the truth that redemption came through Christ alone.

This was the context for their first 'Agreement of the People', published in 1647, which among its proposals urged freedom of conscience and freedom of worship for sects and separatists. It stated that 'matters of religion and the ways of God's worship are not at all entrusted to any human power.' It was argued that a group of believers, small or large, could constitute itself as a 'gathered church' with its own covenant to bind and direct it. The Levellers also desired to repeat this exercise on a national scale, with England as a 'gathered' nation bound by covenant with God. In the 'Agreement' they argued that after the defeat of the king 'all legal Authority in England was broke', and that a new covenant should guarantee the full rights of the people. It can be said that the Levellers were the first of the sects to be truly democractic.

It is therefore significant that some members of the New Model Army were imbued with sectarian piety, since Lilburne and the Levellers maintained that religious imperatives were also political principles. Yet, as the political situation changed with the rise of the army grandees in the Council of State, the Levellers began to lose influence. 'We were before ruled by King, Lords and Commons,' one wrote, 'now by a General, a Court Martial and House of Commons, and we pray you what is the difference.' They were accused of wishing to abolish private property and the entire social hierarchy. In truth, their demands were more specific but no less powerful, with the plea for legal reform, for the redistribution of electoral boundaries, for a larger franchise, for the lifting of all censorship and for a revision of the system of taxation to favour the poor. Most interesting, perhaps, was their demand for a written constitution. But if they are deemed to anticipate later movements of political protest, the danger of anachronism becomes evident. It might be more pertinent to suggest that they applied the theology of General Baptists to the secular sphere. Their central claim was for liberty of conscience, with the dissolution of external religious authority. They believed that the institution of the Commonwealth, and subsequently of Cromwell's Protectorate, was no more than a new system of authority that would in time become a tyranny. They had been betrayed by those in whom they had placed their trust.

In the spring of 1649 Lilburne and other prominent Levellers were arrested after the publication of a pamphlet entitled 'England's New Chains', which called for an association between 'the People' and 'soldiers and others'. Lilburne came before a committee made up of members of the Council of State, and was sent to the Tower to await trial for high treason. Once more the clamour rose in London to release him, with his supporters wearing ribbons of sea-green to mark their loyalty. Lilburne was taken to the Guildhall for trial in October 1649, but, to general surprise and popular jubilation, he was found not guilty of any treason. He and three other Levellers were released on 8 November and were escorted to a dinner of celebration in a tavern on Fish Street.

Lilburne's official tribulations were not over, however; he had a strong and rebarbative character that seemed to delight in dispute and confrontation. Throughout his adult life he had attacked every government and authority set above him, and he was not about to relinquish that stance. He was in and out of court, in exile and in prison, accusing his accusers, defying the authorities, confronting his enemies and condemning those who opposed him for corruption and fraudulent hypocrisy.

But Lilburne was no longer a Leveller. That particular sect had all but dissipated after the arrest of their members in 1649. Many now drifted into covert opposition or uncomfortable conformity. Lilburne himself became a Quaker. He remained true to the principles of sectarianism and religious separatism, and to the ideals of conscience and religious liberty, to the end of his life. He died in August 1657, and it is reported that 4,000 people escorted his coffin to the New Churchyard in Moorfields.

✠

WHAT MAY BE DESCRIBED as the gradual fragmentation of Protestantism into varied and disparate sects was evident throughout the seventeenth century. Despite the fact that these separated faiths never did command general or popular support, and that moderate orthodoxy had become the foundation of the Church of England, local and particular creeds continued to spring up in sects wild or tame. With the demise of the Levellers, for example, there emerged the Diggers, under the guidance of Gerrard Winstanley.

In the second week of April 1649, a group of five men gathered by some uncultivated land on St George's Hill in Weybridge,

Surrey, some 17 miles south of London. A letter of complaint to the Council of State, set up after the execution of Charles I, reported that 'they began to dig on that side of the Hill next to Campe Close, and sowed the ground with parsnips, and carrots, and beans.' They came back with increasing numbers on the following two days, when they proceeded to burn some ten acres of heath, 'which is a very great prejudice to the town'. Two days later twenty or thirty arrived and continued the digging, at which time they invited 'all to come in and help them and promised them meat, drink and clothes'. The writer added, 'it is feared that they have some design in mind.' In this supposition he was correct. That design came from the suggestion of their informal leader, Gerrard Winstanley, who hoped and believed that the land of England might become 'a common treasury of all, without respect of persons', such persons including the landowners themselves.

Winstanley seems the most unlikely proponent of what was one of the most radical sects in that period of confusion in the mid-seventeenth century. He was born in Wigan on 19 October 1609, but little or nothing is known of his formative years. He first comes to light in 1630 as an apprentice of a dealer in cloth, Sarah Gater, who worked in the London parish of St Michael Cornhill. The main business of Wigan was cloth, and Winstanley's father was engaged in that trade; Gater may well have been a relative and connected to Wigan itself. Winstanley stayed with her until 1638, when he started as a clothier on his own account, and became a member of the Merchant Taylors' Company.

Winstanley recalled that he was then 'a strict goer to Church, as they call it, and a hearer of Sermons', who 'never questioned what they spake'. He was one of the large majority who were faithful to the orthodox Church of England, in other words, and in 1640 he was married in conventional fashion to Susan King. It should have been a time of prosperity for a London tradesman, but the fissure between king and Parliament, and the succeeding civil war, rendered his trade precarious and his future prosperity uncertain.

The Winstanleys therefore moved from London to the safer environs of Cobham in Surrey, where the King family owned an estate. Winstanley complained later that 'by the cheating sons in the thieving art of buying and selling and by the burdens of, and for, the Souldiery in the beginning of the war, I was beaten out both of estate and trade,' and that he was compelled 'to live a Countrey-life'.

The change of circumstances may have induced in Winstanley a profound dissatisfaction with the world as he knew it, and with the conventions of religious belief in which he had been raised. He was no longer convinced that spiritual truth and authority were to be found in the ministers of the Church or in the scriptures, and affirmed instead that true faith could spring only from the acknowledgement of God's indwelling spirit in each man and woman. It is difficult to trace the path of his belief, but it has been surmised that he moved from the orthodox Church to the Baptist faith before pursuing the further reaches of millenarianism. In this he embodies the sectarian and separatist imperatives of the 1640s.

From 1648 onwards Winstanley published a series of texts through the agency of a London bookseller who favoured radical writings. In the first of them, *The Mysterie of God, concerning the Whole Creation, Mankinde,* he plots the course of divine and human history with its culmination in the awareness of God within every person. Restoration after the original Fall of Man can come only from 'free discovery within'. He also called for the dissolution of the entire legal system, and the abandonment of a national Church. His creed was inspired by what he believed to have been some revelation or mystical understanding. In a text of 1649, *The New Law of Righteousness*, he recalls that 'as I was in a trance not long since, divers matters were present to my sight, which must not here be related. Likewise I heard these words. Worke together.

Eat bread together; declare this all abroad.' He was tapping into the English visionary tradition that runs from Julian of Norwich to William Blake and beyond.

In particular Winstanley invested great significance in the so-called possession of the land. This may in part have been inspired by local preoccupations, since the area of Cobham was beset by division between landlords and tenants, but it was part of a wider vision of longing and belonging. The earth, the land or soil, was owned by humankind and not by any proprietor. As long as the land was divided according to 'mine' and 'thine', 'the common people shall never have their liberty; nor the land ever freed from troubles, oppressions and complainings,' which will provoke the wrath of the Lord. Private property, buying and selling, were anathema; pride and greed should be replaced by community and fellowship that would create 'Onenesse'. Winstanley did not call himself or his followers 'Diggers', but rather 'true Levellers'. They were concerned not so much with the liberty of the individual conscience, as were Lilburne and his associates, as with a version of communal utopia. Winstanley also wrote of 'the true Levelling which Christ would work at his most glorious appearance'. This was a religious, not a political, movement. It was one of the few attempts at what we might now call communism with a spiritual or otherworldly mission, anticipated by William Langland's late fourteenth-century poem *Piers Plowman*. It is a proper and perceptible aspect of the English soul. It is to be found in writers as diverse as John Clare and Thomas Hardy, for whom the land is sacred.

The Digger experiment itself was a failure. After their encampment on St George's Hill, its adherents were beset by angry interventions from local labourers and landowners, as well as official and military disquiet. Many of the Diggers had come from Winstanley's own parish of Cobham, but the residents of the neighbouring parish of Walton dragged them to their local church and beat them. A few days later, 'above a hundred rude [common] people' broke their spades and hoes before marching them into the parish lockhouse. A few of their improvised dwellings were burned or pulled down.

Other small colonies of Diggers were soon confronted by better-organized attacks from the local authorities, and were pursued by court actions for trespass and by economic boycotts in the areas close to them; some of them were confined to the White Lion Prison in Southwark. The New Model Army had at first followed a policy of benign neglect towards these fellow radicals, but turned against them when they believed that property rights were threatened. Nevertheless, groups of Diggers emerged in other counties, made up largely of local inhabitants, and the essential message of communitarianism spread among the Baptists and the Quakers.

Winstanley finished his last tract, *The Law of Freedom in a Platform*, in November 1651, in which he outlined the nature of the commonwealth he had wished to create. In this text he reiterated his profound belief that 'God dwells in every visible work or body,' close to a pantheism that most of his contemporaries did not accept. But he wrote no more, and in the summer of the following year he returned to Cobham and to conventional farming. He might have been exhausted by the years of dispute and hostility, since he took up conventional parish duties as an overseer of the poor and a churchwarden. After the restoration of Charles II he conformed to the Church of England. By 1665, after the death of his wife, he married again and with his new partner returned to London, where he resided in the parish of St Giles-in-the-Fields and took up business as a corn chandler. The light had failed. It is evident that he became a Quaker, and in 1676, brought down by 'gripes & vomiting', he died and was buried in the Quaker burial ground of Long Acre. But he died in body and not in spirit. His vision of communal possession and the joint ownership of common land was one of the enduring legacies of the mid-seventeenth century.

✠

THERE WERE LESS FAMILIAR sects that emerged in the same period, among them the Grindletonians and the Seekers. The Grindletonians were named after the parish of Grindleton in the West Riding of Yorkshire, where its curate, Roger Brearley, formed a small congregation in the belief that to the pure all things are pure and that 'the Christian assured can never commit gross sin.' It was not a new doctrine, but it is evidence that local groups and local convictions could spring up anywhere.

The Grindletonians in turn were said to spring from the Familists or the Family of Love. These were in a sense a secret congregation among the larger communion of Protestants, who practised outward conformity and deference to external authority while holding diverse and unorthodox beliefs. They had begun as a loose group or groups in the 1560s, but had grown into something close to a 'family' united by ties of love and faith.

The faithful believed themselves to be infused with the spirit of Christ, and could commit no sin. This was to be 'godded with God'. The perfection of the true believer was the perfection of Christ within him, and the laws of Moses and of human government were not valid. The true believer was maintained in a natural state of grace that would lead to salvation. Prayers had no significance, and the Sabbath need not be observed. Men and women might attain, by the indwelling of the divine spirit, the innocence that prevailed before the Fall. The gifts of nature come from God's bounty, and so should be shared equally. The critics of this congregation suggested that that last precept was also applied to their wives. In practice the Familists were characterized by humility, meekness and toleration in a fractious world that was often bereft of these qualities.

The Seekers seem to have been the heirs of some of these beliefs. They were a loose group who asserted that no existing

Church, of whatever persuasion, could enshrine the grace and power that Christ had given to his Apostles. The visible churches were to be shunned as sinful and the faithful must wait for God to provide a new race of apostles. All existing rituals, ordinances and practices are invalid. One of their proponents, William Erbery, declared, 'in that apostasy we now are, we cannot company with men, no not with saints, in spiritual worship but we shall commit spiritual whoredom with them.' You must not enter their churches. You must not worship their God. You must sit still and wait.

The Seekers represent a fervent, and sometimes almost desperate, spirituality in the face of religious conflict and confusion. They represent a religion of the spirit rather than a religion of scripture, and in that sense are to be sharply distinguished from the mainstream of Protestantism.

✠

THE MOST PROMINENT of the radical sects, for a while, were the Ranters, whose leading light was Abiezer Coppe. He was born in Warwick on Sunday 30 May 1619, and baptized two days later at the local church of St Mary's. From his early youth, by his own account, he was marked out by zealous devotion, together with prayers and fasting; at the age of thirteen he began to compile a catalogue of his sins, and two years later, while at the town's free school, he began to study the Greek New Testament. Such a conscientious young man might go far, and very soon afterwards he was admitted to All Souls College in Oxford, before moving on to Merton College in that city.

But Coppe's time at university was relatively short and, perhaps for financial reasons, he left Oxford without a degree in order to become an unlicensed minister or preacher in his native town. In 1644 he was enlisted as chaplain to the military officer in charge of the Parliamentary forces in that area, where he became known as a vehement proponent of the need for 'Re-baptizing, and

Independency, and was a sharp Reproacher of the Ministry'. He had become a sectarian of Baptist or even Anabaptist tendency. As a result of his public 'rebaptizing', he was sentenced to close imprisonment for fourteen weeks.

In 1647 Coppe experienced a conversion, or revelation, that led him away from all forms of religious observance. In his later text *A Fiery Flying Roll* (1649), he recounts that he lay 'trembling, sweating, and smoking (for the space of half an houre)' in the presence of the divine. In this trance he was promised salvation, but not before he had imbibed a 'bitter cup; whereupon (being filled with exceeding amazement) I was throwne into the belly of hell'. These visions endured 'for the space of foure dayes and nights, without intermission', in which period 'the life was taken out of the body (for a season)' as if 'a man with a great brush dipt in whiting, should with one stroke wipe out, or sweep off, a picture upon a wall'. One of his great strengths lay in the power of his writing.

Coppe was altogether changed, and began to promulgate a doctrine that was considered by most of his contemporaries to be worse than blasphemy. The man of true faith, he said, cannot sin and is therefore at liberty to indulge in all fleshly desires. In *A Second Fiery Flying Roule* (also 1649) he declared that 'it's meat and drink to an Angel (who knows none evill, no sin) to sweare a full mouth'd oath.' The Oxford memoirist Anthony à Wood reported that Coppe would preach 'stark naked' by day and lie drunk with a woman 'stark naked' at night.

In his writing and in his actions, Coppe began to collect a body of followers who were known as 'the Attainers', 'Mad Crew' or, most pertinently, 'Ranters'. He was the principal member of a Ranter group that called itself 'My One Flesh'. The various names covered a heterogeneous group of people, perhaps numbering a few hundred or a few thousand, who were scattered over the counties, with the largest concentration in the Midlands. They may have been previously imbued with Anabaptism or Familism.

Their beliefs were varied and often contradictory. The world of flesh has no real existence, but is like a reflection upon water. Matter was eternal, and God did not create the universe. Sin has no reality outside the minds of men and to God all things are the same; therefore, there is no judgement or punishment. No man could commit a sin once he had committed that sin as if it were not a sin. The soul dies with the body, so there is no heaven and no hell. Humankind is God in consequence of Christ's incarnation. All the creatures of the world are one Being. 'God', as a follower put it, is in 'this dog, this tobacco pipe, he is in me and I am him'. It was a form of pantheism, all the more powerful for being aligned with anti-clericalism. It was also in keeping with the spirit of antinomianism that was common among the various sects, with the belief that the recipients of divine grace are exempt from conventional human laws.

Another Ranter argued that just as a stream is distinct and recognizable in itself until it enters the ocean, 'so the spirit of man whilst in the body was distinct from God, but when death came it returned to God, and so became one with God, yea God itself.' These precepts certainly overturned the prevailing doctrines of Calvinism, in particular, in which sin and guilt are the true heirs of the world. The Ranters offered the negation of the Protestant spirit, and their often jubilant sayings were therefore welcome to those who distrusted or despised the Calvinist ethic.

Coppe was commanded in a vision at the end of 1648 to 'go up to *London*, to *London*, that great City, write, write, write'. This was a period of English history when the number of divine visions and commands rivals that of the Old Testament. But Coppe did more than write. On his arrival in the capital at the beginning of 1649, he recalled, he prostrated himself before cripples, beggars and lepers, kissing their feet and 'resigning up' his money to them. He also remembered how at a prison in Southwark he sat, ate and drank with gypsies, embracing them and kissing them, putting his hand 'in their bosomes, loving the she Gipsies dearly'. To the pure, all things are pure. To the holy, all things are holy. That was his belief. It was an extreme response to extreme times. He believed that the world was coming to the end of time and to 'the dreadfull day of JUDGEMENT'.

In January 1649 Coppe was permitted to preach at the ancient church of St Helen's, Bishopsgate. Before the usual large congregation he mounted the pulpit and was said to have cursed and blasphemed for an hour, declaring at one point, 'a pox of God take all your prayers hearing, reading, fasting.' He then went into hiding, but he could not elude his pursuers for very long. The Council of State ordered his arrest and the seizure of his 'mad and blasphemous' books, and at the beginning of 1650 he was arrested and eventually confined in Newgate Prison.

Coppe wrote to his adherents that 'Newgate . . . is noe prison to mee while I am inthroned in my Triple heart wch is but one & triangular, which is as firme as a stone, when I my selfe (heere & there and everywhere) raise uppe my selfe.' When he was brought before a Parliamentary committee, he refused to take off his hat – also a custom of Quakers to defy or deny official rank – then seemed to feign madness by talking to himself continually and throwing apples, pears and nutshells around the room.

Yet by the summer Coppe had prepared a recantation of his previous doctrines and professed sincere repentance for his words and actions. It is not certain whether this was feigned or genuine, but he was released from confinement and seems to have been forgiven by some Baptist congregations. In 1657, however, he reappeared in print as 'Hiam the prophet', claiming to have seen 'the Lord, the King' and proclaiming the 'consuming fire' to come. The resulting silence was broken ten years later when one Abiezer Hiam was granted permission to practise medicine and surgery. This was no doubt his profession until the end of his life. In 1672

'Hiam' was buried at St Mary's Church in Barnes. Wood ended his account of Coppe's life by remarking that he was 'brought low by certain infirmities which he had contracted in his rambles by drinking and whoring'.

The Ranters themselves had already dispersed or become attached to other sects, in part because of the Blasphemy Act of August 1650, which suppressed 'abominable and corrupt Opinions and Practises, tending to the Dishonor of God, the Scandal of Christian Religion, and the Professors thereof, and destructive to Humane Society'. Their meetings had been violently dispersed, their adherents whipped or imprisoned. Soon enough, like the Levellers before them, they ceased to play any part in what many of them had expected to be a new age.

✠

THE SEVENTEENTH-CENTURY theologian Lawrence Clarkson was perhaps the epitome of the fervent separatist and sectarian. He became in turn an Independent and an Antinomian, a Baptist or Dipper, a Seeker and a Ranter, until he eventually became a Muggletonian. This was one of the more obscure sects of the period but, paradoxically, one of the longest-lasting.

The honour of being the first Muggletonian can be claimed by Lodowicke Muggleton himself. The son of a farrier, he was born in July 1609 in a corner house, part of Walnut Tree Yard along Bishopsgate Street, just north of the City wall of London. At the age of fifteen he was apprenticed to a tailor working in the same small yard, but a year later he contracted the epidemic plague that killed some 40,000 Londoners. He did not succumb to the pestilence, however, and after his recovery he claimed that he never experienced any other sickness. His consistent advice was to keep away from doctors. That counsel was still being given to Muggletonians in 1941.

At the age of twenty or twenty-one Muggleton worked for a

William Wood, *Lodowicke Muggleton*, 1674, oil on canvas.

pawnbroker, but he subsequently returned to tailoring with his cousin William Reeve, who would in time become a Ranter. It is clear that Muggleton was raised in what might have been called a 'hot' ambience. He married for the first time in 1634 or 1635, and he described his oldest daughter, the first of three, as 'the most experimental and knowingest Woman, in Spiritual Things'. Three years after the death of his first wife in 1639, he married again, but the children of the second marriage all died young; he explained the mortality by virtue of the fact that they had inherited his wife's 'melancholy and dropsical nature'.

In 1651 or 1652 Muggleton experienced what might be called a spiritual awakening and a sense of renewal after a long period of self-doubt and melancholy; by his account it was a mystical revelation, lasting for approximately six hours, from nine in the evening to three in the morning, and recurring over the next four days. His younger cousin James Reeve claimed that he been vouchsafed a similar epiphany in the same period. Both of them became 'prophets'. Reeve, in particular, announced that God had spoken into his 'external ear' and revealed that he and Muggleton were the 'two witnesses' mentioned in the eleventh chapter of Revelation as 'the two olive trees, and the two candlesticks standing before the God of the earth'; they are the true prophets 'and if any man will hurt them, fire proceedeth out of their mouth.' This was taken to mean that they might curse or bless, both of which they proceeded to do with some frequency.

Some of their central beliefs were not unfamiliar. They held that each person possessed two seeds, of faith and of reason. In this third 'age of the spirit', only the seed of faith was full of grace. The doctrine of the 'Two Seeds', as it became known, signified that the true seed came out of Abel and the false out of Cain. God has a body in the form of a man, between five and six feet in height, so it was literally true that he created Adam in his own image. When he came to Earth in the figure of Jesus, Moses and Elijah were the custodians of heaven on his behalf. The devil was a phantasm of the human imagination, and hell resided in oneself. Heaven was six miles upwards in the sky. The soul dies with the body, only to rise again at the Last Judgement. As the two men spread their gospel – it might be called, as with other sects, the 'everlasting gospel' – they attracted hostility, and Reeve was chased by children shouting, 'There goes the Prophet that damns people.' But their more obviously blasphemous tenets, such as that denying the Trinity, led to their arrest and confinement for six months in

September 1653. They continued their joint ministry until Reeve, constantly moving from place to place in fear of arrest, was reduced to a 'sick, wasting condition' and died in 1658.

Muggleton was now the leading member of the sect that had assumed his name. Its membership was probably limited to hundreds rather than thousands, who met as small groups in private houses or in taverns where they ate, drank and sang verses of their own composition. There was no formal worship, no preaching or praying, and no reference to scripture except in the form of general discussion. One recalled, after his conversion to Quakerism, that 'no, we had no more to do but believe Muggleton and be saved.' It is worth noting that approximately 40 per cent of the members were female, suggesting that women played a larger part in radical religion than is generally assumed.

Muggleton himself seems to have been a man of some common sense and of humane character, happy to ignore or avoid controversy over matters of discipline. He renounced Reeve's belief that God had 'immediate notice' (signifying the belief that God scrutinized every human action), and relied instead on the doctrine that virtue lay in acting according to conscience. He did not concur with the Calvinist doctrine, shared with many sects, that only the elect would be saved, but believed that more than half the world would find grace. This was appropriate for an age of rapidly changing affinities, and it concurred with his often announced desire to remain 'quiet and still'. The survival of this sect into the twentieth century is puzzling in one respect. The Muggletonians never tried to find or make converts to their creed. They did not proselytize, and did not even tell their families or friends of their faith. It was said that they opened their door to those who knocked, so that only those who sought them out could be enlightened. They were not evangelists.

Muggleton had always said that he sought quiet, but that was not possible. He fought a constant and bitter pamphlet war with the Quakers, perhaps on the old principle that we hate the thing we most resemble. In 1663 he was confined to the Cornmarket Gaol in Derby on the charge of blasphemy, and seven years later his books were seized. On 17 January 1677 Muggleton was once again tried and convicted for blasphemy at the Old Bailey, where he was sentenced to three days in the pillory and a fine of £500. He was then remanded to Newgate Prison for seven months. In later years his memory 'much failed him', but he was 'sencable [sensible, or open to reason] to the last'. He died on 14 March 1698 at the age of 88 and was interred at Bethlem burial ground in the presence of 248 mourners.

But Muggleton's faith was not buried with him, and, almost by a miracle (if such a term can be allowed in this context), survived for several centuries. In Dickens's *The Pickwick Papers* of 1836 there is a cricket team called 'the Old Muggletonians'. In *The Origin of the Muggletonians*, published in 1869, it was asserted that 'they are, I believe, as numerous now as ever they were.' In fact the last surviving Muggletonian, a Kentish farmer by the name of Philip Noakes, died in 1979. In the calendar, at least, the sect endured almost as long as Anglicanism.

OTHER RELIGIOUS SECTS, born out of this time of division, should be included here. Among them are the Dissenting Brethren and the Seventh Day Baptists, who had separated from the Congregationalists and Baptists respectively. The Fifth Monarchy men and women seem to have emerged just after the Battle of Worcester, in 1651, when Cromwell's decisive victory over the Royalists encouraged millenarian hopes of a national transformation and a new age. The ungodly, minister or magistrate, Member of Parliament or military officer, would be the dust under their feet. The godly would rise up to lead and to rule; in this respect the Fifth Monarchists did not at all share the egalitarian spirit of, for example, the Levellers. They were actively preparing for the reign of Christ and his saints; the execution of Charles I two years before represented the collapse of the fourth great monarchy, as foretold in the Bible by Daniel, and they were waiting for the fifth. The reign of Jesus would begin in 1694. They used to clap their hands, jumping up and down, calling out 'Appear! Appear! Appear!' They may even be seen as part of a period drawn to prophecy or astrology as a token of things to come in a world otherwise doomed to uncertainty. Cromwell himself was associated with them until the end of 1653, when the dissolution of the 'Barebones Parliament' turned them against him. The reign of the saints had been postponed.

After the restoration of Charles II one Fifth Monarchist, Thomas Venner, began an insurrection in the middle of London. This was in accordance with the sect's belief that violence was permitted in order to subvert an evil government. His desperate attempt was foiled, and as a result the Fifth Monarchists retreated into the shadows, from which they never re-emerged. Venner declared, before his execution by hanging, drawing and quartering, that 'if they had been deceived, the Lord himself was their deceiver.'

The fierce belief and religious zeal of this period in English spiritual history have never since been equalled, but their presence in the national character should be acknowledged. Some sects, such as the Seekers and Ranters, ceased to exist; others, among them the Baptists and Congregationalists, survived and prospered.

Albert Newsam, *George Fox*, 1835, print.

Twelve

Religion as Transformation
George Fox (1624–1691)

At the end of the English Civil War the millenarian hopes for a new age or a third age faded in the light of the social and political realities that accompanied the Commonwealth and Oliver Cromwell's Protectorate. The strident rhetoric of such sects as the Ranters and the Fifth Monarchists was replaced by the more subdued and quietist piety of other groups. That transition or transformation is perhaps most apparent in the history of the Quakers and of their mentor, George Fox.

Fox was born in July 1624 in the Leicestershire village of Drayton-in-the-Clay (now Fenny Drayton), near a farm that is today deemed to contain the geographical centre of England. The village was steeped in a Presbyterian tradition to which his family was deeply attached. His father, Christopher, was a weaver and a churchwarden who earned the nickname of 'Righteous Christer', so perhaps he bequeathed his spiritual earnestness to his son. Little is known of George's childhood, except that which he reveals in the first chapter of his *Journal* (published posthumously, in 1694). He notes, 'I had a gravity and stayedness of mind and spirit not usual in children,' where 'stayedness' means seriousness; he goes on to disclose that 'when I came to eleven years of age I knew pureness and righteousness, for while a child I was taught how to walk to be kept pure.'

Some of Fox's relations believed that he might become a minister, but at an early age he was apprenticed to a shoemaker, a profession well known for its radical Protestantism. On one occasion during this period of employment he was invited into an alehouse by his cousin and another young man. When they decided that the one who did not drink a full measure would pay for all, he took a groat out of his pocket, placed it on the table and left them for one of his long and solitary walks. In this solemn and earnest youth, who was ready to flee the world in order to save his own soul, is a measure of the man.

The incident seemed to open Fox's eyes to the corruption of the world, as he saw it; the voice of God, in his account, told him that he must be 'a stranger unto all'. He broke off his apprenticeship and travelled the hundred miles to London, stopping along the way in Parliamentary towns or garrisons that were in readiness to fight the king. But the capital offered him no respite; believing that it was bound in a 'chain of darkness', he became afflicted by 'great misery and trouble'. Bouts of melancholy despair would occur for most of his life. Still much troubled by the sins of the world, he returned to Leicestershire, where he was restless and fearful, but it is clear from his *Journal* that he already had intimations of divine power. He believed that he heard a voice, warning and advising him. He might say that 'it was opened in me' or that 'it was opened unto me'.

From this time forward Fox was always a traveller. He made his way through Nottinghamshire, Lincolnshire, Derbyshire and other counties in order to seek assistance or advice, but none was to be found. He often walked in the night, with only his Bible for consolation. Then, in a Nottinghamshire town in 1647, a change came upon this 23-year-old pilgrim. A voice told him that 'there is one, even Jesus Christ, that can speak to thy condition.' It seemed to be a revelation that Christ was spiritually present within him, however extravagant that might seem to others, and that Christ would guide him beyond the reach of scripture and all forms of worship. He felt the urgent desire to speak out and, possessed by a new spirit, he became an itinerant lay preacher in the part of the Midlands from which he came. Like John the Baptist, he had come 'to bear witness of the Light'.

Fox was a tall young man, burly and big-boned; he wore a leather jerkin, leather breeches and a broad-rimmed white hat, and kept his hair long, in implicit defiance of Puritan custom. His eyes were so bright, when he was exalted, that many commented upon them. He spoke out of his own experience, to which he gave spiritual meaning and definition, and that for him was truth enough. He preached the light of salvation within each human being, at a time when most people looked for certainty. Elated by his enthusiasm, he may have spoken more than he knew. Sensing the light of Christ within him, he believed that he was Christ in essence. He was in effect the Son of God, a claim he maintained all his life. The 'light within' or, at a later date, the 'inner light', as he called it, burned so brightly that he believed he had become a spiritual power. There was no need for priests, or for churches, or for sacraments and ceremonies. It was not long, therefore, before he attracted a small but faithful number of followers, who called themselves 'children of the light' or 'friends of the truth' (later to become known simply as 'Friends'). These followers, too, became the 'flesh and bone' of Christ, sensing the presence of God within them. One of the new 'children of the light' addressed him as 'thou god of life and power'. The behaviour of the first Quakers, as they came to be known, with their rapturous language and their ecstatic bearing, was very different from that of the later 'saints'.

Yet soon enough Fox acquired enemies as well as friends. Here was an excited young man who called himself the son of God. This was blasphemy of the most egregious kind. He felt called upon to interrupt services after the sermon, when he denounced the ministers and the worship in their 'steeple-houses' or churches. Some believed him to be bewitched. This disruption, and others like it, became a common practice among his loyal supporters. He also castigated drink and dancing, music and song, which may bear some relation to his Puritan background.

In 1650 Fox was arrested during a service at Derby, under the provisions of the new Blasphemy Act. He could also have been prosecuted and condemned for denying that scripture was the word of God, and for claiming that the sacraments of baptism and communion were not the work of God. At his subsequent trial he declared that he was sinless and perfect, a statement that was in itself enough to condemn him. He is also recorded as having performed 170 miracles of healing. One of the justices in that town was the first to call him in derision a 'quaker', because, as Fox put it, 'I bade them tremble at the word of the Lord.' He was confined in the local prison for almost a year. He was in and out of such fetid and noisome dungeons for much of his life, forced to sleep in puddles of filth, with excrement poured on him. He was deprived of warmth, of food and of water, but he was never subdued or in fear. He fought back against his accusers and – guided by what he described as 'the Openings of the Power' – claimed divine sanction for his behaviour and his beliefs.

A few days after his release from the common gaol in Derby, Fox approached Lichfield, where the three steeples of its cathedral 'struck at my life'. He went into the town and cried out through its streets 'Woe to the bloody city of Lichfield!', in the manner of the Old Testament prophets whom he venerated. He may also have worn his hair long from their example. He travelled on to Yorkshire and Lancashire – as yet he had no horse – and then to Cumbria. In that county he was introduced to Margaret Fell of Swarthmoor Hall, who became one of his most ardent supporters; her husband, Thomas Fell, a judge and vice chancellor of the Duchy of Lancaster, tolerated and helped to protect the inspired traveller. Swarthmoor Hall, under Margaret's guidance, became the centre of a nascent Quaker organization. She was later to be Fox's wife.

But for Fox there was no abiding city. He was always restless, ready to move on, eager to preach at meetings in barns, in fields, in marketplaces and in private houses. In his *Journal* there are snatches of speech that throw light on his progress: 'George, what! Wilt thou never have done? . . . Hold thy tongue, George . . . Stand up again, George.' From Swarthmoor he travelled throughout the northwest of England, where his name was becoming well known. His meetings were larger, and his followers increased in number. Some of them became preachers also, to act as missionaries in the 'darker' parts of the country.

The Quakers discarded all external forms of worship, and waited in silence for the Spirit to descend. Fox first derived this practice from the Seekers, a radical sect that bore much resemblance to the early Quakers; the Seekers were taught to 'sit still, in submission and silence' until the Lord descended. For the Quakers, the partaking of the Eucharist was denied in favour of inner experience, so that 'true Baptism' came from the Holy Spirit and 'true Communion' meant inward union with Christ. God existed in each person, and this 'inner light' was not to be found in the church or chapel. Men and women were spiritual equals, therefore, who would not assume any titles or degrees of honour. Quakers always used 'thee' or 'thou' in address. They would not take off their hats to salute so-called superiors. They would not pay tithes (a tenth of their crops and animals) to the established Church, and they would not swear oaths before judge or magistrate, since the practice was forbidden in scripture. They also urged the abolition of lawyers and universities.

✠

THE JOURNEYS OF George Fox through the north of England, and elsewhere, left a trail of fire. He denounced Presbyterians, Papists, Independents, Ranters, Fifth Monarchists, 'Prayer Book Protestants' and all others who did not recognize the truth of the 'inner light' that he experienced. As a result he provoked argument, anger and violence against himself and his supporters. He was beaten with clubs, staves and rods; he was thrown into ditches or thrust into ponds, beaten unconscious and left for dead, the crowd urging on his assailants with calls of 'Kill him! Kill him!' or 'Knock the teeth out of his head!' or 'Bring the cart and carry him to the churchyard!' The age of civil war was also the age of savage violence and of mob rage. Yet Fox survived, just as he survived the conditions of the filthiest prisons. He was physically strong enough to withstand assault, but his real strength came from his unconquerable will and his powerful self-belief. He trusted the divine life within him.

One event shook Fox, however. His principal comrade in faith had become James Nayler. Nayler was born in the West Riding of Yorkshire, and was a farmer before he enrolled in the Parliamentary army. Towards the end of his nine years of service he became a preacher to the soldiers in the army commanded by John Lambert; Lambert described him as 'a member of a very sweet society of an independent church', which suggests his sectarian origins, while another officer confessed, 'I was struck with more terror before the preaching of James Nayler than I was before the battle of Dunbar.'

When he left the army Nayler returned to his family and to his life as a farmer, but, while ploughing one day, he was struck by a voice calling, 'Get thee out from thy kindred, and from thy father's house.' This was his 'convincement', as the Quakers put it, and after an encounter with Fox he became a welcome and gifted follower. The two men began a joint missionary endeavour, and he accompanied Fox to Swarthmoor Hall. They were also imprisoned together in a gaol in Appleby. Nayler was a prolific writer as well as a striking preacher, and more than fifty pamphlets were credited to him. He was second only to Fox in spreading the Quaker word, and he was soon considered by many to be the true leader of the movement. This was anathema to Fox himself, whose self-absorption may have been the source of his self-belief. At a bitter meeting in Exeter in September 1656, he refused to shake Nayler's hand and offered his foot instead.

Fox's doubts seemed to be confirmed in the following month, when Nayler and a few followers entered Bristol. Nayler rode on a horse, while the others threw garments and flowers before him, chanting 'Holy, holy, holy, Lord God of Sabbaoth.' This was a clear imitation of Christ's entry into Jerusalem on Palm Sunday, and the offence was compounded by Nayler's claim that he was possessed by the inner light and was the Son of God. Fox had made similar statements, but in the interim the Quaker movement had become much larger and, to the authorities, more threatening.

Nayler and some of his associates were summoned to London, where they were questioned by a Parliamentary committee. Within a month he was convicted of blasphemy, the sin of sins, for which he could have merited the death penalty, but he was sentenced instead to a whipping through the streets of London; his tongue was to be bored through with a red-hot iron, and his forehead branded with the letter 'B'. He was also imprisoned for two years of hard labour. The ensuing furore and condemnation severely damaged the Quaker cause, and Fox later wrote in his *Journal* that 'James ran out into imaginations, and a company with him; and they raised up a great darkness in the nation.'

The alarm was sounded against the Quakers as seditious heretics and, as a result, Fox and his close associates felt compelled to follow a path of conciliation. In his epistles to the faithful he counselled them to 'go not forth to the aggravating part . . . let your

moderation, and temperance, and patience be known to all men.'
Where other radical sects, such as the Ranters or the Levellers,
scattered after persecution, the Quakers maintained themselves by
forming a more coherent organization. Fox, together with Margaret
Fell, organized monthly meetings for the faithful, so that 'Friends
be kept in order'; quarterly meetings, as well as larger assemblies,
were also instituted to provide discipline and curb excessive manifestations of godliness. Fox had already ensured that all Quaker
texts came to him for approval before publication.

In these early days, however, and in the violently changing
period from 1640 to 1660, the Quakers were by no means secure.
The restoration of Charles II, and the subsequent uprisings by such
radical sects as the Fifth Monarchists, left once favoured groups
in confusion. The Quakers had, of course, never been favoured,
but now they felt the full force of official hostility. Acts of 1661
and 1662 demanded that all receive Anglican communion and
swear allegiance to the king, neither of which was possible for
the Quakers. Religious gatherings of more than five people were
prohibited, and the measure of 1662 was directed against 'cer-
taine persons under the names of Quakers and other names of
Separation'.

Fox and his associates had already composed a 'peace testimony', declaring that 'all wars and fightings with carnal [physical]
weapons we do deny, who have the sword and the spirit; and
all that wrong us we leave them to the Lord. And this is to clear
our innocency from that aspersion cast upon us, that we are plot-
ters.' But it was not enough. Fox was confined on three separate
occasions for an overall period of four years. His offence lay in
his refusal to swear the oath of allegiance, for the simple reason
that the Quakers never consented to oaths. They would say only
'yea' or 'nay', in accordance with scripture. These long terms of
imprisonment undermined Fox's physical and mental energy to
the extent that, in the latter months of 1670, he suffered from a

depression more severe than any that had afflicted him previously. 'A great weight and oppression fell upon my spirit,' he wrote in his *Journal*. 'I lost both hearing and sight.' It was as if he had become dead to the world.

Yet with long care and attention, principally at the hands of female Quakers, Fox recovered sufficiently to plan new missions. In the summer of 1671 he took ship from Gravesend to Barbados, from where he sailed to Jamaica before passing to North America. There he visited Quaker settlements in Maryland, Long Island and Rhode Island. His path then took him south, as far as North Carolina. He was now a patriarch, if not a prophet.

In the summer of 1673 Fox returned to England, where he immediately faced fresh controversy. In that period Parliament passed a new Test Act directed primarily against Catholics and Nonconformists who refused to join the Anglican Communion. England itself was believed to be in peril from the forays of the Dutch fleet, so that subversion, real or imagined, had to be eliminated. Fox himself was jailed, for the eighth time, but his age and reputation protected him from the worst excesses of his earlier confinements. Nevertheless, in the close air of the county gaol in Worcester his health deteriorated still further; he was afflicted with arthritis and 'dropsy' (now considered to be a symptom of heart failure), but not freed from prison until February 1675.

After his release Fox returned to Swarthmoor Hall under the care of Margaret Fell, now Margaret Fox, and other Quaker women. It was there that be began writing his *Journal*. But by the beginning of 1677 he was stirred once more to go on his spiritual travels. He rode to London, and throughout his slow journey he was welcomed and attended by fellow Quakers. The light of his mission still led him forwards, and in the summer of that year he travelled to Holland and Germany in order to consolidate the movement in those countries. On his return to England at the beginning of 1678 he was greeted by large assemblies of Quakers in the cities and towns he visited. In these last years he visited prisons and attended meetings; he would stand on a chair or table to address those who came to see and hear him in the belief that he was one of the great prophets as great as, or greater than, Moses.

Fox attended his last meeting in Gracechurch Street, London, where he felt cold entering his heart. He lay in bed for two days and then, on 13 January 1691, he died as peacefully as if he had fallen asleep. It is said that 4,000 Quaker mourners followed his coffin to his last resting place, in the Dissenters' graveyard of Bunhill Fields. The exact position of his grave is uncertain, but that part of the burial ground is now known as Quaker Gardens.

George Fox is one of the great religious reformers of English history, and the Quaker movement he established has in many respects an essentially English character. It was at first a faith of fire and fury, filled with fierce apocalyptic warnings. In the face of oppression and persecution, however, the temperature of its activities was gradually lowered. It began in mysticism imbued with radicalism, and ended in pragmatism. It was moved not by dogma or by abstract principles, but by the evidence of individual experience. It was maintained in silence and shared understanding, rather than noise and doctrinal controversy. It advised its members not to be 'loose and airy' in discourse. It advanced the cause of toleration. That has always been the English path.

After Fox's death, the messianic claims of the movement's leadership all but vanished. There were fewer disruptions of church services or tirades beside the market cross. There were no more 'signs and wonders', and there was less interest in 'prophesy-ings' or in fits and trances. There were few now who decided, for example, to 'go naked for a sign', although in truth that had meant going barefoot in a loincloth or sackcloth. The movement's practicality was manifest by the Quaker concern for prison reform and hospitals. The enthusiasm and ecstasy were left behind in favour of reserve and gravity, moderation and restraint. It became respectable in order to become acceptable. In the process, naturally enough, the Quakers became institutionalized. The Children of Light became the Religious Society of Friends. Yet the light was not wholly dimmed. Instead it was transmuted, or refracted, into an implacable force for social and even political change. In time, the Quakers were to become the face, and even the arm, of the great moral crusade of the later eighteenth century to abolish slavery.

Thirteen

Religion as Experience
John Bunyan (1628–1688)

John Bunyan, the tinker, the preacher, the prisoner, the evangelist, the writer of prose and the poet, was born towards the end of November 1628 in the village of Elstow, Bedfordshire. He was part of a relatively poor family. His father was himself a tinker, or brazier, roaming the neighbourhood for pots or kettles to mend. Little is known of Bunyan's early days, except for the suggestion that he attended a school, or at least received enough education to be able in later years to write verse and prose with great fluency. He may, like Charles Dickens, have been largely self-educated, but this is not to be discovered.

At the age of sixteen Bunyan was enrolled in Cromwell's New Model Army, either by choice or by conscription; Bedfordshire was a strongly Puritan area, with a reputation for Nonconformity and dissent. It seems unlikely, however, that he participated in any military action. He was discharged after seven months of service, and returned to his life in Elstow as a young brazier, following in the footsteps of his father.

In this period Bunyan was an avid reader of the romances, chapbooks (pamphlets) and adventures that had flourished in the medieval and Tudor periods. He was also, by his own later account, a desperate sinner. His vices of swearing, lying and blaspheming may seem venial in an energetic young man, but in his memoir, *Grace Abounding to the Chief of Sinners* (1666), they are

Thomas Sadler, *John Bunyan*, 1684, oil on canvas.

considered to be mortal evils that would hurl him into the flames of hell. While playing 'cat', a long-forgotten game with bat and ball, a voice pierced him with the words, 'Will you leave your sins and go to heaven or keep your sins and go to hell?' A more secular age might consider this to be an internal rather than an external voice, but for Bunyan it was the real beginning of all his woes.

At some point over the next two or three years Bunyan married; the date of that event, and the name of his wife, are unknown.

They had for him no significance in his spiritual history. He noted, however, that his wife's father 'was counted godly', and that after their marriage she had brought with her two equally godly books, Lewis Bayly's *The Practise of Pietie* and Arthur Dent's *The Plaine Man's Path-Way to Heaven*; both of them were popular handbooks of Puritan piety, first published early in the century. It was perhaps under their influence that for the next year he attended the church in Elstow, which in the circumstances of the time might have been of a modest Presbyterian or even Episcopalian temper; he conformed to an outward piety even as his first daughter, Mary, was born blind in the summer of 1650.

But that early profession of faith lasted for a year only. Bunyan encountered three or four women talking together in Bedford; they were members of a 'gathered' or Dissenting church in that town, and by his account they were lamenting their failures in the pursuit of godliness. All at once he began to doubt his own piety and was dogged by the belief that he was nothing but 'a poor painted Hypocrite'. He consulted the scriptures avidly, but as he read he was invaded by doubt and guilt, by fear and even despair. The first words of Christian, in *The Pilgrim's Progress*, are 'What shall I do?'

This was not a brief episode. For the following five or six years Bunyan was trapped in spiritual turmoil, doubting that he was saved, believing that he was damned; the flames of eternal judgement flickered around him, and his fear was so intense that sometimes he came close to physical collapse. He was sinking in a marsh of guilt and pollution, as he thought it, which shook as he trembled but would not release him. A voice of temptation or of judgement was sometimes so loud that he turned his head to see who had called to him. He heard 'Sell Christ for that; sell him, sell him.' He carried a burden, like Christian, but he was also an unbearable burden to himself. Even consoling words from scripture were 'a kind of chide for my proneness to desperation'.

At this early date an orthodox psychological analysis would be inappropriate; the seventeenth-century experts in mental health would have been the astrologers or the ministers. Yet it becomes apparent from *Grace Abounding* that the young Bunyan was infinitely scrupulous, infinitely sensitive and therefore infinitely suffering. He always feared the worst. His constant anxiety seems to have stripped away a layer of protection so that he was always vulnerable to the slightest tremor. Words themselves were like lightning strikes that affected him with trembling and nausea. He was so fearful, so obsessive and so literal-minded that he seems sometimes to have summoned damnation and destruction as his only release. That fear took visceral form and, in *The Pilgrim's Progress*, created figures more real than those about him.

Bunyan seems to have found some respite in eventually joining the 'gathered' church of St John the Baptist in Bedford, from the congregation of which came the women who had touched his sensitive conscience four years earlier. It may have included both Baptists and Congregationalists, since in this period the Dissenters, as a result of Restoration hostility, were for safety prepared to mingle in worship. In 1655 he was 'born again' or baptized into the Church. The minister of that church, John Gifford, seems already to have taken an interest in the repentant sinner, who soon became part of his spiritual campaign in the neighbourhood. Bunyan was soaked in scripture, and his own suffering gave him strength and cogency. He became a preacher, at first addressing the local congregation but soon extending his range to the surrounding towns and villages. The unusual sight of a tinker become preacher attracted many, and Bunyan himself wrote that 'they came to hear the word by hundreds and that from all parts.'

By preaching faith, Bunyan found his own. He had begun his mission while still in a state of guilt and terror, speaking 'what I smartingly did feel', but over the next two years his success as a lay preacher of repentance and grace gave him the conviction that he might also be saved. He began to write short religious texts, the first of which was *Some Gospel-Truths Opened*, printed in 1656. But any confidence or ease he had gained was soon relinquished. He had acquired a certain reputation as an eloquent and impassioned preacher of a broadly Calvinist tendency, but, as a result, he had been marked down by the civic authorities who came to power in Bedfordshire with the Restoration.

On 12 November 1660 Bunyan was arrested under the 'Act against Puritans' of 1593, designed to imprison or banish suspected religious separatists. At the quarter sessions Bunyan was given the choice either to abandon preaching or to be consigned to gaol. He chose prison. His time in Bedford County Gaol, at the corner of High Street and Silver Street, was not at first harsh; he was not strictly confined, and even travelled to London in order to preach there. He could also continue to minister to those who came to him for consolation or advice, and earned a small living for his family by making shoelaces.

A few months into his imprisonment, however, Bunyan was no longer allowed to preach. But he could write. In 1661 he composed a series of verses, some in the form of dialogue, entitled *Profitable Meditations*. This was followed by prose texts, with *I Will Pray with the Spirit* in 1662 and *Christian Behaviour* the following year. The latter had the words 'By John Bunyan, a Prisoner of Hope' on the title page and, on the last page, 'Farewell, From my place of confinement in Bedford this 17th of the 4th month, 1663.'

Yet the probability of long confinement and the possibility of death, from gaol fever or the score of different ailments that accompanied the conditions of prison, brought Bunyan again into misery. There were occasions when he believed himself to be 'empty, spiritless and barren'. He was a man in his mid-thirties who had been deprived of wife and family. He believed that, at the promptings of his conscience, he was 'pulling down his house upon the head of his wife and children. Yet, thought I, I must do it, I must do it.' He refused to submit and to gain his release by swearing to abandon preaching. He had the duty, and the need, to convey the voice of the Lord. The county gaol was in fact the lodging for some fifty other persecuted Nonconformists and, in a little room on the first floor that was used as a chapel, he prayed with them and exhorted them.

In the first six years of confinement Bunyan concluded some six religious texts. *Grace Abounding* was published in 1666, and two years later he was released from prison as a result of some temporary amnesty. But shortly afterwards, no doubt as a result of his desire and determination to minister and preach to the Bedford faithful, he was confined for a further four years. It was harsh, but the alternative punishments were banishment or death. Both would bring an end to his self-appointed vocation. And, for him, the experience of imprisonment afforded him further strength and faith. He was also attached to millenarianism, and was involved for an early period with the Fifth Monarchists, who proclaimed the belief or hope that the last days were approaching. If those wished-for days were indeed coming, to be in prison for true faith was a blessing.

Bunyan's years in Bedford gaol are largely blank and obscure, although it can be said with some certainty that in the final period of his imprisonment he began to envision and even to start work on *The Pilgrim's Progress*. In January 1672 the church of St John the Baptist, in Bedford, appointed him its pastor, albeit one still in captivity. Bunyan was released in the spring of that year, after the publication of Charles II's Declaration of Indulgence, which lifted the penal code against Nonconformists.

How did Bunyan appear at this crucial time? A friend, Charles Doe, stated that

> he was tall of stature, strong-boned, though not corpulent, somewhat of a ruddy face, with sparkling eyes, wearing his hair on his upper lip, after the old British fashion; his hair

reddish, but in his latter days, time had sprinkled it with grey; his nose well set, but not declining or bending, and his mouth moderate large; his forehead something high.

He looked, in other words, as English as a Bedford pork butcher or a Clerkenwell watchmaker.

With other Dissenting ministers who had been imprisoned alongside him, Bunyan had already set out a framework for the Nonconformist congregations in the county. This became the setting for his preaching and his ministry. Despite the king's withdrawal of his Declaration in May 1673, Bunyan continued his mission until he was eventually arrested at the end of 1676, under ecclesiastical law, and remained in confinement until 21 June 1677. It seems very likely that, during this relatively short period of further imprisonment, he managed to complete *The Pilgrim's Progress*.

✠

THAT CELEBRATED WORK is part allegory, part narrative, part drama, part sermon and part devotional manual. Bunyan was already known for works of devotional meditation, dogmatic theology and religious controversy, and for the poetry of piety. All these play their part in an English text of comprehensive power. It is a work established upon individual experience, but that word did not have the abstract amorphous meaning that now accrues to it; 'experience' conveyed a practical testing of beliefs or instincts.

It begins with Christian, the pilgrim: 'As I walked through the wilderness of this world I lighted on a certain place where was a den.' In the marginalia Bunyan glosses the 'den' as his prison in Bedford. Prison may in fact have been the training he had to undergo in order to write this narrative. 'And lay me down in that place to sleep; and as I slept, I dreamed a dream.' The dream vision is an integral part of the English sensibility, exemplified by

The Dream of the Rood in the eighth or ninth century and by *Piers Plowman* by Langland in the fourteenth. *The Rood* opens with 'Hwaet, ic swefna cyst secgan wylle' – 'Listen, I will speak to you of a wonderful dream' – and Langland described that 'thanne gan I to meten a merueilouse sweuene', a marvellous dream. Bunyan is not likely to have known these poems, but the deep Englishness of his imagination found similar words and images.

An overwhelming debt was also owed to the King James Bible, published seventeen years before Bunyan was born. It came to him with newly minted phrases to convey the sense of the sublime; the simplicity and directness of its words had struck him at moments of crisis or despair, to the extent that its cadence and vocabulary shaped his own prose. He quoted from it continually, and the speech of his characters is infused with it:

> You make me afraid; but whither shall I fly to be safe? If I go back to my own country, that is prepared for fire and brimstone, and I shall certainly perish there; if I can get to the Celestial City, I am sure to be in safety there: I must venture. To go back is nothing but death; to go forward is fear of death, and life everlasting beyond it. I will yet go forward.

The Pilgrim's Progress continues the line of English music.

There were many other native influences. Bunyan was naturally influenced by his early reading in the chapbooks and romances of his youth, by the ballads and newsbooks of the time, by folk tales and popular fables, by the polemics of the Ranters and the Quakers whom he encountered in the army and elsewhere. Religious debate was the essence of the period. The simple, colloquial tone of his prose reflects the clear stream of the living language, and in that sense it resembles the popular sermons of the period, not unlike those that Bunyan himself gave, which mixed moral instruction with the sugared pills of fable and contemporary satire. The religious atmosphere and traditions of Bedfordshire are also somewhere within the text. It has been said, of Thomas Hardy and others, that the more local the source, the more universal the effect. Everything comes together in this English account of the suffering soul.

✠

CHRISTIAN'S PILGRIMAGE TAKES him from the prison cell of his conventional life to the Celestial City of heavenly salvation. The journey is arduous and even perilous, endangering his own soul. He tells his wife, before embarking upon it, that 'our city will be burned from heaven'; that city is named the City of Destruction. His sense of self is bound up with the experience of agonizing fear. As he leaves he is pursued by two citizens, Obstinate and Pliable, who urge him to go back. But they abandon him when he reaches the Slough of Despond, from the depths of which he is rescued by Hope. He is distracted by Mr Wordly Wiseman, but is then directed to the Wicket-gate by Evangelist. He knocks, and it is opened. That gate signifies redemption by Christ's death. The method and meaning of the book are by now apparent.

This is an allegory written in letters of fire. Bunyan distils his own experience in a series of radiant images and vividly imagined characters. Christian is forced to confront 'the hill Difficulty', 'the Valley of Humiliation', 'the Valley of the Shadow of Death', the town of 'Vanity Fair', 'the Delectable Mountains' and 'the Celestial City'; in the course of his adventure he encounters Timorous and Mistrust, Lord Hate-Good and Giant Despair, Ignorance and Little-Faith, as well as Faithful and Hopeful. It represents the great pilgrimage of humankind.

But it is also a very English journey, directed by emotion and instinct rather than by doctrinal explanation. It follows living experience rather than theology. You would not know, in reading

The Pilgrim's Progress, that its author was a Calvinist. He does not allude to the Calvinist theories of reprobation and election; even though they were central to his life, they were foreign to his purpose here. As Christian says, 'the soul of religion is the practical part.'

In one sense Christian's progress can be read as an account of other seventeenth-century journeys, over rough roads, encumbered by mud and puddles. The traveller must sometimes reconnoitre steep hills, where he may catch 'a slip or two', and sometimes he must go 'out of the way' among 'turnings' and 'windings'. Sometimes dogs will bark at him, or he will be mistaken for a vagrant and placed in the stocks. Snatches of conversation can be heard along the way: 'Is this the way?' 'You are just in your way.' 'Whence came you?' 'What have you met with?' or 'What have you seen?' 'Back, back.' Some travellers might want 'to make a short cut of it, and to climb over the wall'. Does it matter how they reach their destination? 'If we are in, we are in.'

His vivid characterization and colloquial directness, however, cannot obscure the fact that Bunyan sees his characters in the light of eternity. *The Pilgrim's Progress* is the vast arena for Christian's journey towards grace and redemption, and its power and authority come directly from Bunyan's identity as a Dissenter utterly apart from the established faith. He belongs to the seventeenth-century world of dogmatic struggle and debate, in which deeply held religious faith was the only stay against the dark. Bunyan is nothing like Zeal-of-the-Land Busy, from Ben Jonson's play *Bartholomew Fair* of 1614, or the other Puritan caricatures of that century's drama. He is too desperate and determined to be that. Christian embarks on his journey alone 'because none of my neighbours saw their danger as I saw mine'. At the heart of this was the awareness of imminent destruction and everlasting fire. It is a glimpse into the fervent spirituality of seventeenth-century England.

✠

SOON AFTER BUNYAN'S final release from Bedford gaol in June 1677, he resumed his vocation as a preacher. His long confinement had brought him fresh confidence and renewed energy, and he began his ministerial work in earnest, drawing up lists of preachers and choosing suitable buildings as places of worship. In the months after his release he wrote and published his most popular sermon, 'Come, & Welcome, to Jesus Christ', which was issued in six editions during his lifetime. In the following year he composed a short text, *A Treatise of the Fear of God*, which rehearsed his major preoccupation with the nature of salvation, and the fact that fear and trembling are the signs of election to eternal life. That was also the dominant theme of *The Pilgrim's Progress*.

In the summer of 1677 Charles II dissolved Parliament in the hope that his natural supporters, the Tories, would prevail. He was eager to confront the Whigs then pursuing his brother, James, Duke of York, who would succeed him as a Catholic monarch. A declaration condemning 'the factious party' was read from every pulpit. Religious controversy still dominated local and national politics, with consequences that directly affected Bunyan himself. Nonconformity was again becoming dangerous.

This was also the period when Bunyan completed three of his most substantial works; from 1680 to 1684 he wrote *The Life and Death of Mr Badman*, the second part of *The Pilgrim's Progress* with Christiana as its heroine, and *The Holy War*. Mr Badman may be seen as an allegorical adversary of Christian. He is conceived in terms of Bunyan's worst fears. He is an atheist, thief, drunk, fornicator, hypocrite, highwayman and altogether 'one massy body of sins'. In his preface to the work Bunyan asserts that all these vices 'have been acted upon the stage of this World, even many times before mine eyes'. So he gives an anatomy lesson on Restoration England. It is in fact a work of observation and anecdote rather than of imagination, a didactic treatise rather than a work of art, but one still fuelled by Bunyan's intimate sense of overwhelming sin. He severely castigates Mr Badman's swearing and cursing, for example, two vices in which he himself indulged in his unconverted youth. He could draw the figure from his own entrails.

That book was followed, in 1682, by *The Holy War*. It takes the form of allegory, in which the town of Mansoul is besieged by the agents of Satan before being saved by the army of Emmanuel or, in translation, 'God is with us.' It is not an altogether fluent or powerful allegory, as Captains Good-Hope, Charity, Patience and Self-Denial fight against their diabolic adversaries, but in conceiving this narrative Bunyan was able to conflate the plight of the individual soul in a world of wickedness with the persecution of Nonconformists in his own time. The personal and the political were parts of the same religious imperative.

Mr Badman had been written in the form of dialogue between Attentive and Wiseman, and its style strongly suggests that Bunyan was eager to repeat the success of *The Pilgrim's Progress*. In a prefatory verse to *The Holy War*, in fact, he refutes the claim that his most popular book was not written by him. He makes it clear that 'the whole, and every whit, is mine.' It is not surprising, then, that after *The Holy War* he began work on a second part, or sequel, to the adventures of Christian on the path to paradise.

The principal figure here is Christiana, wife of Christian, who together with her family retraces his steps towards the Celestial City. A group, rather than a solitary traveller, is following the path to salvation. Their journey is rendered less urgent and, therefore, less serious. As the twentieth-century theologian Ronald Knox put it, 'Christian goes on a pilgrimage, *Christiana* on a *walking tour*.' It has its cast of characters of various dispositions, including Great-Heart and Mercy, Little-Faith and Timorous, but they are meant to be closer to reality than to allegory: 'So the old gentleman blushed, and said, Not Honesty in the abstract; but Honest is my name.' They are an aspect of the English preference for the individual and the concrete. As an innkeeper who welcomes Christiana puts it, 'nothing teaches like experience.' In the same spirit, the little group of pilgrims 'made a pretty good shift to wag along'.

For all that, Christiana and her children are still shadowy or half-conceived, both real and unreal. Christiana herself is elusive, and is not filled with the same lifeblood as Christian. Bunyan evoked the soul but not the substance, on the clear understanding that this was his preoccupation. In truth he did not seem to believe that women were as fit a subject for contemplation as men. It was a conventional assumption. Even among the ranks of the Nonconformists, females were deemed to be at a lower spiritual level. Bunyan himself opposed the idea of women meeting, without men, to pray or worship together. 'The Holy Ghost', he wrote, 'doth particularly insist upon the inability of Women.'

✠

THE SOCIAL AND POLITICAL situation, for all Nonconformists, became more ambiguous on the death of Charles II and the accession of James II in 1685. How would a Catholic sovereign treat the very large number of Dissenters throughout his kingdom? The first months were not promising. James's army, gathered to prevent a rebellion, spent some of its time harassing Presbyterians and Baptists, who were considered to be enemies of the state. But soon enough, in the face of disaffection from the Nonconformists, the new king chose discretion rather than confrontation. In the spring of 1687 a declaration of indulgence suspended the execution of all penal laws for religious offences. From this time forward Dissenters flocked to their chapels and assemblies without the least hindrance. In *The History of England*, Macaulay remarked that 'an observant traveller will still remark the date of 1687 on some of the oldest meeting-houses.'

This was also the year in which Bunyan, as minister and travelling preacher, was finally free of restrictions and the fear of arrest. In one sense it made no difference. In his last months he continued preaching, travelling and writing with the same urgency as before. He may have extended the range of his own preaching, too, and was heard in Cambridgeshire, Essex and Suffolk as well as in London. His success as a preacher was heightened by his fame as the author of *The Pilgrim's Progress*, and large crowds now gathered to hear him. He was in the capital in the summer of 1688, when he was called to Reading in order to reconcile a father and son as part of his ministry. On his return to London in the middle of August 1688, he was caught in a storm from which he contracted a severe fever. He lay in the house of a friend on Snow Hill, and he died there. John Bunyan, like George Fox three years later, was taken to his grave in the Nonconformist burial ground of Bunhill Fields. It became a resting place for the English soul.

J. B. Longacre, after J. Jackson, *John Wesley*, before 1869, engraving.

Fourteen

Religion as Revival

John Wesley (1703–1791)

A few yards from the burial sites of George Fox and John Bunyan arose, almost a century later, the building that became known as Wesley's Chapel. The closeness may be considered fortuitous, but there are no coincidences in the world of faith. Just as Quakerism and Methodism bear striking similarities, so Fox and Wesley resembled each other in many respects. Both came from deeply religious families; both established faiths on principles completely different from those of their devout parents. Both of them travelled, on foot or on horseback, the length of Britain for most of their lives; they were on an English pilgrimage. Both were guided by what they believed to be the Spirit, by the 'inner light' or by the pursuit of 'perfectionism'; they were both so ambitious and disciplined that they were able to create national and even international movements.

Both men began with a form of spiritual mysticism, but ended in practical and pragmatic ministries. They proclaimed the truths of individual experience over doctrine or abstract principle. They were both involved in matters of social reform and concerned with the improvement of schools, hospitals and prisons. They both performed apparent miracles of healing, and they both wrote journals of their spiritual progress. They both suffered attacks from violent mobs, until age and familiarity prevented the blows. Here, perhaps, is an outline of the English soul. In addition, they both took their missions to America. And both wore their hair long in the manner of the prophets.

✚

JOHN WESLEY WAS BORN on 17 June 1703 in the small market town of Epworth in north Lincolnshire, where his father, Samuel, was the minister. Samuel Wesley was a devout 'Church of England man' or 'churchman' who believed in the hierarchies of Church and state and who practised the established religion, which, if not exactly 'high', was steadily moving upwards as a beacon of Anglican faith markedly different from the Dissenting or separatist congregations. His principles were so exacting that for a while he separated from his wife, Susanna, on the grounds that she had refused to pray for the new king, William III, who had supplanted the exiled James II in 1689. In many respects John Wesley resembled his mother in her unswerving will and sense of religious duty. It is perhaps worth noting that both of his parents had come from strict Dissenting families.

Wesley's early life, as one of ten surviving children, all but three of which were female, was remarkable only for accidents that were later granted supernatural status. When he was five years of age, his family's Epworth rectory was deluged with fire and the young boy himself was rescued at the last minute; so the phrase concerning 'the brand plucked from burning' was applied to him. It had been plucked from the book of Zechariah. A later incident at the rectory was more curious. When Wesley was sixteen years old a persistent and ubiquitous poltergeist haunted the family. It became known as 'Old Jeffrey', and its knocks and groans, together with the noises of shattering glass and gobbling turkeys, caused great consternation. Everyone in the house heard them, including Samuel. It is believed by some that the energy of young females – of which there were many in the Wesley household – may provoke strange disturbances, but in the eighteenth century supernatural explanations were altogether more credible.

The young Wesley first comes into focus as an undergraduate at Oxford. He entered Christ Church in 1720, and was considered a pious and dutiful scholar to the extent that he was granted a fellowship at Lincoln College six years later. It was a predictable progression for one with a will to work and a desire for advancement, but it was greatly intensified by a zeal for religious improvement.

At the age of 22, in 1725, Wesley was granted what may be called his first revelation. He studied Jeremy Taylor's two books of Christian devotion and contemplation, known together as *Holy Living and Holy Dying* (1650–51), which persuaded the impressionable young man to dedicate himself to a life of faith and grace. In a diary entry for that year he wrote to himself that 'whenever you are to do an action, consider how Christ did or would do.' This ambition was strengthened by his reading of the *Imitation of Christ* (c. 1390–1440) by Thomas à Kempis and William Law's *A Practical Treatise upon Christian Perfection* (1726). He was drawn to the inward faith and assurance of these texts as a harbour for his restless soul; in them he found, as he put it, 'simplicity of affection and purity of intention'.

Wesley began to draw up lists of tasks for a life of piety, and carefully calculated the hours of his day for that pursuit. He became an inveterate compiler of lists, which is sometimes regarded as a symptom of anxiety. He was ordained a deacon in 1725, as the necessary preliminary for acquiring a fellowship, and three years later became a minister in the Church of England. But, of more enduring significance, he became attached to a group of three or four young men at Oxford who formed a little religious society of their own. The Holy Club had been assembled under the guidance of Wesley's younger brother, Charles, who matched him in devotion if not in discipline.

It can be seen as one of many religious societies that emerged in the period, as an ardent alternative to the more conventional presence of the established Church. The name of the club might seem presumptuous, but it was given to the group as a token of irony rather than respect. They were also known as the 'Bible-moths' or the 'Bible-bigots'. But 'Holy Club' stuck. Its members prayed together, read together and took communion together; they also decided to fulfil their Christian principles by visiting the poor and comforting the sick as well as the men and women confined in the two Oxford prisons of the Bocardo and the Castle. They inspired other small societies in the university and may be seen as a model, in miniature, of the 'connexions' between groups and individuals that Wesley would later establish. They also became known as 'methodists' because of their ordered regimen of devotion.

What was known by Wesley as the 'second rise' of Methodism occurred more than 3,000 miles away. The colony of Georgia was established in 1732; it was in fact the last of the North American colonies, and was the project of James Oglethorpe, a former army officer who wished to provide land and a new home for impoverished or indebted Londoners. After consulting friends and family, Wesley agreed to lead a mission that seems to have been devoted to the new settlers and to the Indigenous people who inhabited that region. In the autumn of 1735 he took ship across the Atlantic to revive in a pagan land what he considered to be the essentials of 'primitive Christianity'. He was also intent upon 'saving my own soul', in the belief that he was still in need of true faith. It was a doubt that often assailed him in these years. The mission itself could not be described as a success. He found the settlers to be stubborn and refractory, and described the Indigenous people as 'gluttons, drunkards, thieves . . . implacable, unmerciful'.

Wesley was also fatally involved in a mysterious relationship with a young woman, Sophy Hopkey, that was the harbinger of other difficulties with women. It was never clear to him where pious counsel and religious instruction might become touched by affectionate feeling and even mutual love. He had very little understanding of human nature in its more private forms.

In the case of Hopkey, Wesley's attempts to educate her were replaced by an intimacy that he recorded in his *Journal*. He confessed, 'I put my arms around her waist, sometimes took her by the hand, and sometimes kissed her'; he seems to have come close to proposing marriage, but something held him back. Tired of his dalliance and indecision, she married someone else. He was seized with despair and then, without thought of the consequences, refused to give communion to the now married woman. This was an open affront to her, all the more blatant in a small community of settlers, and her uncle forced him to stand trial for a number of alleged offences that violated the religious scruples of the colonizers. Wesley did not face a jury, but fled. He made his secret way to the port of Charlestown, from which he sailed back to England after an inglorious episode and a failed mission. He landed at Deal, Kent, on 21 February 1738.

✝

WESLEY CAME BACK in a mist of uncertainty about his future role as a minister. He was invited to preach in certain London churches, but his sermons were so strident that he was often asked not to speak again. The ministers and their congregations were not accustomed to 'enthusiasm', which was considered to be akin to the fanaticism of the previous century. While on board ship, however, Wesley had encountered a group of Moravian immigrants from Germany, whose simple piety and assurance of divine love impressed him greatly. They had also established a form of communal living to which he had aspired in the Holy Club at Oxford. On that model, then, in the spring of 1738, he formed 'our little society . . . which met afterwards in Fetter Lane'. The idea of a religious society, a close association of fellow believers, was always crucial to him.

Another revelation deepened Wesley's vision. In the same spring, he had gone somewhat unwillingly to the meeting of Moravian faithful in a chapel on Aldersgate Street in London; someone began to read out Martin Luther's *Preface* to Paul's Epistle to the Romans, whereupon,

> about a quarter before nine, while he was describing the change which God works in the heart through faith in Christ, I felt my heart strangely warmed. I felt I did trust in Christ, Christ alone, for salvation; and an assurance was given me that He had taken away my sins, even mine, and saved me from the law of sin and death.

It was a moment of conversion, and marked Wesley's profound realization that he might be justified by faith alone. This was the first stage in what became known as 'the awakening', the moment when, in his words, 'God began His great work in England,' and which gathered its fruit in the Methodist movement.

Where previously he had considered himself to be still a cold Christian, in need of abundant grace for salvation, Wesley now felt himself assured of redemption. Like Fox and others, he believed that he had the inward experience of divine love to guide him through the world. What was Methodism for him but an impassioned plea for the simple truths of what was known as 'primitive Christianity'? This was the good news he wished to impart, and he aligned himself with other religious societies. 'Come poor, lost, undone sinner!' he called out to those who came to hear him. 'Come just as you are to Christ!' For Wesley this represented a return to the basic principles of redemption, or saving grace; salvation came through Christ alone, and was wholly dependent upon true faith. It brought with it absolute assurance. In this assurance lay the novelty of his movement; it was the birthright, as it were, of every believing Christian. The crux for Wesley himself came when he observed to a Moravian, 'I know Christ has died for us,' and the other replied, 'Yes, but do you know that He has died for *you?*'

This was a message apparently more striking and more inspired than that which came from the pulpits of the national Church. It is often noted that the early supporters of Methodism came largely from among artisans, craftspeople, tradespeople and the 'middling' workers of the industrial towns, who had generally been neglected by the ministers of the established Church. They were now promised the chance of justification and salvation, by which 'faith after repentance is ease after pain, rest after toil, light after darkness'; they were to experience 'peace, joy, love'. It opened the prospect of a new life that never before had been vouchsafed to them.

Wesley began to preach with more certainty and greater fervour. Crowds assembled from local neighbourhoods in order to listen to what they believed to be the voice of God. The group of Methodist followers grew ever larger.

One of them, George Whitefield, was already an inspiring and almost mesmeric preacher. Henry St John, 1st Viscount Bolingbroke, a leader of the Tories, believed that he possessed 'the most commanding eloquence ever heard'. David Garrick, the actor, told a friend that he would give £1,000 to utter an 'Oh!!!' like Whitefield. It was Whitefield who persuaded Wesley to take his preaching out of doors and address the people in fields, on village greens or hillsides, in churchyards or in open markets. That was now Wesley's vocation. He had been told by one Moravian pastor 'to preach faith till you have it and then because you have it, you will preach faith'. This spiritual synergy became the source of his strength, when the new faith of others confirmed his own. In converting others, he could bear witness to the scriptural truth and also nourish the grace given to him. His successful evangelism conquered any of his remaining doubts and anxieties.

Wesley's will was as powerful as his inner faith, and was sustained by it, but his practicality was also of the utmost importance in future years. As Fox had done before him, he set out a pattern and plan for the organization of the small societies of his followers into a coherent national 'connexion'. The societies were grouped into 'bands' and were themselves divided into 'classes'. Wesley considered this to be 'providential legislation'. He had a passion for rules and for the exercise of authority in maintaining them, and was quick, resolute and highly organized. He had always drawn up timetables for his own activities and devotions, with a time for prayer, a time for preaching and a time for every other aspect of the devotional life. Inevitably he wished to apply the same system of control to others. He could never be part of a faith that he could not dominate and manage.

Wesley's deployment and careful guidance of 'field preachers' into thirty 'circuits', for example, set up a body quite different from anything in the established Church. The preachers were predominantly laypeople, known as 'helpers' or 'messengers of God'. In fact they represented the beginning of an independent faith. As part of that process, he instituted in 1744 a national conference of travelling preachers that continued to meet annually. At the conference of 1763 Wesley even outlined a constitution and compiled the articles of Methodist belief. He became known to some as 'Pope John'.

The writer and historian Horace Walpole watched Wesley preach in 1766 and wrote that he was 'a clean, elderly man, fresh-coloured, his hair smoothly combed, but with a little *soupçon* of curls at the end. Wondrous clever, but as evidently an actor as Garrick'. He might have added that Wesley was small of stature, approximately five foot three, with an erect bearing and piercing blue eyes. He had a sharp, angular nose and a powerful jaw, and his eyes were slightly hooded. His hair was long, moving gradually from auburn to white, and looked odd for the period. He often wore full black clerical dress, so that from a distance he might be mistaken for a raven. His resemblance to an actor was also noticed by others, and it is likely that he had assimilated certain theatrical skills in order to improve the effect of his preaching. One observer believed that he had mastered the art of pantomime, too, and could convey his meaning by gesture or mute action.

Wesley's large open congregations, perhaps infected by what was later called the madness of crowds, succumbed to hysteria. What must they do to be saved? Some fell down unconscious, as if they were dead, or were reduced to convulsions. Others groaned aloud or gave way to violent weeping and trembling. The Bishop of Exeter observed 'Shriekings, Roarings, Groanings, Gnashings, Yellings, Cursings, Blasphemies and Despairings'. Wesley himself observed of one Mass congregation that

> the people were half-strangled and gasping for life . . . great numbers wept without noise; others fell down as dead; some with extreme noise and violent agitation. One man hurled himself upon a wall again and again, calling out 'Oh what shall I do? What shall I do? Oh for one drop of the blood of Christ!'

It is worth noting that this was a period that has been described by literary scholars as the age of sensibility, with such works as Henry Mackenzie's *The Man of Feeling* (1771) and the 'graveyard poetry' of Edward Young's *Night-Thoughts* (1742–6). It is sometimes assumed that the poetry of sentiment or passion began with the Romantics of the nineteenth century, but in fact the previous century was one in which vehemence of feeling was generally exhibited. Wesley is representative of a change in sensibility that affected domestic and social as well as religious concerns. No one is separate from the age in which he or she lives.

✝

WESLEY ESTABLISHED SMALL GROUPS of the faithful, or what he
described as Christians 'of like mind who seek fellowship with each
other', and recognized the significance of laypeople rather than
ordained ministers in the spreading of the gospel. The numbers
grew, and the congregations became larger. The Methodist faith
spread in the manufacturing districts of the northeast, the north
Midlands and the Potteries; it flourished in mining areas and in
fishing villages. And it thrived in London, too. As early as 1739,
a year after he established his first society in Fetter Lane, Wesley
renovated an old cannon factory in the area of Moorfields, the
Foundery, and established the first meeting house for a Methodist
congregation. By 1776 it was clear that a much larger meeting
house was necessary, and a year later he laid the cornerstone for
a chapel along the City Road, opposite the Dissenters' graveyard.

Women as well as men became valued members of the small
groups that came together as a result of Wesley's ministry. He
knew, as did other Dissenters, that female spirituality and eloquence were an important aspect of inspiring faith. His own
relationships with women were more ambiguous, and, as with
Sophy Hopkey in Georgia, he was always uncertain or unaware of
the line between pious tutelage and human affection. This involved
him in embarrassment and, sometimes, ridicule. He did eventually
marry, but the union was not a success. His wife was jealous of the
letters he wrote to fellow believers of the opposite sex.

Wesley travelled everywhere, and by the end of his life there
was not one English county that he had not visited. It is estimated
that each year he covered as much as 20,000 miles on horseback
and preached approximately eight hundred sermons to numbers
varying from a few hundred to twenty thousand. Astonishing in
itself, this became part of, and perhaps the inspiration for, what is
known as the evangelical revival. Yet, for those first Methodists,

it was not so much a revival as an awakening or a renewal of old certainties. Wesley himself did not wish to leave the Church of England but to restore it. When accused of preaching outside the traditional parish boundaries, he replied, 'I look upon all the world as my parish.'

It is also true that Wesley shared the popular belief in the supernatural, and was willing to use its agency in the course of his ministry. He resorted to sortilege (the practice of drawing lots) to determine his actions, and believed firmly in the presence of ghosts. He was of the opinion that sickness might be induced by evil spirits, and always claimed that 'Old Jeffrey' was the invisible visitor to Epworth rectory. He trusted the evidence of things unseen. In him, as in other leaders of English faith, pragmatism and mystical spirituality were closely aligned.

In the growth and development of a powerful movement, disagreements and rivalries were bound to occur. It is the law of life. For Methodism this took the form of an old and bitter contention. There were some, Whitefield among them, who professed the Calvinist belief in predestination, by means of which only the elect would be saved and the rest consigned to damnation. Wesley had always rejected that proposition, as leading either to moral anarchy or to despair, and instead held the doctrine that Christ's Crucifixion might merit the salvation of all. This was too wide a breach to be resolved, and soon enough 'Calvinist Methodists' were opposed to the rest. Wesley also came to attest the idea of 'perfectionism', by which he meant that some were so blessed by divine grace that they could no longer sin. Sin held no dominion over them. He called this 'entire sanctification', 'the great salvation' and 'perfect love'. This doctrine was also opposed by the Calvinists, but no force of Earth could hinder or delay his self-imposed mission.

Wesley came to disagree on a minor scale with his younger brother. Charles Wesley had always supported him in the

Methodist ministry, and was previously associated with John in the Holy Club at Oxford, but he was much more circumspect about breaking the bonds with the Church of England. Charles was less vehement, and watched with growing unease the accelerating if still uncertain progress towards an independent faith. He disliked the idea of lay ministers, and disagreed profoundly with John's belief that he could in practice ordain them. That was the role and duty of bishops. But mutual affection and shared belief were enough to keep the brothers from separation, and in fact Charles contributed materially to the nature of Methodism with the hymns he composed for daily or weekly worship. Hymns had not been an aspect of English spirituality before this time, but the Methodist example soon spread until singing became a characteristic part of national devotion.

Forceful opposition also came from outside. Just as the Quakers and Ranters had been vilified and abused in the past, so the Methodists and their preachers came under sustained attack from violent crowds or enraged ministers of the national Church. Wesley himself was often beaten, abused, pelted with stones and bricks, forced to flee or to take refuge. This was a measure of the condition of England, where political and religious passion could swell at any moment and where 'mobocracy' often ruled. It was part of the ready emotionalism of the period.

✠

ON 1 JANUARY 1790 John Wesley wrote in his *Journal*,

> I am now an old man, decayed from head to foot. My eyes are dim, my right hand shakes much, my mouth is hot and dry every morning, I have a lingering fever almost every day, my motion is weak and slow. However, blessed be God, I do not slack my labour. I can preach and write still.

He was now 86 years old, and before the infirmity of age he had been a miracle of health and energy, waking at four in the morning and preaching by five. He had now become a national figure, almost an institution, whose presence drew admiring crowds where once he had provoked abuse and hostility.

Wesley preached his last sermon on 23 February 1791 in Leatherhead, before returning to his house along the City Road, where he was persuaded to take to his bed. He died eight days later, and was buried in a vault behind the chapel he had erected fourteen years before. He believed that all his life he had been led by providential grace, but iron will and self-belief had also led him forwards. 'I am driven,' he once wrote. 'I cannot stand still.'

Wesley's energy and determination can perhaps be estimated in the fact that the Holy Club of four members in Oxford had, by the time of his death, been transformed into a religious society of 70,000 members. Now in Great Britain it has more than 4,000 preaching houses and approximately 165,000 adherents. The world communion of the United Methodist Church is believed to number 12 million.

Luigi Schiavonetti, after Thomas Phillips, *William Blake*, 1808, engraving.

Fifteen

Religion as Individual
William Blake (1757–1827)

William Blake was born on 28 November 1757 in the Soho quarter of London; he was baptized in the church of St James, Piccadilly, close by, and so was formally introduced into the Church of England. But his mother, Catherine, was of the Moravian brethren, who, on the basis of a personal revelation of Christ, formed small groups or communities that practised prayer, piety and good works; they were not separated from orthodox Protestantism, but they were distinct from it. This was the context of Blake's early years, in which he was imbued with a religion of piety, enthusiasm and vision. His house was on the corner of Broad Street and Marshall Street, but he did not attend any of the Dissenting academies in the city. He once explained that 'there is no use in education. I hold it wrong. It is the great Sin. It is eating of the tree of Knowledge of Good and Evil.' It is evident that he had no conventional education at all, and knew only what he learned from his mother and from his incessant reading, with his closest and most significant attachment to the Bible. It would have been the staple of his family, the object of continual meditation and interpretation.

Blake seems by his own account to have been a separate and lonely boy, whose principal childhood memory was of solitary walking. He walked everywhere – to Dulwich and Camberwell, to Lambeth and Croydon. When he travelled north to Hampstead or Highgate, Hornsea or Muswell Hill, he was afflicted by a 'torment of the Stomach'. He was always highly sensitive to the spirit of place. But he also sensed, and saw, other spirits. In later life he described how in Peckham Rye, by Dulwich Hill, he looked up and saw 'a tree filled with angels, bright angelic wings bespangling every bough'. On another occasion he saw haymakers at work and 'amid them angels walking'. He was about to be beaten by his father, for telling lies, but his mother intervened.

At an early age Blake evinced a remarkable skill at drawing, and his parents, in place of a more formal education, sent him to Henry Pars's drawing school in the Strand. He continued his training at the Academy of Painting and Sculpture in St Martin's Lane, and after much labour, practice and study, he was enrolled in the summer of 1772 as the apprentice to an engraver, James Basire, in Great Queen Street. He was destined to become a tradesman rather than an artist and so began the career that, for better or worse, he was to pursue for the rest of his life. On a proof of 'Joseph of Arimathea among the Rocks of Albion' Blake wrote that it was 'engraved when I was a beginner at Basires from a drawing by Salviati after Michael Angelo'. The figure stands on an outcrop of rock along the English coast, lost in thought or vision, isolated and apart; he is looking steadfastly at the ground and, with his arms folded across a simple hooded shirt, there is such an air of intensity and brooding concentration upon him that he might have been taken from a tomb painting or a medieval psalter. He is one of the figures of Blake's early imaginative world. John Foxe believed that Joseph, the principal figure of the Glastonbury legends, was the first begetter of English Christianity; in turn William Blake saw in Joseph the lineaments of the English prophets, just as Blake himself can be placed in that line of Dissenting prophets who comprised the alternative traditional religion of the sixteenth and early seventeenth centuries.

After two or three years as Basire's apprentice, Blake was 'sent out to make drawings in Westminster Abbey' as preparation for a series of engravings. He later told the artist, Samuel Palmer, that 'in Westminster Abbey were his earliest and most sacred recollections.' His poetry and art are filled with images of cloisters and crypts, of tomb architecture and memorial figures that become emblems of a spiritual reality still existing within the material world. Crouching above the ornate sepulchres, and drawing the marble figures that lay upon them, the young man entered into communion with the dead. That communion would never end. After his apprenticeship was completed he was admitted to the Royal Academy Schools, where, despite the best intentions of his fashionable teachers, he became more committed than ever to the pure outline and clearly defined form of such masters as Raphael and Michelangelo. He etched on plate 54 of *Jerusalem*,

> In Great Eternity, every particular Form gives forth
>   or Emanates
> Its own peculiar Light, & the Form is the Divine Vision
> And the Light is his Garment This is Jerusalem in
>   every Man.

✛

SINCE BLAKE WAS brought up principally by a mother who espoused Moravian doctrine, it seems likely that he was imbued early on with similar beliefs. The Moravians were those who had once so impressed John Wesley with their simple piety and their assurance of divine love. In fact Wesley helped to formulate the principles of the English branch of 'Moravian Brethren' in 1738. Several congregations emerged in England, from Yorkshire to Bedfordshire, with the express purpose of restoring the practice of early Christianity. They were of German origin and part of a growing evangelical and pietist movement, but they held certain beliefs that were peculiar to them. They found glory in sexual intercourse as a sacramental act and they venerated human sexuality, and the sexual organs, as gateways to the divine. The Moravians held the belief that union with Christ could be experienced by means of sexual intercourse in marriage or what was called 'conjugial love'. This was enlarged into a veneration of the blood and wounds of Christ upon the Cross, particularly the side wound, which was likened to the vagina. Their conflation of sex and piety was of interest to the young Blake, whose poetry and art would come to celebrate it.

Blake had also been reading the work of Emanuel Swedenborg, the Swedish philosopher and theologian whose startling works circulated among the Dissenters and political radicals of eighteenth-century London. In the spring of 1744, on one of his many visits to London (which would in a sense become his spiritual home), Swedenborg had taken lodgings with a watchmaker, John Paul Brockmer, a Moravian who lived in Salisbury Court near the Moravian chapel in Fetter Lane; in the autumn of the following year, he lodged with another Moravian from the Fetter Lane chapel. In 1783 Robert Hindmarsh, a printer with a Moravian background, formed a 'Theosophical Society', for translating, printing and distributing the writings of Swedenborg. This society was renamed in 1785 'The British Society for the Propagation of the Doctrines of the New Church'. That Church was established upon Swedenborgian precepts.

An affinity between Swedenborg and the Moravians is clear enough, but there was for Blake a more personal connection. In February 1787 Blake had stayed for three days and nights by the deathbed of his younger brother Robert, and at the final moment he saw the released spirit ascending and 'clapping its hands for joy'. Swedenborg had taught that the spirits of the dead rose from the body and reassumed physical form in another world. He wrote that 'for the space of eight months now I have by the pure mercy and grace of the Messiah, been having the same sort of conversation with people in heaven as with my friends on earth.' In a heightened state of spiritual consciousness, which could take the form of trance, dream or vision, Swedenborg travelled to heaven and to hell. He conversed with angels and visited their dwellings, describing them as if they were on an adjacent street. Time is not measured in days or years, but in changes of awareness; distance is measured only by the nearness of God; wherever the angels happen to be, they are always facing God. Swedenborg also believed that sex was a spiritual as well as a physical power; it existed in the spiritual world, therefore, and was continued in the next phase of existence. He brought palpable order and degree to an otherwise numinous and elusive reality, and he was for a while the philosopher who gave substance to Blake's visions. He died at 26 Great Bath Street, Clerkenwell, at the end of March 1772 and was buried in Princes Square, Wapping.

Swedenborg was revered by many in London, which, at the end of the eighteenth century, was awash with mysticism and millenarianism. Many of the tracts and pamphlets sold in the bookshops and on the bookstalls were concerned with occult and cabbalistic beliefs. There were Quakers and Socinians, Freemasons and 'the Ancient Deists' of Hoxton; some of them were astrologers or alchemists, mystics or magnetizers, but all of them believed in the primacy of the spiritual world. This was a phase of the English soul. In the spring of 1789 Blake and his wife, Catherine, attended a general conference of the New Jerusalem Church at the Swedenborgian chapel in Great East Cheap; the New Church had been established to convey Swedenborg's teachings to the world, and Blake's presence at the conference confirms his attachment to them. He became disenchanted with the Church, however, when it went the way of what he called 'old religion', with its organized hierarchy and its own ministers.

Blake told a friend and fellow artist, John Flaxman, that soon after his retreat from Swedenborg 'Paracelsus & Behmen appeared to me.' In respect of any understanding of the English soul, it is

worth making the obvious point that neither of these philoso-
phers was of English origin. England has always been a magpie
or perhaps magnetic nation, adopting beliefs and practices that
come from elsewhere. In the same fashion Blake picked up separate ideas, or fragments of knowledge, as he needed them. He
was a synthesizer and a systematizer, but it was his own synthesis
designed to establish his own system of belief. From the sixteenth-
century Swiss physician Paracelsus he learned the central truth
that 'Imagination is like the sun. The sun has a light which is not
tangible; but which, nevertheless, may set a house on fire.' He
learned that 'God who is in heaven exists also in man, and the two
are but One,' and that 'the human body is vapour materialized
by sunshine mixed with the life of the stars.' From the German
mystic and theologian Jakob Böhme he came to an understanding of the 'One Man', 'Universal Man' or 'Cosmogonic Man' that
was so influential among the mystics of the late eighteenth century. Böhme adumbrated the same great theme, the *mysterium
magnum*, in one of his aphorisms: 'He for whom time is the same
as eternity, and eternity the same as time, is free of all adversity.'
And he reiterated the fundamental belief that 'our whole doctrine
is nothing else but an instruction to show how man may create a
kingdom of light within himself.' This was the context of Blake's
perception in *The Marriage of Heaven and Hell* that 'men forgot
that/ All deities reside in the human breast.'

In Blake's lifetime there was a chapel of Behmenists in Bow
Lane, and in the religious literature of the period we find references
to 'the poor people who love Jacob Behmen'. Six Methodists were
expelled from their churches for teaching his doctrines. Böhme,
like Swedenborg, was highly compatible with Moravian teaching; the Moravians' printer, John Lewis, published a treatise by
the German theologian in 1770. Blake's religion, if that is the right
word, sprang from these sources. One verse of his is in fact profoundly reminiscent of the older theologian. Böhme wrote, 'if thou

conceives a small minute Circle, as small as a Grain of Mustard-seed, yet the Heart of God is wholly and perfectly therein.' He anticipates Blake's 'Auguries of Innocence': 'To see a World in a Grain of Sand/ And a Heaven in a Wild Flower'.

By 1793 Blake had begun to prepare a number of engravings and etchings, combining words and images, in which he copied the numbered chapters and verses of the Bible in order to create an alternative testament. In *The Book of Urizen* (1794), *The Book of Ahania* and *The Book of Los* (both 1795) he wrote his own Genesis and Exodus. In these works he opposes Urizen, the god of rationality and of narrowed perception, to Los, who represents the power of the creative imagination. It was a bold undertaking but not, in the fervent climate of the time, an inexplicable one. Blake may have been acquainted with Richard Brothers, an exact contemporary and vociferous prophet of a new Jerusalem. In these etchings Urizen broods over his books of brass with outstretched hands; Los howls in torment among flames; Urizen is crouched in despair beneath great rocks; from the bowed head of Los a huge globe of blood, like a planet, emerges. Blake was opening the doors of perception to another, greater reality. Henry Crabb Robinson, a lawyer and diarist, noted of Blake that 'he is not so much a disciple of Jacob Behmen & Swedenborg as a fellow Visionary . . . He lives as much as they did in a world of his own.'

Out of these words and images arose the great and complex architecture of Blake's later prophetic books. In *Milton* and *Jerusalem* (both started *c.* 1804) he consummates his vision of human destiny and of eternal salvation:

And all that has existed in the space of six thousand years:
Permanent, & not lost not lost nor vanishd, & every
   little act,
Word, work, & wish, that has existed, all remaining still

For every thing exists & not one sigh nor smile nor tear,
One hair nor particle of dust, not one can pass away.

William Blake died on the evening of 12 August 1827 and was buried in the Dissenters' graveyard of Bunhill Fields. After his death a fellow artist, George Richmond, kissed him and then closed the dead man's eyes 'to keep the vision in'. Yet in truth his vision has never been lost. It is integral to the English soul.

Sixteen

Religion as Established

In an account of religious faith, the common ground – that which is traditional, that which is familiar – can be neglected in favour of less orthodox but more diverting paths. But that ground is still there. The Church of England, the established Church since 1559, was the result of compromise and shared understanding. It was meant to provide reassurance and a middle way between factions. In this it was wholly successful, and proved itself to be durable enough to survive into the present time.

George Herbert's treatise *The Country Parson* was composed in 1632, but more than two centuries later its precepts were still being observed. He had written it to provide 'the Form and Character of a true Pastor, that I may have a Mark to aim at'. The church parson is clean in body and in mind. He is courteous and diligent, ministering to all ranks and degrees among his parishioners. He has a thorough knowledge of the scriptures and possesses a zeal for preaching. He is both 'rewarder and punisher' in his community, and takes on the role of unofficial magistrate in all local disputes: 'Therefore he endures not that any of his Flock should go to Law; but in any Controversy, that they should resort to him as their Judge.' He should therefore read Michael Dalton's *The Country Justice* (1618) and the *Abridgements of the Statutes* (c. 1551). He is also the doctor for his parishioners, acquainted with anatomy as well as physic. He should own a herbal, to find the appropriate cures or salves. In conclusion Herbert noted, characteristically, that the parson 'is a Lover of old Customs, if they be good, and harmless; and the rather, because Country people are much addicted to them'. This parson was, then, the principal figure of his district as magistrate, doctor and spiritual guide. In that he reflected the position of the Church itself in national life. It was permanent and certain.

After the restoration of the monarchy in 1660, the Church of England had been once more in the ascendant. The 'settlement' enshrined by the Act of Uniformity in 1662 penalized Dissenters as 'men of factious, peevish and perverse spirits' and confirmed the prayers and practices of 'the whole Catholique Church of Christ'; this was in effect the Church of William Laud and Richard Hooker. Church and state were thereby reunited in a bond that has never since been broken. Those who did not take communion according to the established rite could be denied the privileges of citizenship. In this general restoration of national faith, churches were refurbished, once-familiar rituals were performed again, and the old feast days celebrated. The new 'auditory' churches were designed for preaching, but the sermons avoided the fire and thunder of the Puritans as well as the convoluted rhetoric of John Donne or Lancelot Andrewes. The style was now plain, simple and direct, suitable for a period that has been called, perhaps unfairly, the 'age of reason'.

The Country Parson offered a paradigm of parish life, but of course conditions varied from place to place. Some clergy held two or three livings, while others were confined to one. The 'pluralists', who held more than one living, commonly employed poor curates to take their place. 'There the old rascal goes,' cries the curate on seeing the vicar, his employer, in Tobias Smollett's *The Adventures of Roderick Random* (1748),

> and the devil go with him. You see how the world wags, gentlemen. By Gad, this rogue of a vicar does not deserve

to live; and yet he has two livings worth £400 per annum, while poor I am fain to do all his drudgery, and ride twenty miles every Sunday to preach; for what? why, truly, for £20 a year.

Some lived in affluence, therefore, in a comfortable parsonage or Georgian house, while others lived in relative poverty in a cottage no larger than those of their neighbours. It was not unknown for the parson to join the ploughman in the fields. A large number of the poorer clergy were ill trained as well as ill paid. They were often married, with an abundance of children, and with few if any opportunities to improve their position. In these conditions many struggled to sustain their duties of visiting the sick, relieving the poor, teaching the children, preaching the gospel and conducting the Sunday services.

It was observed that their richer and grander parishioners treated them with barely veiled contempt. A poor chaplain ministering to a rich family had the status of a servant, and could be found in the middle of dinner 'picking his teeth and sighing with his hat under his arm while the knight and my lady eat up the tarts and chickens'. The divisions of rank and wealth within the clergy were so great that little connection, or communication, was ever possible between them.

There was a more general distinction. The higher clergy of the Church of England were considered to play the largest part in the order and discipline of their communities. Many were magistrates and lived on familiar terms with the local squire, with whom they drank, ate and hunted. In this alliance of Church and state, they were also the masters who might rule or neglect their 'flock' as they wished. It is likely that they were feared rather than respected in a world where social rank or status was of the greatest importance.

For most of the gentry their Church was naturally and inevitably the state Church. It was part of their birthright. In turn the higher clergy were in the early eighteenth century wholly at the service of the political administration, whether that be Robert Harley and the Tories or Robert Walpole and the Whigs. The Archbishop of Canterbury had an official seat on the Privy Council, while the bishops were an intrinsic part of the House of Lords.

Of 12,000 'benefices' or permanent posts in the Church, only 2,500 were in the choice of the Church itself. Six hundred were appointed by the colleges of Oxford and Cambridge, which were in a sense factories for the manufacture of clergy, and a thousand were in the gift of the monarch. All the rest were at the disposal of private patrons who administered livings as part of their property. They might bequeath them to younger sons, relatives or friends. So the pastor emerged as a version of the country squire. He conducted the necessary services and ministered to the sick or unfortunate. But he was also a gentleman who delighted in cards and hunting, drinking and dining. These clergymen became a stock feature of nineteenth-century fiction. Since many of these 'rectors' held more than one living, they were able to collect more than one parish 'tithe', which amounted to one-tenth of the agricultural produce or income of each parishioner. The 'rector' would then appoint a 'vicar' to be his substitute in an individual parish, while also relying on the help of curates.

The bishops themselves were in fact now some of the greatest lords in the land. A few held political or diplomatic positions, while the great majority supported the government of the day. They were often of noble blood, and it was a matter of self-congratulation that after the rule of Cromwell the grandees had returned to their palaces. The Church was considered to be one of the three great professions, alongside law and the emerging art or science of medicine, and the Church of England was primarily a religion of duties and responsibilities that maintained social cohesion. That was of the greatest importance, since religion was

James Watson, after Joshua Reynolds, *Edmund Burke*, 1770, engraving.

the basis of civil society. Edmund Burke noted in his *Reflections on the Revolution in France* (1790) that 'the majority of the people of England, far from thinking a religious national establishment unlawful, hardly think it to be lawful without one.'

Morality, rather than theology, was the guiding presence. Where the parson and the landowner are in agreement, the religious and secular state reflect each other. Habit, and indifference, complete the picture. If this sounds cynical, we may turn to that most English of observers, William Hogarth, who in *The Sleeping*

Congregation of 1762 shows the effect of a universal dullness covering all. In his etching the service is dominated by royal, rather than divine, images. Spirituality has been converted into slumber. That torpor, or passivity, persisted. In the early decades of the nineteenth century religion was the air that the 'respectable' breathed. The established religion was neither hot nor cold. The Broad Church accommodated a wide range of opinions, if not beliefs, in its maintenance of a nationally based religion. Samuel Butler wrote, in *The Way of All Flesh* (published posthumously in 1903 and set in the middle of the nineteenth century), that its adherents were often 'tolerators, if not lovers, of all that was familiar, haters of all that was unfamiliar'. Their preachers conveyed only the dry details of a 'middling' morality. They were scarcely affected by Romanism or ritual, and had in turn stood aside from Dissent and Nonconformity. The French historian Hippolyte Taine remarked that the average Englishman or Englishwoman believed in God, the Trinity and hell, 'although without fervour'. And that was the key. It was not a secular nation but to a large extent it was an indifferent one.

The complacency of the upper classes was not shared by other levels of society. A report by the census-takers of 1851 remarked that

> working men, it is contended, cannot enter our religious structures without having impressed upon their notice some memento of their inferiority. The existence of pews [which were rented by the more affluent], and the position of the free seats, are, it is said, sufficient to deter them from our churches.

As for the indigent poor, and those close to absolute poverty, no one really expected them to attend church or chapel. They would probably have been ejected if they had attempted to do so. The senior clergy did nothing to address this and the bishops, in particular, did not offer any spiritual leadership to the nation at large. They did not pretend to offer any cogent analysis of social change or political development. They may not have considered it necessary, since the largest number of their flock believed, at least, in the certain existence of the Almighty, in heaven and hell, and in the value of prayer and scripture. This was the vague penumbra of their lives. There was no reason to disturb them or to inform them any further.

It is worth reflecting for a moment on the nature of pragmatism in English faith. In the fourth century that curiously English heretic, Pelagius, asserted that Christian worship lay in the sphere of practicality and action rather than in the cultivation of a more exalted spirituality. We read of the Anglo-Saxon theologian Eadmer of Canterbury that he possessed a practical working simplicity in religious matters. From Julian of Norwich to John Wyclif and beyond, there has been an emphasis on simplicity and practicality. As in most features of English spirituality, continuity is the key. The reformed religion, as outlined in the Elizabethan Settlement, was concerned as much with practice and usage as with doctrine. The Church of England, in subsequent years, proved itself to be flexible as well as comprehensive; in matters of faith and theology, it espoused the virtues of moderation and compromise.

As the nation changed in the nineteenth century, therefore, so did the status of the national religion. In the early years of that century the Church was still so largely tied to the political and legal system that it was in effect synonymous with it. But the repeal in 1828 of the Test and Corporation Acts, which had confined public office to those espousing the principles of the Church of England, marked a decisive moment in the history of the established Church. Catholic emancipation followed in 1829, and the entrance of people of Jewish faith to Parliament was compounded by that of the atheist Charles Bradlaugh. The Church of England was no longer the Tory Party at prayer, as was once suggested, and could not even be considered to be the nation at prayer. With the passing of the Civil Registration Act in 1836, Anglican ministers lost their monopoly over the rites of birth, marriage and death. That authority was now a civic, rather than ecclesiastical, requirement. The compulsory church rate, imposed for the benefit of the parish church and its officials, was abolished in 1868.

It should be noted, however, that tradition could not be overturned by legislation; for many people birth, marriage and burial needed the blessing of the traditional Anglican rites of passage. It was a question of custom and loyalty. For the early Victorian family the Bible and the Book of Common Prayer were always close at hand, together with a volume of sermons and an 'improving' book or two. Yet, as a result of all these measures from the 1820s to the 1860s, the Church no longer intruded so noticeably into private and public lives. It had become a national Church set within an increasingly mixed and various nation. It was not to its advantage, therefore, that in many respects it stayed as it was. The majority of its clergy were still graduates of Oxford or Cambridge, and many needed a private income to sustain their roles. Their affinity with the more affluent rendered them less combative and contentious in their battle for souls – on the presumption that they considered it to be a battle at all. For them the parish was a miniature version of the social world, where the maintenance of law and order, combined with paternalistic discipline, was the key. The routine of churchgoing was familiar enough, with regular Sunday attendance in the morning and services in the evening, quarterly or monthly communion services, and special observances on high days and holy days.

Another duty was given to the clergy. A Church organization, the National Society for Promoting the Education of the Poor in the Principles of the Established Church, was, as its name suggests, the principal agency for the education of the less fortunate. Many parishes had organized rudimentary schooling for those who did not care for 'dame schools' or could not afford private schools, but the Society provided the first concerted effort to raise up the children of the disadvantaged. These 'National schools' were in large part staffed by the clergy and parish officers on the understanding that, according to one clergyman, 'when you have manufactured a steady, honest, God-fearing, Church-going population, then you have done your duty as schoolmasters.' This may help to elucidate the novelist Charles Kingsley's remark that 'we have used the Bible as if it were a mere special constable's handbook, an opium dose for keeping beasts of burden patient while they are being overloaded.'

✠

IT WAS CLEAR, then, that the Church of England was for a variety of reasons losing its hold over the population. As early as 1799 the Bishop of Chester, William Cleaver, whose bishopric included areas of the new industries, noted that in one parish of 40,000 not one person attended any church. Church-building was in demand in the early nineteenth century, but the new churches were only half filled. London, in 1836, had a population of almost 1.5 million, but the Church provided seats in its places of worship for just 140,000. In 1851, according to the national census, 66 per cent of the available seats were unoccupied. They were filled, if at all, by the middle class and lower middle class; the working classes were not to be seen. That is why the great towns and cities, marked already by the factories and slums of the new industrial order, were considered to be hostile territory for the clergy. If the established religion was meant to be the foundation of social harmony, its failure – its absence – was the harbinger of disaster.

That did not imply that the working classes were irreligious or pagan, as some observers suggested. They had an understanding of religion quite different from that of their 'betters'. In 1888 the senior cleric of Oxford House, the first settlement 'house' for undergraduates to do social work among the poor of east London, wrote, 'my first surprise about East London was its extreme respectability; in morality and a sense of decency they are far ahead of dwellers in some other parts of London.' That sense of decency and respectability did not consort well with the idea of a pagan working class, but it does suggest that the poorer men and women possessed a sense of morality that was based on a residuum of religious belief. They rejected the established Church because it was the preserve of the upper classes, who either patronized or ignored them.

It would be wrong, however, to overemphasize the restricting power of the Church. Many parish priests in the great towns and cities were involved in welfare work and poor relief as a direct result of the successive waves of industrialization. They believed that social work was directly related to their religious ministry. One bishop told his clergy that 'no man can know the Gospel . . . without feeling for the poor a melting pity.' But pity was not enough. The more zealous clergy tried, as far as possible, to alleviate the ills of their parishes. They presided over philanthropic societies and organized soup kitchens. They superintended orphanages and poor schools. They administered clothing clubs and mutual benefit societies. They sat on the boards of hospitals, Friendly Societies and savings banks. Perhaps most importantly, they engaged in house-to-house visits in order to enquire more closely into the wretched conditions of many of their parishioners. They were often the only visitors in a world of factories, slums and filthy streets. All the ills of the industrial world confronted them.

The number of philanthropic clubs and societies had increased by mid-century, with the growing awareness that poor and unsanitary social conditions were the largest cause of disease and distress. Charles Blomfield, Bishop of London at the time, noted that drunkenness and disease 'were frequently the result of want', and that to alleviate this by any possible means was a Christian duty.

William Howley, Archbishop of Canterbury from 1828 until his death in 1848, went further in his support of factory reform. He told the Lords in 1832 that 'it was a disgrace to a Christian and civilized community to allow such a system to continue merely for putting money in the pockets of master manufacturers.' In the second half of the nineteenth century the established Church was eager to emphasize the importance of slum clearance, factory legislation and sanitary reform. It was now animated by the pressure of social responsibility and the need for moral reform.

This did not mean that the Church necessarily came closer to the working class and the poor, who remained apart from its rites and services. They were still the lost congregation. It is likely that they remained largely unaware of the Church's renewed interest in social welfare. It is also probable that they retained the belief or instinct that the established Church was the voice of the upper and middle classes, a notion that was supported by a bishop at a meeting for working men in 1870 when he remarked that 'the great idea which the Church has to teach men is the idea of duty.' 'Duty' implied deference of an inferior to a superior, and introduced the possibility of social distinction or even social control. This was the dilemma that the Church of England was never able to resolve. The fact that the bishops in the House of Lords, as well as their clergy, were traditionally opposed to Dissenters and Nonconformists also meant that they were considered conservative in political attitude. At least, they tended to support the political party currently in power. It was a question of pragmatism. 'This Established Church', wrote the Archbishop of Canterbury, Archibald Campbell Tait, in 1876, 'is an instrument devised by Providence for welding this great people into one compact Christian body.'

Time and tide were not in the Church's favour. Primary and secondary education gradually came under the aegis of the state, and changes in leisure activities and the rise of organized sports meant that Sundays were no longer the preserve of the churches.

Larger forces were also at work. In 1894 Keir Hardie, a founder of the Labour Party and its first Parliamentary leader, wrote, 'I claim for Socialism that it is the embodiment of Christianity in our industrial system.' The initiatives of the social gospel were to pass into other hands.

✝

AT THE END of one of the annual Oxford–Cambridge Boat Races, the members of the Oxford crew left the bank of the Thames and travelled to the East End in order to resume their social work among the poor of that area. They were, in a sense, missionaries to 'outcast London', as it was often called. Many novels of the mid-nineteenth century contain accounts of athletic, fair-haired young men, based in a 'house' purchased by the Church, who sally forth to fight the twin evils of paganism and poverty. Their efforts were not altogether successful. The divisions between the shepherd and the flock, to use familiar terms, were too great. As one sympathetic clergyman put it, 'a few weeks spent in Bethnal Green during the vacation might benefit the undergraduate, but can hardly have much effect on the East End.' The young men did not understand the principles or beliefs of the working class, and the working class did not know what the undergraduates were doing there. It was a miniature of the Church of England in the nineteenth century.

Seventeen

Religion as Battle

Catherine Booth (1829–1890),
William Booth (1829–1912)

Catherine Mumford was born on 17 January 1829 in the small market town of Ashbourne in Derbyshire. Her father was a carriage-builder and lay preacher of Methodist persuasion, and, since her mother matched him in spiritual intensity, the young girl was raised in a deeply religious household. But the father drifted, began to drink and renounced his former faith. As a result Catherine grew more dependent upon her mother, who instilled in her a fear of the Lord as well as a fear of the world. She had read the Bible eight times before she reached the age of twelve. At that age she also became the 'secretary' of a Juvenile Temperance Society. It may have been a narrow childhood, but in many respects it was an inspiring one.

When Catherine was fifteen the Mumford family moved down to London, where, in the neighbourhood of Brixton, they set up house. Mother and daughter attended the local Wesleyan chapel and Catherine joined its 'class meeting', at which she prayed, sang, and listened to the testimony of others. In the following year she experienced the force of the sudden grace that came with the assurance of salvation; it had come upon her while reading one of Charles Wesley's hymns, which included the phrase 'my Jesus is mine!' It was an epiphany, and it reveals the extent to which the words of John Wesley and his brother had entered the English soul. Yet as Catherine's spirit rose, her physical health sank; in

Catherine Booth, 1889, photograph.

this period she was diagnosed with consumption. The pattern of religious fervour and intermittent illness would be maintained for the rest of her life.

There had been a split in the ranks of the Methodists, between those who adhered to the opinions of the organizing Conference and those who wished for a looser connection between the chapels, with the participation of lay members as well as ministers. It seems to be the fate of English Nonconformism that it creates a central organization with some difficulty, which is then divided into smaller and smaller groups. Catherine herself, with an innate distrust for a separate clerisy, favoured the Reformed Methodists, who wished for a more open Church.

As a result Catherine was expelled from the membership of the established Methodists, but was taken up by the Reformers. She became the teacher of a Sunday school on reformed lines, and remained in that post for three years. She also met a wealthy patron of the Reformers, one Mr Rabbits, a boot and shoe manufacturer from Borough. Soon after they had met, in the summer of 1851, Rabbits invited her to a tea party at which he introduced her to a young evangelist who had also been expelled from the conventional Methodist structure. His name was William Booth. According to both of them, it was love and recognition on first meeting.

✠

WILLIAM BOOTH WROTE that 'for me, as a young man, there was one God and John Wesley was his prophet.' Booth was born on 10 April 1829 in Sneinton, a village a mile east of Nottingham that was being absorbed into the town by the process of industrialization. His father, Samuel Booth, was a nail-maker and then a speculative builder whose fortunes went steadily into decline. His mother, Mary, seems to have withdrawn into herself as a result of her husband's failure. William spoke of his childhood as 'a season of mortification and misery'.

For a while Booth attended the leading academy of Nottingham, but the family's poverty meant that he had to abandon learning – for which he had little, if any, interest – and earn a living. He found employment in a pawnbroker's shop, to which the poorer or more desperate of his neighbours came for temporary financial relief. He knew the area and its inhabitants well, then, and he once said that 'from the earliest days I was thrown into close association with poverty in its lowest depths.' Nottingham was largely devoted to lace manufacturing, and the decline of that trade threw many into distress.

For a while Booth was drawn to the angry denunciations of the 'physical force' Chartists, but another force drove him forwards. In 1844, at the age of fifteen, he joined the Wesley Chapel in the town. He may already have been aware of his aptitude for oratory and, accompanied by a friend of fellow feeling, he began an evangelical mission in the poorer quarters. The message of sanctification and salvation had to be taken everywhere. He carried a chair into the street and, standing upon it, began to sing a hymn, which was followed by an entreaty to join the Methodist services. Some three or four people gathered to watch this spectacle, and were often joined by others. It was a form of entertainment for those who had little diversion in their own lives. For Booth, it was an early education in social ministry. He told one companion, 'I intend to be something great, I don't mean to belong to the commonalty.'

At the age of nineteen Booth was raised from the position of street preacher to that of authorized lecturer in the same cause. This was also the age when he finished his apprenticeship in the pawnshop and, in pursuit of better-paid and more rewarding work, set off for London. The hopes of those coming to the city are generally dashed, and he was obliged to find employment with another pawnbroker in south London. It was the only trade he knew.

Booth was at this time still an orthodox, if fervent, Methodist, but he was now confronted for the first time with a heaving mass of stricken humanity. He jotted down 'loneliness' as his first reaction to the roaring streets, but above the hubbub he seemed to hear the call to preach as if his life depended on it. He delivered his first sermon in London in a Methodist chapel on Walworth Road, and soon became acquainted with the circuit of other chapels in this area; on Sundays and on his free weeknight he was engaged in earnest and impassioned sermons that sometimes disconcerted the more conventional congregations. After one particular meeting in Borough, Rabbits, the shoe manufacturer, approached Booth and urged him to become a minister and preacher for the Reformed Methodists. His persuasion, and his promise to subsidize the young preacher so that he could leave his regular employment, soon worked. It was at this juncture that Rabbits introduced Booth to Catherine Mumford.

✛

THE COURSE OF true love in this case ran relatively smoothly, despite Booth's absence as a newly created minister in Lincolnshire, and his confession to Catherine that 'I am always running before to find doubts and fears; mine has always been a restless and dissatisfied life.' Catherine was a constant source of consolation and encouragement, and acted as a kind of spiritual confessor to one who was uncertain of his destiny. She wrote sometimes censorious letters to him, revealing what her son later described as 'her tendency to decide what is right for others'. She had reservations about the fire and fury of revivalism, to which Booth was drawn, and urged him to attach himself to another group, the Methodist New Connexion, which encouraged the greater participation of the laity. There were other matters that touched her closely, and in the course of their correspondence it became clear that she asserted the rights of women to share equally in the administration and services of the Church. Her first biographer wrote that 'she held that intellectually woman was man's equal,' and that any inferiority came from circumstance or prejudice. She was one of the first and most ardent of the feminists, a position developed both by her experience and by her education, and one that she propounded forcefully to William.

Booth returned from Lincolnshire to London in February 1854 and, on the day after his arrival, he preached in Brunswick Chapel in Newington, South London. He was an impatient evangelist, and soon enough he left London again in order to begin a campaign in Bradford and Nottingham, Sheffield and Manchester, as well as other points of the English compass. His continual preaching did not disturb his relationship with Catherine, however, but seemed to strengthen it. When they were married on 16 June 1855, at Stockwell New Chapel in south London, they embarked upon what was essentially a joint mission. They enjoyed only a week's honeymoon, on the Isle of Wight, before they began a 'revival' campaign on the island of Guernsey. William then travelled on alone, when Catherine was once again incapacitated by illness.

Both husband and wife were in fact prone to depression and, perhaps as a result, both dwelled on the possibility of illness and disease. In particular William suffered badly from dyspepsia or severe indigestion, a condition that was often exacerbated by anxiety and nervous exhaustion. They both resorted to popular if unproven remedies, and placed their trust in hydrotherapy and homeopathy. In the spring of 1856, however, a baby came into the world. The infant was christened Bramwell, and was followed by seven others. Catherine Booth was as strict with her children as she was with herself, and said of Bramwell that 'he must be taught implicit, uncompromising obedience,' a task that she performed for all of her large family. The discipline might seem harsh, but in later life their sons and daughters were never critical or resentful.

The Booths were still poor, homeless and, when travelling, forced to rely on lodgings in the poorer quarters. But their mission continued through the country with greater and greater success. They were uplifted by their combined faith and by their shared trust in the principles of the Methodist faith. In 1858 William was confirmed as a minister at the New Connexion conference, and was sent to evangelize with his wife in Gateshead. They remained there for two years.

That faith, however, came at a price. The dogmatic and authoritarian tone of its leaders, especially in regard to William Booth's insistence on a travelling ministry, alienated him and Catherine. They decided to break off their connection so that he could maintain his independence as a lay preacher. Catherine herself began to play a more active part. At first she assisted at her husband's meetings, but then she expanded her role by working with the poor and the abandoned in the areas they visited. She began to speak out and then fully to evangelize with her husband, but her first call to the public ministry came on Whitsunday 1860 at the Bethesda Chapel in Gateshead. After William had completed his sermon, she rose from her pew and walked to the front of the chapel. 'What is the matter, my dear?' he asked her.

'I want to say a word,' she replied.

William informed the congregation, 'My dear wife wants to say a word.' That evening Catherine delivered her first sermon, 'Be filled with the Spirit', which inaugurated 'the life of publicity and trial', as she put it, that would continue for the next thirty years. The call to preach had become irresistible, and when her husband fell sick, she took his place in the pulpit. 'I spoke', she told her husband, 'with unwavering confidence, liberty and pleasure to myself.' Such was her success as a female revivalist that the Booths became a joint ministry, travelling across the country and eventually leading separate campaigns in the great cities. Over the next four years they travelled to Cornwall, Wales, the Midlands and the North. In 1865 Catherine was invited by a group of Free Church Methodists to visit Rotherhithe, in south London, where the advertising bills proclaimed 'Come and Hear a Woman Preach'. She travelled on to Southwark and Deptford, Bermondsey and Kennington.

Catherine had already proved herself to be a powerful and eloquent speaker, to the extent that her fame in religious circles was larger than that of William. He joined her in London, which soon became the centre of their endeavour, and their first ministry for the city was pursued in Whitechapel, where their services were held in a tent within the Quaker burial ground of Thomas Street. When the tent collapsed they moved to a dancing saloon, where the ragged congregation was exhorted and moved to repentance. It was the beginning of the Booths' true crusade and the inauguration of their East London Christian Revival Society, to be renamed in 1867 the East London Christian Mission, and an early example of urban evangelism. It was for them always a spiritual rather than a social concern, with the emphasis on conversion and salvation. William said that the open air was his cathedral, in which he preached the repentance of sins.

The Booths moved on to a wool warehouse, a stable, a disused penny gaff (popular theatre) and an abandoned music hall. In the process the Christian Mission was transformed from a chance combination of individual sympathizers into a fully-fledged organization. William, its energetic and implacable leader, named himself General Superintendent. His will to conquer sin and Satan, as he saw it, was also the will to mastery; he did not countenance any dissent to his plans. The Booths would be the spiritual guides to all those who joined them. At prayer meetings and open-air services, strict discipline was maintained; there was a time for prayer, a time for song, a time for exhortation. 'Stations' of the Mission were set up across the East End with the purpose of reclaiming sinners. It seemed to some that the spirit of John Wesley had risen again on a new religious crusade. Catherine was instrumental in the success of the Christian Mission by preaching at meetings, serving on committees and attending conferences, as well as 'missioning' in other and more comfortable parts of London. Without her support and active ministry, it is hard to know how her husband would have succeeded.

The Booths then established 'Holiness Meetings', according to their belief that the sinful could be purged and redeemed by sudden conversion and by the instantaneous access of grace. The meetings were the setting for large crowds, who were in turn mocked and assaulted by those who did not view religious fervour in the same kindly light. Publicans were known to pay groups of young men to disturb the proceedings with bricks, dead cats and general refuse. They did not, however, deter those who had come to be saved. They sang and danced, they shouted and jumped uncontrollably, they fell to the ground in fits or trances. It was very similar, if not identical, to the first meetings of Methodists under the tutelage of Wesley.

All this was in sharp contrast to the condition of the Anglican Communion in the same period, with a Church that excited no passion and no enthusiasm. It was made up of generally decent if undiscerning people who, according to Samuel Butler, 'would have been equally horrified at hearing the Christian religion doubted, and at seeing it practised'. That judgement may have been a little unfair, but it is certainly true that the established religion rested on what was comfortable and what was familiar. That has always been the default position of the English soul.

It was not a difficult business, however, to form the Salvation Army out of the Christian Mission. The name emerged as if by accident when, in 1878, Booth crossed out 'Volunteer Army' on a statement of purpose and replaced it with 'Salvation'. It was more appropriate for his aims and, in the context of British militarism, more timely. The Army was part of Booth's answer to the problem of 'How to Reach the Masses', as he put it. So its soldiers put on a show. They dressed in uniform, were divided into ranks from general to corporal, and marched behind a brass band, sometimes accompanied by banjos and fiddles. The fact that many of these soldiers were women, who became known as 'Hallelujah Lasses', only added to their appeal. The introduction of women, under the guidance of Catherine, was as welcome to some as it was profoundly shocking to others. But the women, as well as the men, marched forwards. The posters, advertising the prospect of salvation, were copied from those of the music hall. They announced the imminent appearance of the 'Salvation Midget', the 'Hallelujah Giant' and the 'Converted Sweep'. The hymns were sung to the tune of popular songs. It was a movement derived entirely from its urban environment, and was composed of working-class men and women who might be biscuit-makers or fishmongers, cooks or coal merchants. The orthodox distinction between sacred and secular was erased in the urgent desire to bring the gospel to the poor. 'Is it something new?' William wrote at the time. 'It may be so, and yet it may be none the less true and scriptural, and none the less of divine origin, and made after some heavenly pattern for all that.'

This deeply spiritual purpose was accompanied, in characteristically English fashion, by practical urgency and pragmatic method. William Booth was no theologian, and had an aversion to learning as such, believing that theory and doctrine were no substitute for a fundamental faith based on the Bible. He had no real use for the sacraments, such as baptism and communion, but believed in active service to save souls. 'Go and do something' was one of his favoured phrases, in which he was at one with Gerrard Winstanley and the Diggers, George Fox and the Quakers, John Wesley and the first Methodists. There are other correspondences with the native spiritual tradition. William's mystical sense of sudden conversion and sanctification is akin to the 'inner light' of the Quakers and to Wesley's espousal of 'perfectionism'.

It was clear to Booth that the newly converted were best able to convert others, so the early members of the Salvation Army were those who preached the repentance of sins and the acquisition of grace. They were not the buttoned-up evangelists of a later date. Some of them had been part of what was known as the 'submerged tenth', that part of the urban population living permanently in poverty, and the volunteers or soldiers returned to the lower depths in order to salvage some of their fellow sufferers. 'We are moral scavengers,' William wrote, 'netting the very sewers.' In this pursuit he was encouraged and assisted by Catherine; they were constantly at work and, according to a friend, their household in London was 'like a railway station'. The Salvation Army was soon spreading throughout Europe, America and Australia.

In the autumn of 1890 William Booth published what might be called his first social manifesto, *In Darkest England and the Way Out*, in which he described 'the shambles of our civilisation' with its lost, its outcast and its disinherited. It was not in fact written wholly by him, but by a sympathetic journalist who gathered up his notes and ideas in order to press them into coherent shape. But it marked a change in the Booths' understanding of the urban world, one that recognized the economic and social calamities of late nineteenth-century London. William became as concerned with reform and rescue as with spiritual redemption. There were nine chapters under the heading 'The Darkness', with such titles as 'The Homeless', 'On the Verge of the Abyss' and 'The Children of the Lost', which were followed by chapters of 'Deliverance' concerning such practical remedies as city colonies to provide immediate assistance and farm colonies for training in industry and agriculture. He used the example of the London cab horse by pointing out that 'every cab horse in London has three things – a shelter for the night, food for its stomach, and work allotted to it by which it can earn its corn.' The moral was clear enough.

In the summer of 1888 Catherine delivered her last sermon in the City Temple on Holborn Viaduct; it was the culmination of almost thirty years of service, during which she had promoted the spiritual equality of women and helped to form the Salvation Army. In the autumn of 1890, after two years of suffering, she died of cancer. She was often considered to be the more interesting and accomplished of the pair, and William never took a decision without consulting her. After her death she was described as 'the most famous and influential Christian woman of the generation'.

After his wife's death William embarked on annual travels to the overseas outposts of the Army in America, India and elsewhere.

He became a renowned figure, immediately recognized with his flowing white beard, craggy nose and small, but piercing, eyes. As a result of *In Darkest England*, he and his now enlarged staff established food depots, shelters, rescue homes and labour bureaux in the industrial centres of the country. Even though it came last, this was the aspect of the Salvation Army that the public would come to know best. For two or three years he directed this scheme of social work, elaborate and detailed as it was in operation, but his attention was never very far from his spiritual purpose. 'God must be the central figure,' he said in one interview, 'and His glory the end of any service.'

But age was stealing upon him. William wrote to his son Bramwell, now second in command of the Army, that 'I am very tired – but must on – on – on – I cannot stand still.' He often seemed exhausted, but as soon as he stood up to speak or to spring into action, he was as alive and alert as ever. By the end of the nineteenth century there were 100,000 soldiers, both male and female, in the service of the Army. But increasing blindness, and the attendant frailties of age, eventually slowed him. He died on 20 August 1912, after a failed operation for cataracts, and a few days later 35,000 followers gathered for a memorial service at Olympia. He was buried, next to his wife, in Abney Park cemetery on Stamford Hill.

Eighteen

Religion as Thought
John Henry Newman (1801–1890)

John Henry Newman, in turn Anglican priest and Roman Catholic cardinal, was born in the ancient City of London on 21 February 1801, to affluent parents. His childhood was comfortable, but at an early age he was possessed by a sense of mystery that never really left him. 'I thought life might be a dream,' he wrote in later life, 'or I an Angel, and all this world a deception.' That recognition, or understanding, that the visible world was the veil for a higher reality or, as he put it later, 'the unreality of material phenomena', was always with him. It was the context for his life.

Newman was fifteen when his father, a banker, lost his employment as the result of a financial collapse in the City. The boy was obliged to remain at his school in Ealing during the crisis, when he was afflicted by a serious illness, 'keen' and 'terrible', which prompted him into a form of religious conversion. He was already of a scholarly or bookish temperament, and at the age of fourteen had read Thomas Paine, Voltaire and other 'atheist' writers. But now, under the influence of a classics master, he was swept into Calvinism and believed himself to be born again by faith in Christ and so guided towards ultimate salvation. This led him to the understanding that there were 'two and two only absolute and luminously self-evident beings, myself and my Creator'. This was not self-glorification but self-abasement in the presence of mystery.

He also hoped and believed that he would remain celibate for the rest of his life, which 'strengthened my feeling of separation from the visible world'. He always sensed that he had been marked out for a larger purpose.

In 1816 the studious and determined young man entered Trinity College at Oxford University; he was in avid pursuit of learning and worked for many hours each day but, precisely because of the strain of overwork, he did not perform well in his final examinations. The failure, shocking as it seemed, served only to animate Newman; with the encouragement of friends and tutors he set himself to win a fellowship at Oriel College, where the test was not of what he had learned but of how he had learned it. Originality and perspicacity were required. He had those qualities in abundance, and at the age of 21 he was elected a fellow.

So began Newman's life of learning and enquiry at the ancient university. Oxford was more than just his alma mater, since it elicited from him deep feelings of affection and loyalty. It became his true home, where he was to a large extent protected from a life of unrest and struggle in the world. In that place of safety he pursued a career in the Anglican Church. In May 1824 he was appointed curate or priest's assistant in the local church of St Clement's, and the following month he progressed to be a deacon; soon afterwards, he preached his first sermon and administered his first baptism. He was ordained to the priesthood in the following year. He had lost the elements of his early Calvinism and followed a path towards the 'higher' end of Anglicanism, with a preference for ritual and established liturgy as well as an aversion to liberalism of any kind.

Other fellows of Oriel shared Newman's sympathies, among them Richard Hurrell Froude, John Keble and Edward Bouverie Pusey. In one of those movements of thought and sensibility that seem larger than any individual choice, they all sought a middle way of devotion between the 'high and dry' Tory Anglicanism of

John Henry Newman, *c.* 1888, photograph by Herbert Barraud.

previous decades and the evangelical or Dissenting tradition that had existed since the seventeenth century.

Newman was perhaps the most scholarly of the little group, and, in his pursuit of clear dogmatic principle, he began to study the work of the early Fathers of the Church from the first centuries after Christ. Here, if anywhere, was to be found the apostolic tradition that would confirm the claims of the Anglican Communion to be the true Catholic faith, freed from the trammels of Roman superstition and idolatry. But that patrimony meant that it could not be aligned with any secular authority. Church and state were deemed to be forever separate. So believed Newman and his fellows at Oriel.

The matter reached its climax when, in February 1829, the Home Secretary, Robert Peel, proposed in the House of Commons a bill for Catholic emancipation, allowing Roman Catholics to take up public office in Parliament and elsewhere. At a stroke it undermined the Anglican supremacy, and thus the authority of the Church of England. This was followed, in 1833, by another Parliamentary Act, which removed ten bishoprics from the Irish Protestant Church; it was clear to Newman and his colleagues that the state was meddling in what ought to be spiritual matters. In the summer of that year Keble mounted the university pulpit and delivered a sermon on 'National Apostasy' in which he warned that the Church might be 'forsaken, degraded, nay trampled on and despoiled, by the State and people of England' for the sake of 'popularity and expediency'. For Newman, this was the true source and origin of what became known as the Oxford Movement, which soon enough became a living force in the Church of England. In the autumn of that year Newman composed three 'tracts' designed to reclaim the apostolic foundation of the Church of England and to reassert the purity of its doctrinal development. There were to be ninety such *Tracts*, covering all areas of Church doctrine and practice; the members of the Oxford Movement then also became known as 'Tractarians'.

In the same period Newman's research into the early Fathers of the Church found expression in a volume he completed on the Arian heresy of the fourth century, a heresy in which Christ is subordinate to God the Father. Arius believed that 'If the Father begat the Son, then he who was begotten had a beginning in existence, and from this it follows there was a time when the Son was not.' As a result he was condemned by the Council of Nicaea in AD 325 and sentenced to exile.

In his account Newman emphasized the indisputable authority of the true Church as opposed to scepticism or doubt, and was implicitly condemning the same tendencies in his own period. For him, the past was always to be seen in living relation to the present. The principles of his historical scholarship, and the dangers of contemporary controversies, therefore came together in a striking condemnation of liberal errors and in defence of the guiding principles of the Church of England. He sought dogmatic certainty and the golden chain of tradition. In his disquisition on Arianism he also laid stress on the incapacity of language before the mystery of the divine. This was the prevalent note of the Tractarians themselves, who dwelled in reverent tones on that mystery, as opposed to the enthusiasm of the Evangelicals and the 'dry' expositions of orthodox Anglicans. Newman was now preaching at the University Church of St Mary the Virgin, of which he had been appointed vicar in 1828, and Matthew Arnold recalled him 'gliding in the dim afternoon light through the aisles of St Mary, rising into the pulpit, and then, in the most entrancing of voices, breaking the silence with words and thoughts which were a religious music – subtle, sweet, mournful'.

Towards the end of 1836 Newman's lectures on the Church were published, in which he criticized what he called 'popular Protestantism' or evangelical enthusiasm. He also composed a tract in which he wrote that 'the glory of the English Church is that it has taken the VIA MEDIA . . . It lies between the (so called) Reformers and the Romanists.' Here he propounded the middle way in matters of faith. This was in fact one of the defining elements of the English soul in its aversion to extremes and its close colloquy with human experience. It was a way of avoiding conflict and resolving controversy. It was the foundation of the Elizabethan Settlement propounded almost three hundred years earlier.

For Newman, however, that middle way was chiefly to be found in the practice and principles of 'Anglo-Catholicism'. That term, new-minted by the members of the Oxford Movement, meant not compromise or equivocation but, rather, a living stream of tradition from the days of the Church Fathers. In Newman's words, 'it is latent, but it lives. It is silent, like the rapids of a river, before the rocks intercept it. It is the Church's unconscious habit of opinion and sentiment.' Certainly it was becoming stronger in Oxford itself, and his university was, for Newman, a touchstone of integrity and truth. In a volume of lectures published in 1838, he elaborated on the middle way as the path between justification by faith alone, the evangelical doctrine, and justification by obedience to the Catholic tradition. When a proposal was put forward to build a monument to Cranmer and Latimer on the site in Broad Street where they had been burned during the reign of Mary I, Newman demurred. He did not believe that these reformers, martyred though they were, were representative of the English Church. He was well aware that obloquy would fall upon him for his unpopular stance, but, as he told a colleague, 'clamour makes our principles known.' In his spiritual autobiography, *Apologia pro vita sua* (1864), he recollected that in the spring of 1839 'my position in the Anglican church was at its height. I had supreme confidence in my controversial *status*, and I had a great and still growing success, in recommending it to others.' But that status was soon changed. This was also the year in which he delivered 'the last words which I ever spoke as an Anglican to Anglicans'.

Even as he wrote about the development of the Oxford Movement, he was preparing to leave it for an unknown future in another Church. He was obliged to choose between Anglicanism and Roman Catholicism.

Newman wrote in a letter to Keble that 'one cannot stop still.' The process of thought itself was, for him, a line of fire that led him forwards. That was the time when he began to doubt. All his scholarship, his prayers and his contemplation, guided him towards one conclusion. He had turned once again to the study of the fourth century and of the early Fathers, and had realized that the heresies of that age had been rebuffed only by Rome and that the Roman Church was the bulwark of the true faith. As it was then, so it was now. He saw present conflicts in the mirror of antiquity, and knew that he could no longer walk upon the *via media*. That would make him akin to a heresiarch, a promulgator of heresy. He had no choice in the matter of his soul's allegiance.

Some words of Augustine convinced Newman finally. He had read that '*Securus judicat orbis terrarum*', the verdict of the whole world is conclusive, and now the words tolled for him. This brief justification of the Roman Catholic faith, as well as the long course of ecclesiastical history, meant that, in his words, 'the theory of the Via Media was absolutely pulverised.'

Newman could not hide or deny this crisis of faith. In the last 'tract', *Tract 90*, published in 1841, he attempted to interpret one of the foundations of English Protestantism, the Thirty-Nine Articles of 1571, in a Catholic sense. He examined each article in turn, to demonstrate that at the least they were 'not uncatholic'. This was considered a rebuff to conventional Anglicanism, and the university authorities delivered a public censure. The Bishop of Oxford argued that the *Tracts* should be discontinued, and in the autumn of 1843 Newman left his post at the University Church. His last sermon was on 'The Parting of Friends'. The final separation, however, was inevitably slow. In the autumn of 1845 Newman resigned from Oriel College, and in that period he published his *Essay on the Development of Christian Doctrine*, which in itself was a meditation on the growth of his own understanding.

On 9 October 1845 Newman was received into the Catholic Communion. It was for the majority still an alien faith, often despised or rejected. The history of English Catholicism, from the sixteenth century, is itself elusive and fragmentary. It remained a living faith, but a half-concealed one. It was the faith of the Irish working class, who migrated to Liverpool and elsewhere, but it was also the religion of the local gentry in the North, who had withstood the advances of the Reformation. Never the twain could meet. It had remained divided, and on the defensive, until the middle of the nineteenth century, when it returned to prominence partly as a result of the 'higher' principles of the Oxford Movement.

In the autumn of the following year Newman travelled to Rome in order to attend the College of Propaganda, where he prepared for the priesthood. He remained in Rome until his ordination. While there he visited the Roman Oratory, a community of priests and lay brothers united in prayer, scholarship and pastoral care. He believed that such a foundation could be established in England, where it might become the focus of his work as a newly converted Catholic priest, and Pope Pius IX favoured the idea. As the acknowledged Superior of a new English Oratory, Newman returned on Christmas Eve of 1847.

✛

PERHAPS NEWMAN MOST resembles his fellow English saint, Thomas More, since in the years after his conversion he was obliged to unite his deep spiritual awareness with the practical detail of his temporal life. He had wanted to set up his Oratory in London, but the papal Bishop Apostolic in England had considered Birmingham to be more suitable. It was one of the first towns of the industrial and scientific revolutions, as well as a centre for political reform. Newman had already established a small community of priests and lay brothers in the parish of Littlemore, just outside Oxford, and with these he moved in 1848 to the new Oratory of Birmingham, where the chapel was a converted gin distillery. Two years later it removed to the outlying district of Edgbaston. He was to remain there for the next 42 years.

On coming to Birmingham Newman had immediately become immersed in administrative detail, a fate that was compounded in 1851 by an invitation from the Archbishop of Armagh, John Beresford, to become rector of the new Catholic University of Ireland, in Dublin. Newman had, from his early days at Oxford, always been assiduous in the pursuit of learning, and the offer provided the opportunity to put his devotion to scholarship into practice. Almost at once he was involved in arguments over the proposed lecturers, students and syllabuses of the new foundation.

This activity found expression in *The Idea of a University* (1873), made up of sermons, lectures and occasional papers. In this book he argued that no form of knowledge should be excluded from a life of study; both science and theology should be admitted, since 'to erect a University . . . [it] is pledged to admit, without fear, without prejudice, without compromise, all comers, if they come in the name of Truth; to adjust views, and experiences, and habits of mind the most independent and dissimilar.' In the same spirit of enquiry, the pursuit of truth must not be hampered by questions of utility or presumed social benefit, since

> an assemblage of learned men, zealous for their own sciences, and rivals of each other, are brought, by familiar intercourse and for the sake of intellectual peace, to adjust together the claims and relations of their respective subjects of investigation. They learn to respect, to consult, to aid each other.

Everything must come together to form the conditions for intellectual development.

The university was for Newman a secular version of the Roman Church, taking up the principles and perceptions of traditional disciplines and gradually turning them into a coherent body of thought that could then be transmitted to the next generation. The nature of these enquiries, from the new sciences of statistics and economics to the awakening of geology, would, of course, alter in time, but all would be admitted in the pursuit of knowledge and enlightenment. Catholic theology was the key, but its claim to universal knowledge must be sustained by the embrace of change as the law of life. The student then 'apprehends the great outlines of knowledge, the principles on which it rests, the scale of its parts, its lights and its shades'.

That was the theory, but the practice was very different. The preparations for the Catholic University continued over the next two or three years, and Newman himself became increasingly exasperated with the tactics of the archbishop. It had become a long negotiation, or series of negotiations, and Newman was installed as rector only in the early summer of 1854. He was often infuriated by the machinations of the higher Roman Catholic clergy, but of course he could not say so. Obedience was the most important of the moral virtues.

Newman had to measure out his time between Birmingham, Dublin and London, where another branch of Oratorians had been established. The two Oratories were often at odds, each of them vying for ascendancy. He wrote, 'as a Protestant, I felt my religion dreary but not my life – but, as a Catholic, my life dreary, not my religion.' As a Protestant he savoured battle, and as a Catholic he knew submission. He was by now spare and emaciated, with deep furrows upon his face and sunken eyes. He looked as if he had been scorched by thought. He continued his mission in Birmingham, but 'people are strange to say, so watching me, that I find I must be most cautious, for everything I do is known.' Many of the old Catholics considered him a parvenu, stirring up unnecessary hostility towards their faith, while many Protestants considered him a papal agent and a betrayer. In turn he often found his fellow Catholics, among them the most senior, to be untrustworthy and ambiguous, showing the two faces of England and of Rome.

In some sense, like the salamander, Newman lived in fire. His next controversy came upon him at the end of 1863, when he received a copy of *Macmillan's Magazine*, a monthly literary periodical. In it was an article by Charles Kingsley, the well-known author of *Westward Ho!* and *The Water-Babies*; in the course of his review of Froude's *History of England*, Kingsley noted that 'truth, for its own sake, has never been a virtue with the Roman clergy. Father Newman informs us that it need not, and on the whole ought not to be.' He was in effect accusing Newman of lying for the sake of his Church. Newman wrote a formal letter of complaint, but the allegation touched a sensitive spot. In the spring of 1864 he started work on a history of his beliefs and opinions. Standing at his high desk, he wrote from morning to night, sometimes working for 22 hours at a stretch, missing meals, weeping and crying out in distress at his memories. It was to be called *Apologia pro vita sua*, in translation *A Defence of His Life*, and was first published in weekly instalments. He confessed that it was 'the most arduous work I ever had in my life', and 'one of the most terrible trials that I have had'.

Such was the appetite for religious works in this period that the *Apologia* became an immediate success, and its large sales meant that Newman would never again have to be concerned about his finances. It is in many respects a tour de force, a chaste and fluent account of his theological development in which the ease and elegance of his words become the music of his thought. He recites in meticulous and chronological fashion the phases of his belief from childhood onwards, but also touches on theological enquiry and dogmatic truth. It is in effect an autobiography of his mind, in which he traces 'the succession of thoughts' to their ultimate conclusion. It may be in part familiar, but it is never dull. It is circumstantial, but it centres on what for Newman was an inner and living truth.

In the summer of 1866 Newman began making notes on what would become his last substantial work. On the nature of religious certainty, *An Essay in Aid of a Grammar of Assent* would take him four years to complete. It may have been in part inspired by the forthcoming Vatican Council, during which, Newman suspected, the doctrine of papal infallibility would be defined. He argued in this book that the belief in an abstract principle is merely notional or intellectual. It can become certain only when it assents to propositions of which we have had real experience in a particular and concrete sense; truth is discovered as the direct result of a chain of probabilities that come to an unerring conclusion. You walk forwards step by step into the light. This was in essence the meaning and direction of his entire life. You cannot understand the world by means of logic alone. We can assent fully only to that which we have experienced as true.

Newman had hoped that he could spend the rest of his life in sorting and publishing his essays and lectures, or, as he put it, 'sweeping up, dusting, putting my house in order'. But at the beginning of 1879 he was offered the red hat of a cardinal. He was at first nervous of the honour, with all the duties it might entail, but who could refuse the Pope? It was his duty to obey and to serve. After being received into the College of Cardinals, and being excused from residence in Rome, he continued his devotional life at the Birmingham Oratory. He sketched out proposals for further writing, but his physical powers were waning. He became ill from a bout of pneumonia in the early morning of 10 August 1890, at the age of 89, and on the following evening he died.

Newman's was an English spirituality and, as he wrote of a contemporary in the *Apologia*, 'he was an Englishman to the backbone in his severe adherence to the real and the concrete.' He rested not on abstract truths or theoretical systems, but on the practical experience of the world. He fought, and suffered, to be true to himself. He helped to renew the spirit of Anglicanism, and to assist in the natural development of Roman Catholicism. It could be said that, from his youth as a Calvinist to his old age as a cardinal, his whole life was in pursuit of religious certainty. As a child he had considered the world to be a veil, or an illusion, and on his tomb were inscribed the words *Ex umbris et imaginibus in veritatem*. From shadows and images into truth.

Charles Spurgeon, 1859–70, photograph.

Nineteen

Religion as Evangelical
Charles Spurgeon (1834–1892)

By the nineteenth century the evangelical tradition was as firm and as strong as the established Church. The word itself signifies one who is filled with the spirit of the Gospels, or that which pertains to the Gospels, and so accommodates many of the men and women already described in this volume, Gerrard Winstanley and John Wyclif among them. John Wesley was the most prominent, and it was he who inaugurated 'vital religion', which changed the understanding of Christian faith in the late eighteenth and early nineteenth centuries. He preached the power of the Holy Spirit in awakening a new life, and proclaimed the supremacy of holy scripture. It was a lesson that touched and invigorated the Dissenters and Nonconformists outside the established Church. By the nineteenth century it had also come to dominate the Church of England. It became part of its soul.

The number of evangelicals grew among the middling and lower ranks of the English people, especially among artisans and shopkeepers, and among the inhabitants of the great towns and cities who were already experiencing the travails of the new industry. Women, more than men, were ready to step into a new life. The presence of these newly awakened faithful had already inspired a gradual change in the Church of England, which came to accept them as part of its communion. They were evangelicals but they were also Protestant, often more Protestant than many

Anglicans. By the early decades of the nineteenth century they were not dissenters but assenters, affirming the sacred role of the established Church.

The evangelical movement can also be seen as coextensive with the Romantic movement in English poetry, with a similar emphasis on private revelation and numinous experience. The affirmation of the poet John Keats that 'I am certain of nothing but the holiness of the Heart's affections and the truth of the Imagination' might have been shared by many evangelicals who would have interpreted the Imagination as the Holy Spirit.

✠

CHARLES SPURGEON, NOW FORGOTTEN but once revered, was the quintessence of popular evangelicalism in the nineteenth century. He was born in the summer of 1834 in the Essex village of Kelvedon. Hs father was a lay preacher and Dissenting minister; his grandfather was also an independent minister. The chapel and the pulpit were his inheritance. He attended schools where, according to his brother, he received 'the best education that nonconformity could command', and devoted himself to the study of John Foxe, John Bunyan and other stridently religious writers. He is said to have delivered his first sermon at the age of fifteen, and a year later he experienced that sudden and overwhelming conversion that was the touchstone of evangelical faith, just as Wesley had done when he felt his heart to be 'strangely warmed'. Spurgeon dated his own conversion to 6 January 1850, when in Colchester a preacher of the Primitive Methodist faith led him towards salvation. Five months later he was distributing Congregational tracts; then he entered a Baptist congregation. The fact that in these early months he moved within the combined influence of Baptism, Methodism and Congregationalism suggests that in this period dissent might have exerted a unifying force.

Spurgeon soon recognized that he had the inner power of preaching, and he delivered his early sermons at Waterbeach Baptist Church in Cambridgeshire. By one means or another his skill and reputation were soon known elsewhere among the godly, and in 1854 he was invited to become the pastor of the Reformed Baptist church in New Park Street, Southwark, London, where his sermons attracted larger and larger numbers. His brother noted that he seemed to step fully grown into the pulpit, and a historian of evangelicalism, Edward Poole-Connor, wrote later that 'crowds began flocking to hear him, editors to make his preaching front-page news, comic-song writers to render his name familiar to the music halls, caricatures to burlesque his appearance.' Spurgeon's appearance was perhaps not in his favour; he was stocky, his head on the large side and with what was described as a 'heavy' countenance with two prominent front teeth. But, as the poet Richard Monckton Milnes, Lord Houghton, recalled, he might have been taken for a hairdresser's assistant when he entered the pulpit, but when he left, 'he was an inspired apostle.' John Ruskin and Lord John Russell were among his congregation.

Those congregations became too large for the chapel in Southwark, and in 1855 Spurgeon leased Exeter Hall in the Strand and then, at intervals, the Surrey Gardens Music Hall (on the site of what is now Kennington Park), which could hold 12,000. Spurgeon was billed as 'the Cambridgeshire Lad'. On the first night at the music hall, in the autumn of 1856, a false alarm of fire provoked a stampede in which eight people were crushed to death. It was reported in the newspapers that at the height of the disaster Spurgeon had called out from the stage that 'there is a terrible day coming when the terror and alarm of this evening shall be as nothing.' But this may have been a rumour spread by those who wished to malign his ministry. He continued his work at the Surrey Gardens, having been, as he put it, 'hardened in a burning furnace', but in 1861 he built his Metropolitan Tabernacle in Elephant and

Castle, a little to the north. It was the largest building in England designed expressly for public worship, and despite its extent, it was always filled. It was testimony to the power of evangelical religion in mid-nineteenth-century England.

A Sunday service at 'Spurgeon's' was one of the attractions of the capital, although for many it was a form of pilgrimage. It also became known as 'the second evangelical awakening' or 'the revival', in reference to the work of Wesley and George Whitefield; Spurgeon himself was considered to be the true successor to Wesley. 'Fancy a congregation of ten thousand persons', *The Times* reported,

> streaming into the hall, mounting the galleries, humming, buzzing and swarming like bees, eager to secure, at first, the best places and, at last, any place at all . . . To the hum, and rush, and trampling of feet, succeeded a low concentrated thrill and murmur of devotion, which seemed to run at once, like an electric current, through the breast of everyone present; and by this magnetic chain the preacher held us fast bound for about two hours . . . It is enough to say of his voice that its power and volume are sufficient to reach everyone in that vast assembly.

That voice was also described as 'clear and musical as a silver bell', but it was a bell that could summon a multitude. Spurgeon used only notes scribbled on one side of a sheet of paper, but one observer recalled that 'he did with ease and spontaneity mental feats which men of name strive in vain to accomplish. He could grasp all the bearings of his subject, hold his theme in hand, and display his thoughts, like troops, at the tactical moment.'
Busts and prints of Spurgeon were placed in many homes, meeting houses and assembly halls. He was one of those who in the closing decades of the nineteenth century raged against the scepticism

about the supernatural and against the critical analysis of scripture that were being proposed in the more advanced circles. Spurgeon wished to turn back the tide of 'liberalism' that was affecting even the faithful. In the summer of 1887 he protested in an evangelical periodical that 'the Atonement is scouted, the inspiration of Scripture is denied, the punishment of sin is turned into a fiction, and the Resurrection into a myth.' This sense of loss, and of grievance, characterized the last years of the nineteenth century, when all the forces of the world – scientific, political and social – seemed to be opposed to the received faith. For the evangelicals, too, it was considered to be an evil time. Spurgeon died on 31 January 1892, and was buried in Norwood cemetery in south London.

✠

SPURGEON HAD LIVED, however, in a century of unparalleled evangelical success. By its early decades, the evangelicals had attained an unusual level of public importance. Their earnestness and self-discipline, their seriousness and sense of duty, their utter respectability, helped to fashion the ethos of the early Victorians. William Gladstone noted that the movement 'did by infusion profoundly alter the general tone and tendency of the preaching of the clergy'. It was what one historian of the period described as 'the imponderable pressure of the evangelical discipline'. In these early years the evangelical party, among both Anglicans and Nonconformists, set up 'missions' to assist as well as to convert the floating population in the poorest areas of London and other cities. The evangelicals would visit the public houses and the gin palaces, the music halls and the penny gaffs, the street markets and the pleasure gardens, with a stock of cheap Bibles and assorted free tracts on the evils of drink or the perils of indolence.

The *Edinburgh Review* noted that these urban missionaries 'have not hesitated to preach in filthy courts and alleys, the haunts of vice and infamy, to audiences which could not be tempted to listen under any roof but the sky', and that as a result 'the profound darkness in which the English peasantry were enveloped at the beginning of the century has been gradually dissipated.' On New Year's Day 1860, the Britannia, the old Garrick and Sadler's Wells theatres were opened for Sunday evening services, which attracted 'overwhelming' and 'immense' congregations; the Britannia was in Hoxton, in the East End of London, and an evangelical minister remarked,

> if this work is done, we shall see some unknown Luthers and Whitefields excavated out of this dark mine, to spread the Gospel farther and wider than we have any idea . . . I believe we are on the eve of a greater work than England ever saw, and the East End of London is the right place to begin.

But perhaps the most remarkable contribution of the evangelicals in the early nineteenth century lay in the establishment of the 'ragged schools', the schools of last resort for the poorest and most neglected children who had no chance of education elsewhere. In 1843 Charles Dickens visited an early ragged school in Saffron Hill, Clerkenwell. An advertisement had appeared in *The Times* seeking charity for this establishment, stating that, in his words, 'a room had been opened and supported in that wretched neighbourhood for upwards of twelve months, where religious instruction had been imparted to the poor.' It had been set up by evangelicals primarily to reclaim the souls of the errant young, but at the same time trying to inculcate in them the rudiments of learning. Dickens knew Saffron Hill very well. It was the area in which he had placed Fagin's den in his novel *Oliver Twist*.

His companion, on entering the school, found the smell too much and quickly left, but Dickens persisted. He discovered that 'the close, low chamber at the back, in which the boys were

crowded, was so foul and stifling as to be, at first, almost insupport-
able.' Yet he found some trace of hope. The ragged school was of
recent date and starved of funds, but its teacher 'had inculcated
some association with the name of the Almighty, which was not an
oath, and had taught them to look forward in a hymn (they sang it)
to another life, which would correct the miseries and woes of this'.

Dickens was not necessarily well disposed to philanthropy in
general or to evangelicals in particular, as the caricatures in his
fiction reveal, but here he reveals the enormity of the urban challenge and the evangelical earnestness in confronting it. In the year
after his visit, the Ragged School Union was established by some
prominent evangelicals; funds were raised and volunteers found.
By 1867 some 204 day schools as well as 207 evening schools had
been organized. It was a measure of the power and effectiveness of
the evangelical middle class in affecting English society.

This was nowhere more evident than in the rise of the 'Clapham
sect', a group of second-generation evangelicals who lived in that
neighbourhood of south London and who combined practical
piety with philanthropic zeal. It demonstrated the appeal of that
movement to what were called professional men, to the bankers,
civil servants, merchants and lawyers; they were in effect the un-
announced rulers of Victorian society, and all were to be found in
the Clapham sect. They were also to be found in large numbers
within the clergy. The members of the sects were called, perhaps
ironically, 'the Saints', but their political and philanthropic work
was influential in prison reform, factory reform and the removal of
such social evils as the exploitation of 'climbing boys' or apprentice sweeps. Their influence was maintained by the power of the
new steam presses, and at the time of the fiftieth anniversary of the
Religious Tract Society in 1849, it had printed 500 million copies
of 5,000 separate titles.

The most prominent member of the group was William
Wilberforce, whose campaign against slavery was one of the most

important crusades of the nineteenth century in which the principles of evangelical piety were put into practice. He helped to establish a society for improving the conditions of child workers, and established the Association for the Relief of the Manufacturing and Labouring Poor. This emphasis on practicality and pragmatic action has always been of English provenance, but the Victorian evangelicals were the first group to translate it into political terms. Legislation, guided by the Houses of Parliament, could be seen as an aspect of Christian morality. It embodied the great purpose of the evangelical movement.

This was also the age of the evangelical societies, of which the most successful were the Society for the Suppression of Vice (1802–85) and the Lord's Day Observance Society (1831–; now the Day One Christian Ministries). No other organizations had so great an influence on English life in the nineteenth century. The campaign against 'vice', which was effectively a campaign against the eighteenth century, had some notable victories. The 'Vice Society', as it became known, had been established by Wilberforce and other members of the Clapham set with the express intention of prosecuting 'excessive drinking, blasphemy, profane swearing and cursing, lewdness, profanation of the Lord's Day, and other dissolute, immoral, or disorderly practices'. The worst excesses of prostitution, male and female, were removed, many brothels were closed and the unlicensed places of entertainment were shut down. Obscene books and prints were removed from sale and the hours of public houses were restricted. Naked bathing in the Thames and elsewhere was prohibited, and the statues adorning the Great Exhibition of 1851 were duly covered. Wilberforce also persuaded the administration to give up the national lottery. It is clear enough, however, that moral earnestness might in turn lead to moral censoriousness, with the ever-present opportunity for prudery. The assurance of personal salvation did encourage spiritual arrogance or at least complacency, together with a tendency to rebuke the conduct of others. Manuals of proper conduct, and of appropriate Christian behaviour, were readily available for every class.

Wilberforce was also instrumental in promoting the inviolability of the Sabbath when he argued that 'Sunday is intended for strengthening our impression of invisible and eternal things; and that as such, people can only innocently recreate themselves on that day by attending to their religious duties.' As a result the seventh day of the week became a byword for vacancy, gloom and monotony. As William Lamb, Lord Melbourne, told the new queen, Victoria, in 1837, 'nobody is gay now, they are so religious.'

At the height of evangelical success, there were still many who challenged it. In his treatise *On Liberty* of 1859, the philosopher and economist John Stuart Mill asked,

> How will the remaining portion of the community like to have the amusements that shall be permitted to them regulated by the religious and moral sentiments of the stricter Calvinists and Methodists? Would they not, with considerable peremptoriness, desire these intrusively pious members of society to mind their own business? This is precisely what should be said to every government and every public, who have the pretension that no person shall enjoy any pleasure which they think wrong.

It would be a mistake, however, to dwell on the perceived faults in any profession of faith. Much evangelical work was necessary and admirable. Thomas John Barnardo, who opened a ragged school in the East End two years after arriving in London, and Elizabeth Fry, who was ordained a Quaker minister at the age of 31, are sufficiently well known. They turned philanthropy into a mission. Anthony Ashley-Cooper, the 7th Earl of Shaftesbury, another convinced evangelical, did more to alleviate the human lot than any other Victorian. He has been described as 'evangelical of the evangelicals' and, in that role, he considered himself the true successor of Wilberforce. He took the leading role in most aspects of social reform, from prisons to hospitals, mines to law courts, schools to factories. He stated, 'I believe it is my duty to God and the poor . . . to me it appears less a matter of policy than of religion.' He was concerned primarily with the souls of those whom he wished to help, but that impelled him to take care of their material condition as well. He also remarked, in characteristic English fashion, that 'Christianity is not a state of opinion and speculation. Christianity is essentially practical.' In that spirit he fought against what he called 'the three Rs' of ritualism, rationalism and Romanism.

Many other worthy or pious enterprises flourished in this age of duty and responsibility. There were societies for every conceivable purpose and good cause, societies for alleviating distress and preventing misfortune, societies for promoting this and prohibiting that. On the death of Shaftesbury, some five hundred different societies attended his funeral service, from the British and Foreign Bible Society to the Protestant Reformation Society.

To cut costs and eliminate overheads, the evangelical societies congregated in the same building, Exeter Hall on the Strand, which soon became the centre for pious endeavour. Sir James Stephen, a distinguished lawyer and member of the Clapham sect, concluded that 'ours is the age of societies. For the redress of every oppression there is a public meeting. For the cure of every sorrow there are patrons, vice-presidents and secretaries. For the diffusion of every blessing of which mankind can partake in common, there is a committee.'

By the middle of the century, more than a third of all clergymen were believed to be evangelicals. It was they who encouraged the singing of hymns during services, and such was its success that churchgoing became more popular. Nonconformists, for example, who had previously avoided the prayers and ritual of the established Church, returned to a more sympathetic ministry. It was reported, too, that the female members of the congregation were more inclined to the passionate preaching of a 'serious' incumbent. The heavy and often dull atmosphere of the parish church might thereby be lifted.

The evangelical influence helped to shape the culture of the period in less expected ways. The aptitude for missionary work and zeal for the conversion of the 'heathen' had a direct influence on the colonial enterprise in Africa, India and elsewhere. One evangelical leader noted, 'I believe from my heart that India has been placed in our hands to be Christianized, and that we shall not be allowed to leave it till we have done our work.' So piety and power might march in step. Politics, both national and international, was a crusade or it was nothing. That was, in part, the legacy of evangelicalism in England.

Twenty

Atheism as Religion

Charles Bradlaugh (1833–1891), Annie Besant
(1847–1933), Richard Dawkins (1941–)

C harles Bradlaugh was born in Hoxton, part of the East End of London, on 26 September 1833. His father was senior clerk to a firm of solicitors in the City of London, and the law in all its guises would dominate Bradlaugh's later career. Charles attended local schools until the age of eleven or twelve before he was taken up as a junior clerk and general factotum to the solicitors who employed his father. His education was brief, therefore, but his life of study had just begun. He was a voracious and attentive reader, as were so many in this period; in his moments of leisure he liked to fish in the River Lea, close by, and attend the political and religious gatherings in the adjacent Bonner's Fields, where he became accustomed to strident debate on the issues of the day. He was at this stage a committed Christian, and attended St Peter's Church, off the Hackney Road, where his intelligence and earnestness impressed the vicar, Reverend Packer; he was appointed Sunday School teacher there and encouraged to study the Thirty-Nine Articles and the Gospels. This was to prove his nemesis.

On carefully studying the New Testament Bradlaugh discovered what he thought to be discrepancies or 'discordancies' between the four Gospels. This was a time when any questioning of established doctrine was considered close to heresy, and, on revealing his doubts to Packer, Bradlaugh was suspended for three months from his Sunday School post and asked to consider the matter. But, after due consideration, his scepticism grew. He attended the religious debates on Bonner's Fields, read volumes on the mixed origin and meaning of Christianity, and even became a teetotaller – a stance that, at the time, meant that he was danger-ously unorthodox. Packer wrote to the young man's parents, and suggested that, if he did not renounce his new opinions, he should be barred from his home and his employment within three days. To be a blasphemer, and even perhaps a heretic, was in conventional society to be an outcast.

But the power of Bradlaugh's will and determination then became manifest, as he left home and his job in order to pro-ceed towards a new life. At a meeting in Bonner's Fields he had been introduced to Austin Holyoake, a 'freethinker'; the term itself covered a whole register, from scepticism to unbelief. With Holyoake's encouragement and assistance, Bradlaugh delivered a lecture in the autumn of 1850 on 'Past, Present and Future of Theology'; he was seventeen years old. The young lecturer, who quickly proved himself to be as articulate as he was intelligent, had found his calling.

In December 1850 Bradlaugh enlisted in the army of the East India Company. By some strange arrangement he was shipped not to India but to Dublin, where he was enrolled in the Dragoon Guards stationed in that city and where as a private soldier he wit-nessed the sharp end of authority inflicted on the people. A small family bequest allowed him to purchase his release after three years of service, and on his return to England he resumed his previous employment. He started work as a clerk in a solicitor's office on Fenchurch Street, and such was his knowledge of the law that he was soon acting in an almost managerial capacity. But his real work was just beginning. He was giving lectures on 'freethought' in various halls and institutes of the capital, and soon acquired the reputation of a young 'infidel' on the rise. This was for his employer, a conventional man of law, a startling development. In deference to the solicitor's feelings, Bradlaugh lectured under the name of 'Iconoclast', and concealed his real name. For the majority, however, he was propounding a still forbidden subject. He might have been arrested under the Blasphemy Act of 1650, which was designed to prosecute those publishing or spreading 'blasphemous and execrable opinions' that might endanger national stability; the whole of society was established on oath-taking, addressed to the Almighty, which permeated down from Parliament and the army to every level of social life. As a result Bradlaugh was always at a disadvantage in a court of law, and this exchange is typical:

> Magistrate: Do you believe in God?
> Bradlaugh: I do not.
> Magistrate: Do you believe in a future state of rewards and punishments?
> Bradlaugh: After death, certainly not.
> Magistrate: Then I must refuse your evidence.

✠

ATHEISM, AS A FORMAL and defined belief, was of recent date in England. An entry in the *Encyclopaedia Britannica* of 1771 stated that 'it is justly questioned whether any man seriously adopted such a principle.' It may have been considered, and even sometimes tacitly accepted, but it was not openly professed until the 1780s and 1790s. From the 1820s onwards, however, there was a steady stream of books, pamphlets and lectures promoting atheism and extolling the virtues of freethought. Atheism was propagated under many names – Rationalism, Secularism and Naturalism among them. It was discussed at meetings in committee rooms, coffee rooms, temperance hotels, halls, reading rooms and public houses, and of course in the open air. It was in general a working-class movement, with a few rich or noble bystanders, but a small one. By the time Bradlaugh began his public mission, in 1850, there were many in implicit but unspoken sympathy. The advances in biblical scholarship had cast doubt on the reliability of both Testaments, and the acceptance of Darwinian theory further undermined the orthodox faith. The fact that the established Church made little effort to address the problems of massive industrialization and social change served only to emphasize its weakness and, even, its irrelevance.

As a young lecturer Bradlaugh began a course of private study that would have done justice to a student at a theological college; he became in the *process* a biblical scholar with immediate recall of any chapter or verse and, armed with this knowledge, he widened his career of lectures and debates to encompass the entire country. He had become an imposing figure. At a height of six foot two, and dressed entirely in black with a white shirt-front, he might have been a Dissenting preacher. He may even have wished to emphasize the likeness. His voice was loud, rich and subtly controlled so that it could reach the length and breadth of any hall. Sometimes he wore a black silk top hat. The *Northern Echo* wrote, 'in some respects he reminds us of a Puritan who has lost his way. The apostolic zeal, the vehement impatience with false doctrine, the abiding faith in great principles . . . are all characteristic of the Puritan.' A pile of books lay beside his desk or lectern, so that he could turn to any sentence he wished to emphasize. He might announce, for example, that 'the atheist does not say "there is no God" but he says "I know not what you mean by God; the word God is a sound conveying no clear or distinct affirmation. I cannot war with a nonentity."' The impression he made was strong and enduring. He had an extraordinary fluency and vigour in argument. He was a debater, and a polemicist, but he was also cogent in logic and philosophical enquiry.

In the spring of 1858, at the age of 24, Bradlaugh was elected President of the London Secular Society, and after a time he emerged as the most famous atheist in the country. In 1860 he founded and became the editor of the weekly *National Reformer*, promoting its 'antagonism to every known religious system, and especially to the various phases of Christianity taught and preached in Britain'. This was a monumental act of courage or of folly, posing a challenge to every form of authority. In 1866 Bradlaugh established the National Secular Society, which allowed him to organize and administer all its local clubs and groups. His atheism also had wider ramifications. In his war against external and established authority he was ready to embrace political radicalism and republicanism, and to advocate the doctrine of 'malthusianism'; this was named after Thomas Robert Malthus, the early nineteenth-century economist who believed that the rate of population would naturally outstrip the food supply. 'Malthusianism' became, in effect, the word used to denote methods of birth control that were either unmentioned or unmentionable at the time.

Bradlaugh had already come under attack from the political and legal authorities, which were using any legal means to fine or prosecute him, citing various acts and statutes in order to do so. But he decided to fight back, and in the general election of 1868 he stood as prospective Member of Parliament for the borough of Northampton. This was then the centre of the shoe industry, and shoemakers or cobblers had always been known for their radical sympathies. It was said that they had time and opportunity to think. His first electoral campaign was not a success, but he had so much confidence in himself and in his beliefs that he never accepted failure or defeat. He stood for the same seat again, and then once again, each time unsuccessfully. He had a will as ferocious as his temper.

Bradlaugh's republicanism was also integral to his subsequent campaigns, and on the inauguration of the London Republican Club in the spring of 1871, he delivered a speech in celebration of its purpose. In the autumn of that year, when Queen Victoria was rumoured to be ill, he stated, 'I have repeatedly declared my most earnest desire that the present Prince of Wales should never dishonour this country by becoming its King.' He also began a series of lectures on the same theme, which was eventually published as a pamphlet entitled 'The Impeachment of the House of Brunswick' (1872), replete with legal and historical detail; he had already studied enough to become a skilled constitutional expert. As a result, there were many calls for his arrest and imprisonment, so that the atheist seemed to become the enemy of the people. Bradlaugh provoked violence and ferocious attack, as well as constant heckling and obstruction. A journalist on the *Newcastle Weekly Chronicle* noted that 'no public man within my recollection was the mark and object of more calumnies and falsehoods than Charles Bradlaugh.'

Yet for others Bradlaugh became an ally and support. He was editing and contributing to the *National Reformer*, while delivering lectures across the country. He also began to lecture on Sunday mornings and evenings, no doubt in deliberate imitation of church services, at the Hall of Science on the City Road in London; this became his traditional venue, in the same spirit as Wesley's Chapel along the same road, and was where he spoke on such subjects as 'The Existence of God' and 'The Theory of Evolution'. In the Hall of Science, also, Bradlaugh first became acquainted with Annie Besant. Of this first meeting she wrote in her autobiography that 'eloquence, fire, sarcasm, pathos, passion, all in turn were bent against Christian superstition, till the great audience, carried away by the orator's force, hung silent, breathing soft.' He had found a follower.

✠

ANNIE BESANT WAS BORN on Fish Street Hill, within the City of London, at the beginning of October 1847. Her family was of Irish origin, and she wrote later that 'all my heart was Irish.' Her father died when she was five years old, and in the autumn of 1855 her mother, Emily Wood, moved with her and her brother to a house on Harrow Hill. It was there that Annie Besant began her true education. She read *Paradise Lost*, and spoke aloud the sonorous words of Milton's Devil. Her mother took in boarders from the public school, Harrow, but it was not believed proper for Annie to grow up in a house of young men, and within a few months she came under the tuition of Ellen Marryat, who nurtured her well. Annie was a not particularly pious child, but after a visit to Paris with Miss Marryat, she became attached to the theatre and ritual of Roman Catholicism. This was the prelude to her first attachment, to 'high' Anglicanism, and after she returned to her mother in 1863 she evinced a profound faith in Christ and his Passion. She read the New Testament intently and, like Charles Bradlaugh, noticed the inconsistencies between the four Gospels. But she chose to ignore them in favour of a fulsome piety. At the same time she was reading deeply in poetry and philosophy, guided by her mother, who no doubt sensed Annie's love of learning.

But the happy family was about to break up. Annie, again under the guidance of her mother, was betrothed to the young deacon at her local church. Just before their marriage, Frank Besant was ordained a minister in the Church of England; it seemed likely that Annie would continue her pious vocation as a clergyman's wife. The hope was not fulfilled. A month after their marriage, in January 1868, her new husband was engaged as an assistant mathematics master at Cheltenham College. It was a respectable position, but not in any sense a rewarding one; the role of the wife was in turn neither interesting nor valuable. Annie seemed always to need a purpose, or a direction, in order to justify herself. In these early years of frustration she began to write, and by indirection or accident she discovered that she had a gift for prose. She wrote short stories and composed her first novel, but her gift was checked by two pregnancies in the space of two years; it was further delayed when Frank was appointed minister in the parish of

Annie Besant, *c.* 1897, photograph.

Sibsey, Lincolnshire. It was a rural area, which Annie had never before known, and her shock at the conditions of the agricultural labourers turned to anger. It was an early sign of her identification with suffering.

The Besants began to quarrel, and after some severe arguments Annie took herself off by train to London, where she attended the religious meetings at St George's Hall, off Regent Street; this was a place where the more radical preachers testified to a faith quite different from that of her conventional husband. Annie was never afraid to put herself forwards, in the pursuit of what she considered to be 'truth', and she became acquainted with some of the speakers. Soon enough she became attached to a group of freethinkers and theists, who denied the divinity of Christ in order to celebrate an undivided and omnipotent God. After discussion and much scriptural exegesis she accepted their arguments.

Once Annie took up a principle or belief she became wholly absorbed by it, at whatever personal or social cost. She was guided by the ideas of others, which she adopted as her own, and pursued them with a certainty as strong as her will. This was the pattern of her life and work. On her return to Sibsey she confronted her husband with the dilemma of a vicar's wife who had abandoned orthodox religion, and the solution was in effect a compromise. He worked in his study, and she set up her books and papers in the drawing room. It was agreed that she would attend services in which Almighty God was the object of worship, and avoid those that emphasized the divinity of Christ. The agreement could not last. In 1872 Annie published a pamphlet entitled 'On the Deity of Jesus of Nazareth', which seriously compromised the position of the Reverend Besant. In the autumn of 1873 the couple obtained a deed of separation, and Annie began what she considered to be her new life. It was nourished by the time she spent in study under the dome of the Reading Room in the British Museum, where she earned a precarious living by writing religious pamphlets for a radical publisher, Thomas Scott, with such titles as 'Inspiration' and 'The Religious Education of Children'. This was the period when she entered the Hall of Science, on the City Road, to hear the words of Charles Bradlaugh.

✝

IN HER *AUTOBIOGRAPHICAL SKETCHES* (1885) Annie Besant recalled that occasion, when she first saw 'the grave, quiet, stern, strong face, the massive head, the keen eyes, the magnificent breadth and height of forehead – was this the man I had heard described as a blatant agitator, an ignorant demagogue?' It was the man. She had even anticipated her conversion to his cause by joining the National Secular Society only days before. On hearing of her turn from theism to atheism her publisher, Scott, observed that 'Mrs Besant is an ambitious woman, and when the fit is on her will do and say any mad thing. She is very young and, in all worldly matters, very foolish.'

Besant and Bradlaugh soon became acquainted; almost at once he realized that, as a skilled pamphleteer, she could be enrolled in the service of atheism. Her commanding, but pleasing, voice suggested that she might also be useful on a public platform. She agreed to write articles for the *National Reformer*, with a weekly salary of one guinea, and very quickly she took a central role in Bradlaugh's mission. She gave her first lecture on atheism at the Princess's Theatre on Oxford Street. It was billed as a 'discussion', but the *Reformer* praised it as 'probably the best speech by a woman to which we have ever listened'. Soon after joining the newspaper she was happy to begin a national lecture tour on the virtues of freethought. 'I don't care for life', she said, 'if I can't fill it with work.' There speaks a quintessential Victorian. She later wrote in her autobiography, 'I used every weapon that history, science, criticism, scholarship, could give me against the Churches.'

In February 1875 Besant visited the north of England and Scotland in order to continue her campaign, and in both areas she was a palpable success. She met attack and abuse, some of it personal, but she did not waver. She was now 27; she dressed demurely, in dark silk, and she did not gesture much while speaking. She was, in a sense, a medium for the novel doctrines of the age. Bradlaugh's daughter Hypatia remarked that 'she had a really wonderful power of absorbing the thoughts of others, of blending them, and of transmuting them into glowing language.' There was such novelty in a young woman preaching that Besant attracted an audience wherever she travelled, while the stamp of atheism gave her a further and more sensational appeal. A journalist noted

> what a beautiful and attractive and irresistible creature she was then, with her slight but full and well-shaped figure, her dark hair, her finely chiselled features, her eyes with their impenetrable depths of emotion and thought . . . making her a mixture at once of soft and warm and intellectual femininity.

Bradlaugh and Besant, the twin agents of infidelity, became part of the Victorian consciousness.

But their increasing fame came at a cost. In early 1877 they agreed to reprint Charles Knowlton's treatise *The Fruits of Philosophy* (1832) under the imprint of their recently established Freethought Publishing Company. This was a work that appealed to their Malthusian principles, since it advocated the practice of birth control. It had already been banned in the United States on the grounds of obscenity, but Besant, in particular, urged its republication on the simple argument that it was a medical text with a legitimate purpose. In a preface Bradlaugh added that it concerned 'the most important social question which can influence a nation's welfare'. The book sold rapidly in the first weeks, but their sanguine expectations were not fulfilled. The two most notorious atheists in the country could not be allowed to publish such sensitive material without consequences. In early April they were arrested under the provisions of the Obscene Publications Act of 1857, and on 18 June they were brought to trial in Westminster Hall with the charge that they did 'unlawfully, wickedly, knowingly, wilfully and design-edly' publish and sell 'a certain indecent, lewd, filthy, bawdy and obscene book'. All references to contraceptive devices were at that time illegal, but the text also contained details of sexual inter-course and fertilization, together with detailed descriptions of the external and internal reproductive organs. The Solicitor General conducted the case for the prosecution, but Besant and Bradlaugh were permitted to address the jurors in their own defence.

They were both now practised public speakers, and their speeches were frequently interrupted by applause. After much legal wrangling they were found guilty as charged, but the pre-siding judge – after congratulating Bradlaugh on the presentation of his case – waived the punishment of imprisonment and fine on condition that they pledged not to republish the offending material. It was for them a victory. Bradlaugh's legalistic mind, undertaking the close reading of precedent (his study of the Old Testament) and the cross-examination of witnesses (his study of the New), had led him towards atheism; now the same procedure offered him protection against its legal consequences. 'The Bradlaugh', as he sometimes called himself, had taught himself to become a master of law, and so was able to circumvent its niceties.

At the beginning of April 1880, after twelve years of trying and failing, Bradlaugh was elected Member of Parliament for Northampton. His eventual victory may have been the result of his reputation, which some would call his notoriety, or it may have been a sign that atheism itself was no longer distasteful to the gen-eral public. But the reaction of Westminster was quite different from that of his constituency. Each was obliged to take the oath of

allegiance to the queen before becoming a member of 'the faithful Commons', but that oath had to be sworn by placing the hand
upon the Bible. How could a professed atheist perform what was
for him a meaningless and indeed nonsensical act? He would be
asked to swear by an 'Almighty God' that did not exist. Bradlaugh
was quite aware of the problem, and advised the Speaker of the
Commons that he was prepared to affirm, without using a religious
text, rather than to swear. He had already done so in various courts
of law. But the legal authorities of Parliament judged that this was
not permitted under the Parliamentary Oaths Act of 1866. The
matter was referred to a select committee, which quickly decided
against him. Bradlaugh then decided that, in order to serve his
constituents, he would take the oath. In this, he misjudged. At
the moment he was about to swear, a fellow member stood up
and objected. It would be a mockery, and even a blasphemy, for
any atheist to swear the oath. A further select committee, and
then another, was chosen to adjudge the issue. It was decided
that Bradlaugh could neither affirm nor swear. When he stepped
forwards once more for the formal ritual, he was told to withdraw
from the chamber. In a loud voice he declared, 'I admit no right on
the part of the House to exclude me and I refuse to be excluded.'
This had now become a grave constitutional matter, and the
members voted by a majority of 274 to 7 to imprison him in the
Clock Tower of Westminster. All these proceedings were observed
by Besant, and reported by her in vivid terms for the *National
Reformer*. But the affair had now absorbed national attention, and
Charles Bradlaugh became the name of the day.

Bradlaugh was released from the Clock Tower on the day
after his detention. Gladstone prepared the way for his return
to Parliament by bringing forward a standing order that allowed
any member to affirm if he had the right to do so. Did Bradlaugh
have that right? He took his seat in the chamber and, on the
following day, voted in the customary manner. But one of his

Parliamentary opponents then issued a writ against him, arguing that he was not entitled to vote and should incur a severe financial penalty for so doing. He was once more before the courts, even as he carried on his work as a new MP in his usual scrupulous manner. The issue came to trial in March 1881, and on losing his case Bradlaugh decided to appeal against the verdict. At this point a motion was proposed by his opponents that his Northampton seat should be 'vacated' and a fresh election in that constituency held. Bradlaugh managed to retain his seat in the contest, but commented in the *National Reformer* that 'the election just ended has been the most bitter I have fought, and some of my foes have been more foul than ever I thought possible.' Large crowds greeted him with cheers as he again walked into Parliament. He entered the chamber and was about to take the oath when the Speaker forestalled him. The Commons must decide if he could continue. Bradlaugh was allowed to address the members. 'You think I am an obnoxious man,' he said, 'and that I have no one on my side.' The Parliamentary process began again with claim and counterclaim, objection and interruption, as if it had never happened before. A vote to exclude him was then passed, and he embarked upon a speaking tour of the country in order to assert his rights.

These were the first stages in a Parliamentary affair that lasted for six years. In the interim Bradlaugh stood for election for Northampton a further three times, and was duly elected three times. He was charged and tried for blasphemy, but found innocent. He had described the controversy as a battle between Parliament and the people, not as Christians against an atheist. He had gone to court many times. He had become the favourite target of the press. He had been beaten and abused when trying to enter the Commons. He had conducted national tours and addressed mass rallies. In 1885 he eventually succeeded in taking his place, after a new Speaker allowed him to take the oath without the intervention of fellow MPs. It was the obvious solution after years of bitter acrimony.

But if the controversy had come to an end, Bradlaugh soon faced a challenge of a different kind. Besant had forsworn her atheism. She had now found, or was in the process of discovering, a solution to the world's ills in socialism. She had become acquainted with the leaders of the Social Democratic Federation as well as the Fabians, and followed their lead. One of Bradlaugh's colleagues wrote that 'she seems to be very much at the mercy of her emotions, and especially at the mercy of her latest friends. A powerful engine, she runs on lines laid down for her.' In defence of her, however, it should be admitted that at this time of doubt new theories and new beliefs were always circulating. But she acted on impulse and instinct rather than on judgement, and was so absorbed in her own feelings that she did not consider those of others. Hypatia Bradlaugh considered her 'the most tactless person I ever knew'. Besant began writing pamphlets on her new socialist creed, and introduced references to it in the weekly column she was still writing for the *National Reformer*, even though Bradlaugh himself was adamantly opposed to its principles. He despised political dogma as an assault upon the individual. In 1887 their joint editorship of the *Reformer* came to an end when Besant declared in its columns that 'the partial separation of my policy from that of my colleague has been of my own making and not of his.'

Bradlaugh himself was very busy with his Parliamentary duties and was giving five lectures a week. In one of his last essays he wrote that 'the gradual and growing rejection of Christianity – like the rejection of faiths which preceded it – has in fact added, and will add, to man's happiness and well-being.' But his own 'well-being' was not always equal to the tasks he still set himself. He caught a chill in the autumn of 1889 that affected his kidneys, and became dangerously ill. Early in the following year he resigned as President of the National Secular Society. He declared in one of his last speeches, 'I may have stood still, but I have not changed.' When Besant visited him during his last days, he scarcely spoke a word. She had already abandoned atheism and in later years would venture into theosophy, occultism and Indian mysticism. Bradlaugh died from the effects of Bright's disease on 30 January 1891, at the age of 57.

✠

CLINTON RICHARD DAWKINS was born in Nairobi, Kenya, on 26 March 1941. His father was a civil servant in the British Colonial Service, but the family returned to England in 1949. He was brought up in a conventional Anglican culture, and attended private schools until he entered Balliol College, Oxford, in the autumn of 1949 to study zoology. After graduating he began research work for his doctorate and submitted a successful thesis on 'Selective Pecking in the Domestic Chick'. After a year of further research and lecturing at Oxford, he took up the post of assistant professor of zoology at the University of California at Berkeley in 1967; three years later he returned to Oxford as lecturer in zoology and fellow of New College.

Dawkins's more popular work was initiated in that period with *The Selfish Gene*, published in 1976. Its argument, in abbreviated form, was that

> we, and all other animals, are machines created by our genes . . . I shall argue that a predominant quality to be expected in a successful gene is ruthless selfishness. This gene selfishness will usually give rise to selfishness in individual behaviour. However, as we shall see, there are special circumstances in which a gene can achieve its own selfish goals best by fostering a limited form of altruism at the level of individual animals.

Most people were familiar with the rudiments of Darwinism, with the survival of the fittest (or 'the most stable', as Dawkins pointed out), and the cumulative shifts over many aeons that gradually create new species. Some were also aware of the genetic theory of inheritance developed by Gregor Mendel, and even knew that it had complemented and helped to elucidate Darwin's theory of natural selection. Dawkins's innovation was to present natural selection from the point of view of the gene. This became known as the 'gene's-eye view' of evolution. And this point of view, it turned out, was remarkable. Dawkins explained that the gene was the true 'replicator', the unit in the organic composite that really mattered and the one on which, although indirectly, natural selection operated. The individual was merely the 'vehicle'. In his preface to the first edition of *The Selfish Gene* he wrote, 'we are survival machines – robot vehicles blindly programmed to preserve the selfish molecules known as genes.' It seemed to many scientists to be an intriguing tilt in neo-Darwinian thought, rather than a complete revolution. To the general, educated public, however, it came as lightning from a clear sky. The book helped to create Dawkins's reputation as a formidable proponent of scientific theory. His great skill as a scientist was combined with his gifts as a propagandist and, later, as a polemicist.

Dawkins has described himself as a 'cultural Christian' and, significantly, 'a cultural Anglican'. In some ways he fits well within this tradition, one that reveres the mind that reads as much as the Word that is read. Anglicanism has never been ashamed of thought.

Dawkins is not a Christian, of course. Indeed he is perhaps England's most celebrated, and certainly most ardent, atheist. And yet, as he acknowledges, he is in some ways an unlikely unbeliever. He has spoken many times of his conviction that, had he been born before 1859, when Charles Darwin's *On the Origin of Species* was first published, he would probably not have become an atheist.

Before that date, creation itself in its very complexity seemed to demand a Creator. Although he might resist or even resent the term, Dawkins's true gift lies in the realm of mythopoeia. When people speak, as they do so often now, of the all-encompassing influence of genes on anything from addiction to an aptitude for mathematics, or when they suggest that 'memes' are to blame for certain tenacious fallacies, they are – whether consciously or not – invoking Richard Dawkins.

It was for his notion of the 'meme', in the eleventh chapter of *The Selfish Gene*, that Dawkins became most influential. He was adverting to the fact that 'the new [primordial] soup is the soup of culture. We need a name for the new replicator, a noun that conveys the idea of a unit of cultural transmission, or a unit of imitation.' He called this replicator the 'meme', after the Greek but with a nod to the French. The meme can be anything that convention might term a habit. Even 'habit', however, is too specific. It is an element of human behaviour or practice that passes by imitation from one person to another. As Dawkins explains, a meme can be a custom but also a tune, an urban legend, a catchphrase, a recurring image or logo. It can be, and often is, an entire system of thought, one that survives, unexamined, unquestioned, even when the evidence is against it. Religion, for Dawkins, is a meme, or rather a collection of mutually supportive memes. It is what he calls 'the God-meme'. The gene therefore emerges as the real power in the organic universe as a whole.

The Extended Phenotype, the book that followed *The Selfish Gene* in 1982, elaborates on Dawkins's argument. He suggests that a meme 'should be regarded as a unit of information residing in a brain . . . it has a definite structure, realized in whatever medium the brain uses for storing information.' In *The Blind Watchmaker*, published in 1986 and one of his most celebrated books, God – as an explanation for the complexity of creation – is seen as superfluous. Darwinian natural selection has prised off that cumbrous chrysalis and the truth is now on the wing. The living design of the biological world is in fact a blind process that has no purpose in view and proceeds only by the arcane workings of 'natural selection'; it is not devised or directed by a creative God. Dawkins argues that 'the universe we observe has precisely the properties we should expect if there is, at bottom, no design, no purpose, no evil, no good, nothing but blind pitiless indifference.'

The God Delusion, published in 2006, represents Dawkins's most extended defence of atheism. He lays out his case against God, with some peculiar, if entertaining, forays into physics and philosophy. If *The Blind Watchmaker* should be taken as the work of Dawkins's heart, this is perhaps the work of his spleen. He claims that 'in any of its forms, the God hypothesis is unnecessary.' The possibility of a god, specifically a creative god, is a hypothesis like any other and, as such, subject to enquiry. He concludes that God is unnecessary, and, for the scientist, what is unnecessary is wrong.

Dawkins considers the question of what constitutes an atheist, and writes, 'I have found it an amusing strategy, when asked whether I am an atheist, to point out that the questioner is also an atheist when considering Zeus, Apollo, Amon Ra, Mithras, Baal, Thor, Wotan, the Golden Calf and the Flying Spaghetti Monster. I just go one god further.' On the consolations of atheism, he quotes his own words from *A Devil's Chaplain* (2003): 'There is more than just grandeur in this view of life, bleak and cold though it can seem from under the security blanket of ignorance. There is deep refreshment to be had from standing up and facing straight into the strong keen wind of understanding.' This sentiment may have been shared by Charles Bradlaugh, and by other atheists over the intervening years.

Twenty-One

Religion as Argument
G. K. Chesterton (1874–1936),
C. S. Lewis (1898–1963)

Gilbert Keith Chesterton was born on 29 May 1874 in the prosperous London district of Kensington; his father was an estate agent by trade but by choice an amateur artist, and his mother was of intriguing French and Scottish ancestry. They were middle-class in a comfortably middle-class world. Of his childhood Chesterton recalled that 'anything in it was a wonder. It was not merely a world full of miracles; it was a miraculous world.' That sense of wonder never left him, and may account for the fact that he was often said to resemble a child in spirit. One of his first memories was of a scene in his father's toy theatre, of a young man walking across a bridge with a gilded crown on his head and a golden key in his hand. It was a precise and singular image, the meaning of which was unknown, but it represented for the adult Chesterton 'the boundary line that brings one thing sharply against another. All my life I have loved frames and limits.' He had to see an object, or an idea, clearly and as a whole before he could identify it. Another vivid memory was of a no less enchanted Kensington High Street, where he saw a crowd of people fall to their knees when a 'little dark cab or carriage had drawn up . . . and out of it came a ghost clad in flames'. This was Cardinal Manning, dressed in the scarlet robes of his office, but for Chesterton it was a first glimpse of the miraculous or the supernatural in the realm of the ordinary. It resembled something

G. K. Chesterton, 1915, photograph.

out of a fairy tale, and Chesterton would later believe that fairy tales are the beginnings of faith. It was all the more significant for a boy who had been brought up in what was essentially an agnostic household. It demonstrated the theatrical power of an old religion.

As a child of affluence, Chesterton was sent to a public school, but not a boarding school; St Paul's School in Hammersmith was chosen for him because of its reputation and its closeness to home. He did not seem to be an enterprising or studious schoolboy, and acquired a reputation for untidiness and absent-mindedness. He possessed a voice of a higher pitch than usual, together with a loud laugh. He was also considered 'sleepy', but in fact he was an avid and voracious reader; the difference was that he devoured the books he wished for and not necessarily those the masters required. There was another difference. He did not follow the conventional path from public school to Oxford or Cambridge; instead, his father enlisted him on a fine-arts course at the Slade School attached to University College, London. The boy had already exhibited great skill as a draughtsman and caricaturist, and the amateur artist wanted to encourage his son. This also meant that Chesterton avoided the trammels of a conventional education and so escaped the straitjacket of the age.

In fact Chesterton ranged from art to French and English literature at the college, picking up what seems to have been vast swathes of knowledge at a glance. He had a genius for rapid assimilation. To friends and contemporaries he appeared to be a cheerful companion, avowing the theory that 'existence was extraordinary enough to be exciting,' but in this period he was also beset by the morbid fears of early maturity. He flirted with the contemporary 'Decadent' movement in literature, composed in equal parts of ennui and artifice with the additional doctrine of 'art for art's sake', and he dabbled in spiritualism or mysticism with the equally fashionable use of the planchette for automatic writing. He may even have considered himself to be a blasphemer, except that blasphemy is a sure sign of faith. 'If anyone doubts this,' he once wrote, 'let him sit down seriously and try to think blasphemous thoughts about Thor.' He confessed later that this was the period when he became acquainted with 'the Devil', but it may also have been the time when he first recognized his sexuality, which was for him always a troubling condition.

Chesterton put his doubts and fears to one side in the honourable pursuit of earning a living. He never graduated from University College with a degree, and seemed fated for inconsequential employment. He worked for one or two publishers while amusing himself with exercises in verse, 'nonsense' and otherwise. He also met a young lady, Frances Blogg, with whom he felt an immediate rapport and who would after a decent interval become his wife. He was not perhaps the most promising of husbands, and described himself to her as an 'aimless, tactless, reckless, unbrushed, strange-hatted, opinionated scarecrow'.

Chesterton had already begun writing occasional book reviews, principally by advertising his existence to possible editors, and it soon became clear that journalism was for him the trade or profession of choice. With the help of friends he was given a regular role on *The Speaker*, a radical journal that attacked British imperialism and which at that juncture supported the Boers. But his polemics were concerned with art and literature; his first review, on John Ruskin, appeared at the end of April 1900. In the autumn of that year his first book, a volume of nonsense verse, was also published. He had been launched or, rather, he had launched himself. Early in the following year he was employed by the *Daily News*, a liberal and anti-imperialist newspaper, to be 'manager of the literary page'. It was a career that, in one form or another, he pursued for the rest of his life. He fully shared the principles of the newspaper. He was a fierce opponent of capitalism and its extension in imperialism; he was convinced that both issued from the creeds of secularism and materialism.

At the close of 1901 Chesterton published his first book of prose, *The Defendant*, which, like many of his later books, consisted of a collection of articles. They were boisterous and opinionated, but some reviewers noticed another common element in Chesterton's use of paradox as a pillar of his argument. He took the conventional opinions of the time, and turned them upside down on the principle that 'there really is a strand of contradiction running through the universe.' It became his familiar device, too, in the discussion of religious matters. In a faith that believes that Christ is both God and man, it was absolutely necessary. It was sometimes said that his use of paradox was novel and unfamiliar, perhaps somehow 'un-English', but this is to forget that paradoxes and riddles were at the heart of Anglo-Saxon literature.

By 1903 Chesterton was writing a weekly column for the *Daily News*, and had become one of the most widely read journalists of the period. He informed his mother, 'I might almost say that I am becoming the fashion.' His style was unique, and his opinions acted as a restorative for those who were tired of modern truisms. He liked to demolish 'claptrap' employed in the service of contemporary humanism or rationalism, for the sake of clearing the air.

This was an age avid for firmly stated opinions because it was avid for certainty, and so, as did other journalists of the period, Chesterton became a public figure – to which his height (6 ft 4 inches), his bulk (20 stone and rising), his cape and swordstick all contributed. In the same period he composed his first biography, on Robert Browning (1903), in the same style as his essays. He approached the work not as a scholar enquiring after facts, but as an enthusiast sharing his opinions.

Chesterton used the method that his detective, Father Brown, employed in solving crime. The demure priest relied on his experience of the confessional and on a sympathetic imagination, which allowed him to enter the mind and spirit of his subject. Browning was of course a poet rather than a priest, but Chesterton followed the same path of sympathetic collaboration in order to understand Browning and to make him live. For him the act of intuition was also the act of imagination. In *Dickens*, composed and published three years later, his account of Charles Dickens must in part be an account of himself; he could not separate the two in his description of the fire and energy, the sheer plenitude, of the earlier novelist.

He wrote that the art of Dickens was 'like life because like life it is irresponsible, because, like life, it is incredible'. In that sense the serious genius of Dickens, and perhaps of Chesterton himself, was the comic genius.

IN 1904 CHESTERTON engaged in one of his first attempts at Christian apologetics in a controversy with a noted socialist and atheist, Robert Blatchford, who had denied the spiritual claims of religious faith. Chesterton made his case in a series of apophthegms and startling propositions. 'If Moses had said God was an Infinite Energy,' he wrote, 'I should be certain he had seen nothing extraordinary. As he said he was a Burning Bush, I think it very likely that he did see something extraordinary.' In similar fashion he argued that 'Christianity, which is a very mystical religion, has nevertheless been the religion of the most practical sections of mankind.' On another occasion he noted that 'Christ did not love humanity. He never said He loved humanity. He loved men. Neither He nor anyone else can love humanity.' It was the form of argument he always used in which ostensible common sense and unusual paradox are combined. To be a Christian in the 'modern world' was to be a heretic; to argue with the secular world, and to convince the sceptical imagination, it was necessary to celebrate the unfamiliar in familiar terms. He believed that Christianity is as mysterious as the light of the sun, since 'the one created thing we cannot look at is the one thing in the light of which we look at everything.' Christians should be as proud of their faith as scientists are 'proud of the complexity of science'. So it is that 'the believers in miracles accept them, rightly or wrongly, because they have evidence for them. The disbelievers in miracles deny them, rightly or wrongly, because they have doctrine against them.' In his study *Orthodoxy* of 1908, Chesterton wrote of Archbishop Thomas Becket that 'he wore a hair shirt under his gold and crimson, and there is much to be said for the combination; for Becket got the benefit of the hair shirt, while the people in the street got the benefit of the crimson and gold. This is the thrilling romance of orthodoxy.'

This was also the period in which Chesterton completed his first and most memorable novel, *The Napoleon of Notting Hill* (1904), in which that region of west London becomes a feudal state with its own borders and army. It adverts to the spirit of place and territory that is primeval and therefore, for Chesterton, most pertinent. He believed in myths and old legends as an aspect of the national inheritance, imparting far more truth and power than any current scientific or political nostrum. He once said, 'I am the man who with the utmost daring discovered what had been discovered before.' As a result he took no interest in contemporary waves of fear or optimism, so pronounced in the late Victorian and early Edwardian periods, which were in truth no more than ripples on the surface. He believed in the 'common man' and in his 'ordinary' opinions because, for him, ordinariness bore the marks of truth.

This was, of course, the 'secret' of Father Brown, the priest and detective whom Chesterton created in a short story of 1910. In the many stories that followed Brown was an unremarked appraiser of the most remarkable matters, who understood the mind of the criminal or murderer by intuition rather than mere evidence. He knew that the greatest sinner is also a human like himself. With the knowledge of good and evil, he was calm in the face of sin but unrelenting in its pursuit; but, with the innocence of faith, he looked upon the world as if seeing it for the first time. In *The Secret of Father Brown* (1927) he explains,

> you see, I had murdered them all myself . . . I had planned out each of the crimes very carefully. I had thought out exactly how a thing like that could be done, and in what style or state of mind a man could really do it. And when I

was quite sure that I felt exactly like the murderer myself, of course I knew who he was.

Father Brown refuses to divide the material world from the spiritual world, and reason from faith. Chesterton fought against this dichotomy throughout his life, and in the 'Father Brown' stories he tries to demonstrate that human reality can be understood only with reference to spiritual belief. Rationalism is not at war with faith; they exist in a symbiotic relationship. 'You attacked reason,' Father Brown explained to one criminal who was unsuccessfully pretending to be a priest. 'It's bad theology.' The essence of Father Brown must be that he appears inessential, and his most important characteristic is to seem unimportant. Chesterton wrote that Brown's 'conspicuous quality was not being conspicuous'. In that respect he was quite unlike Chesterton himself and might be seen as the avenging ghost or, more benignly, the spiritual presence of the author.

In the summer of 1921 Chesterton took the final step of his journey to the Roman Catholic Church, since for him Catholicism was the only 'creed that could not be satisfied with a truth, but only with the Truth, which is made of a million . . . truths and yet is one'. It was his witness against what he believed to be the meretricious beliefs and opinions of his age, by means of which 'scientific imagination and social reform between them will quite logically and almost legitimately have made us slaves.' They were the pressing weight of materialism that would stifle any vision of an alternative reality. His right-minded and right-thinking contemporaries were for him moles burrowing ever deeper into the dark earth: 'We do not, as the newspapers say, want a Church that will move with the world. We want a Church that will move the world.'

Chesterton's newly revealed faith was evident in the works that followed his conversion. In 1923 his short work *St Francis of Assisi* was published, in which he praised the saint's virtues of penance and self-denial: 'It was not self-denial merely in the sense of self-control. It was as positive as a passion; it had all the air of being as positive as pleasure. He devoured fasting as a man devours food.' It was the cheerful and optimistic way in which he recommended Christian practice that accounts for much of his effectiveness as a lay theologian. Chesterton believed that Francis of Assisi was joyful for the simple reason that he saw the supernatural as part of the natural world, so that 'a bird went by him like an arrow' in the drama of divine purpose.

In the autumn of 1925 Chesterton published his last major work, *The Everlasting Man*, which he had written partly in reply to H. G. Wells's *The Outline of History* (1920), which had recorded the triumphant advance of humanity and 'the indisputable progress in the power and range of the human mind'. That general assumption could be seen as an extension of Darwinian evolutionary theory, which was accepted at the time as a principle of faith not to be challenged, and so became the object of Chesterton's scorn. Of *On the Origin of Species* he wrote that 'it does not, in the conventional phrase, accept the conclusions of science, for the simple reason that science has not concluded.'

Chesterton was truly a heretic in the early twentieth-century world. In *The Everlasting Man* he argues that the 'evolutionary mania' had persuaded people that 'every great thing grows from a seed, or something smaller than itself. They seem to forget that every seed comes from a tree, or from something larger than itself.' For him, therefore, the supernatural precedes the natural. This truth was as complex as any scientific or biological maxim. At the moment of Incarnation and the birth of Christ, for example, two heterogeneous ideas were yoked violently together in 'the idea of a baby, and the idea of unknown strength that sustains the stars'. But this does not cause ambiguity or confusion, since 'the Christian creed is above all things the philosophy of shape and the enemy of shapelessness.' This is reminiscent of his childhood vision of the toy theatre, where everything had its boundary and its distinct outline. Chesterton went on to argue that the purity of the Catholic creed was 'preserved by dogmatic definitions and exclusions. It could not possibly have been preserved by anything else.' Unlike new orthodoxies, such as those that Wells maintained, 'the Catholic Church is the only thing which saves a man from the degrading slavery of being a child of his age.' It could be said that Chesterton's simplicity of tone, and the directness of his argument, did not consort well with the complexity and ambiguity of belief. But his purpose was to act as a beacon rather than a torch. The weight of work and journalistic routine eventually grew too much for him, and he died of heart failure on 14 June 1936.

CLIVE STAPLES LEWIS was born in Belfast on 29 November 1898; he was the younger son of a local and influential solicitor, Albert Lewis, and of a mother, Florence, who had distinguished herself in mathematics and logic at Queen's University. They were part of what was known as the 'Protestant Ascendancy' in Ireland and were naturally members of the Church of Ireland, which provided the young Lewis with his first awareness of religious faith. His mother died of cancer when he was nine years of age, so instilling in him a sense of unhappy abandonment. His older brother, Warren or 'Warnie', had already been sent to a preparatory school in Watford, Hertfordshire; it was believed by Irish Protestants that an English education, together with the acquisition of an English accent, was a sign of social progress. In the autumn of 1908 Lewis followed his brother to the same school, which he later called a 'concentration camp'. He described it as 'a good preparation for the Christian life, that it taught one to live by hope'. He left the school in the summer of 1910 and was later moved to Malvern College, for which he had no great liking; he detested sports and the school's system of discipline. He wrote of life in an English public school that 'to get on well at one of these, one needs to have a constitution of iron, a hide so thick that no insult will penetrate it, a brain that will never tire, and an intelligence able and ready to cope with the sharp gentlemen who surround you.' He may have learned that lesson at Malvern, since in later life he exhibited some, if not all, of these characteristics.

In these early days Lewis wanted to study, to acquire knowledge and, most importantly, to read. Books were his refuge, and his strength. They were the fountain of his youth. He read widely and voraciously. He read Robert Browning and George Bernard Shaw, Matthew Arnold and Rudyard Kipling. In this period, too, he became acquainted with Celtic literature and the Norse sagas, a double blessing that guided him within the bracing world of epic poetry to which he was immediately drawn. He loved the pounding metre and the heroic adventure of the ancient stories. He read Hélène Guerber's *Myths of the Norsemen* (1909), and came upon Arthur Rackham's illustrations used in the translations of Wagner's *Siegfried* and *The Twilight of the Gods*, where the powerful and flowing images captured what was for Lewis a different and superior reality. He was possessed by 'a vision of huge clear spaces hanging above the Atlantic in the endless twilight of Northern summer, remoteness, severity'. It was a moment of what he would call 'Joy', a sudden uplifting of the spirit in recognition of what has been longed for but not yet experienced.

In this moment came the awareness or sensation of that which is close and familiar, yet at the same time unapproachable. It was, as Lewis described later, 'the scent of a flower we have not found, the echo of a tune we have not heard, news from a country we have never yet visited'. He came to believe that this desire was an unambiguous token of the divine in human consciousness, and he described the experience as one of intense longing. 'It is distinguished from other longings', he wrote, by two things. In the first place, though the sense of want is acute and even painful, yet the mere wanting is felt to be somehow a delight. Other desires are felt as pleasures only if satisfaction is expected in the near future . . . But this desire, even when there is no hope of possible satisfaction, continues to be prized, and even to be preferred to anything else in the world, by those who have once felt it. This hunger is better than any other fullness; this poverty better than all other wealth . . . In the second place, there is a peculiar mystery about the *object* of this Desire.

It is precisely this 'mystery' that leads the unwary, inexperienced or crudely sensual to what Lewis calls 'the spurious satisfactions'. You might imagine that this longing was provoked by a landscape, so you revisit the landscape, but the longing has shifted its ground. You might imagine that it lies in a sweet memory, but if you dive into that memory you find only a whisper where before there had been a song. It is the spirit of 'if only . . .' If only you could recapture that longing. But it can never be caught. The landscape, the memory, the 'fairy lands forlorn' are all only casements through which the longing shines. It has no nest, no permanent resting place anywhere on Earth. For of course it is not earthly.

✝

LEWIS'S LOVE FOR Norse epic was shared, surprisingly and providentially, by a young man across his street in Belfast. When Lewis made the acquaintance of Arthur Greeves, he found the young man reading the same book with illustrations by Rackham. He, too, fed the flame. They talked endlessly of Odin and Thor, Loki and Balder. They had both been pierced by what Lewis called the arrow 'struck from the North'. That time of shared enthusiasm, or obsession, led to a friendship that lasted for the rest of Lewis's life.

After a time at Malvern Lewis was withdrawn from the school and placed under the guidance of a private tutor, W. T. Kirkpatrick, who had been the headmaster of his father's public school in County Armagh but who now lived in Surrey. 'Kirk' was of a rigorously logical temper, and the young Lewis was obliged to question and justify his opinions with the same rigour that was required to parse and translate the classical authors. He was brought up in an atmosphere of debate, discussion and argument to which he contributed an astute intelligence and a capacious memory. Kirk was also a sensitive tutor. He soon realized that his pupil had an understanding of texts and literature far beyond the range of his contemporaries, and told Lewis's father that the young man 'was the most brilliant translator of Greek plays' Kirk had ever encountered. In his judgement, Lewis was destined for the academic life. He added,

> he has singularly little desire to mingle with mankind, or study human nature. His interests lie in a totally different direction – in the past, in the realm of creative imagination, in a world which the common mind would call the unreal, but which to him is the only real one.

This was astute. Kirkpatrick was alluding to Lewis's enthralment with the much earlier writers Thomas Malory and Edmund Spenser, whose shared themes of quest and courtly love became the context for much of his later composition.

In December 1916 Lewis was examined for and awarded a scholarship to Oxford University, and at the same time he was accepted for military service in a significant period of the First World War. At the age of eighteen he went up to University College, Oxford, and also entered the Officer Training Corps based at the university. In the summer of 1917 he was moved to Keble College, where the cadet battalion had been billeted; he shared his rooms with another young recruit, Paddy Moore, and in the comradely circumstances of the time they pledged to look after each other's family in the event of sudden fatality. This oath of fidelity would have interesting consequences.

By the close of 1917 the war had engulfed Lewis. As second lieutenant in the First Somerset Light Infantry he was sent to the front in northern France, where, after a period of trench warfare, he was injured in the chest by shrapnel in what became known as the Second Battle of Arras. When he was discharged from hospital, and demobilized on 24 December 1918, he already had companions. Moore had become a victim of the conflict and, to honour their oath, Lewis had decided to take care of his friend's mother and sister. Mrs Moore was twice his age, but it is clear that she and her young protector soon became closer than might have been expected. She and her daughter took lodgings in Oxford to be near him, for example, when he resumed his studies at the beginning of 1919. He would live with them whenever circumstances allowed, and this domestic intimacy would continue until the time of 'Janie' Moore's death. Their relationship has often been discussed, but no definite conclusions can be reached; it is safe to assume, however, that it entailed more than the 'mother and son' affection that has sometimes been supposed. It was closer, and more puzzling. He concealed it from his father, and was obliged to pursue a 'double life' in order to hide it from his contemporaries at Oxford.

Lewis's career at the university was flourishing. In 1922 he was awarded a first-class degree in classics, and after only a year's further study he received the same in the relatively new discipline of English literature. All the reading of his youth, and of his early maturity, propelled him forwards. In 1924 he was given a temporary appointment as tutor in philosophy at University College, his own college, and a year later he became fellow and tutor in English literature at Magdalen College. It was the start of his real academic life, and he filled that position for almost thirty years.

In February 1926 Lewis completed a long poem in rhyme royal, entitled *Dymer*, which describes a young man's journey through the experience of death and loss. It is of no lasting interest except for its outline of the distinctive path of Lewis's imagination in the form of a quest, by way of Spenser's *The Faerie Queene* and other literary models. It embodies his belief that fantasy is neither real nor unreal, since it is outside the sphere of reality. He never lost his fascination with 'other worlds'. He was also a great joiner of literary clubs or groups at the university, among which were the 'Kolbitars', who gathered to discuss the Icelandic sagas. Lewis was part of a philosophic club, in which he navigated himself away from a Hegelian 'Absolute' to a belief in an undetermined and indeterminate 'God'. This was the path that eventually led him to the Christian faith. It began in a conversation with an Oxford colleague who, despite being a professed atheist, was convinced that the account of Christ in the New Testament was based on fact. It was a myth that happened. From there Lewis moved forwards in slow steps, by means of contemplation and intuition. He carried on an internal debate until eventually he argued himself into faith. As a result, he was to become the best and most persuasive Christian apologist of his generation.

Lewis was also much influenced by G. K. Chesterton. In *Surprised by Joy: The Shape of My Early Life* (1955), he noted that while recovering from trench fever during the war he found 'a volume of Chesterton's essays'. In reading Chesterton, 'I didn't know what I was letting myself in for. A young man who wishes to remain an atheist cannot be too careful of his reading.' In the same account he wrote, 'I read Chesterton's *Everlasting Man* and for the first time saw the whole Christian outline of history set out in a form that seemed to me to make sense.' Lewis also declared that *The Everlasting Man* was 'the best popular defence of the full Christian position I know', and he placed the book in a list of ten works that 'most shaped [my] vocational attitude and philosophy of life'. The two men were in some respects alike, and reflect an aspect of the English soul; both affirmed the life of the spirit, but kept their spirituality concealed behind a sometimes pugnacious or argumentative manner; both evinced an intense interest in the supernatural but expressed it in the practical terms of common sense; they shared a trust in the 'ordinary', but put their faith in the mysterious and miraculous elements of Christianity. They were deeply susceptible to the vagaries of emotion, but in their private dealings were reticent and reserved. It can be said that, in general, the English have a modesty, even perhaps an embarrassment, in spiritual matters on the understanding that faith bears fruit in practice rather than principle.

LEWIS'S CONVERSION CAME upon him by degrees, and he remarked that his search for God was akin to 'the mouse's search for the cat'. In the early summer of 1929 'I gave in, and admitted that God was God, and knelt and prayed: perhaps, that night, the most dejected and reluctant convert in all England.' But his journey was far from over. On the morning of 5 October 1931 he experienced a more complete revelation. In his words, 'I was driven to Whipsnade zoo one sunny morning. When we set out I did not believe that Jesus Christ is the Son of God, and when we reached the zoo I did.' It was the peace after much conflict. But it had not involved an emotional, or an intellectual, struggle. The conclusion to all his doubts and hesitations had come upon him or, rather, had come from him. It had made itself known.

In the period of this conversion to Christianity, Lewis began writing *The Allegory of Love* (1936), in which he traces the tradition of courtly love from the first century to the late medieval period. He discusses those poets whom he loved best, including Chaucer and Spenser, and celebrates the sum of his early reading by giving it a context and a history. He creates a narrative in which the medieval vision can be understood, but at the same time he reveals something of his aspiring nature. This was to be true of many of his published works. He writes that 'if our passions, being immaterial, can be copied by material inventions [such as a bronze figure of Eros or Psyche] then it is possible that our material world in its turn is the copy of an invisible world.' On the nature of the classical gods, he remarks that 'monotheism should not be regarded as the rival of polytheism, but rather as its maturity.'

These explanations reveal Lewis's direction of travel, and that was outlined by a study he wrote over two weeks in 1932, *The Pilgrim's Regress*, which is subtitled 'An Allegorical Apology for Christianity, Reason and Romanticism'; for Lewis the three were united in recognition of one reality, reached by argument and understood by the imagination. For him, 'romanticism' meant the old world of romance with its belief in the marvellous and its tales of quest. It was the 'other world' he had always sought, since it would impart what he called 'an enlargement of our being'. *The Pilgrim's Regress*, Lewis's spiritual memoir, is of course modelled on Bunyan's *The Pilgrim's Progress*; but where Bunyan's allegory shows a soul on a journey towards God, Lewis's work shows a soul searching for anything except God.

The narrator dreams of a young man named John. He lives in a land called Puritania, whose inhabitants live in fear of 'the Landlord'. The cast of characters is both peculiar and familiar. One of the first meetings is with 'Mr Enlightenment', a brisk and self-important gentleman who convinces John that the Landlord does not exist. There follows a sometimes bewildering journey through the intellectual and artistic movements of the 1920s and 1930s. Freudianism is here a giant whose eyes make the skin translucent, Reason a young woman in complete armour, and Wisdom an old man whose children, or students, have a curious need to supplement their diet elsewhere. Although Puritania itself, with its dark mountains, recalls Lewis's native Northern Ireland, the landscape evoked elsewhere is unmistakably English. When John journeys north, on to the tableland of the 'tough-minded', we find ourselves somewhere distinctly Nordic, even Arctic. John finds nothing of what he was looking for. It seems that, with each step, he is moving further and further away from any useful or satisfying destination.

Lewis himself had begun to attend the chapel of Magdalen College during the week, and his parish church on Sundays. He was neither 'high' nor 'low' in the Church of England; he did not believe that such distinctions mattered in the slightest. In this period he became one of the 'Inklings', a group of Oxford colleagues who met regularly to discuss one another's work and to engage in more general conversation or debate. They eventually set a pattern for their conviviality, with meetings on Tuesdays at midday in a local public house, the 'Eagle and Child', and meetings on Thursday evenings at Lewis's rooms in Magdalen. But they were never a 'club'. They were too diverse. One of their number was J.R.R. Tolkien. Tolkien was professor of Anglo-Saxon at the university, and in the first years of this informal society he was at work on *The Hobbit* (1937). He and Lewis had much in common. They were both professed Christians – Tolkien being an ardent Roman Catholic – and both were entranced by the sagas of the Norse and the Anglo-Saxons. They were also of the opinion that 'modern' literature was bankrupt of inspiration and purpose. Lewis argued that the two of them must fill this deficiency, and proposed that Tolkien should compose a novel of time travel and that he himself should write of a journey through space. Tolkien's fiction of time travel came to nothing, but Lewis's project came to fruition with *Out of the Silent Planet* (1938) and its sequels, *Perelandra* (1943) and *That Hideous Strength* (1945). These were not allegories but fantasies, as Lewis suggested, for those who 'wish to visit strange regions in search of such beauty, awe or terror as the actual world does not supply'.

Yet they had another purpose. In each of the three books, to different degrees, Lewis was exploring contemporary problems and analysing relevant responses; he used the fables of science fiction to convey opinions about more Earthbound matters. *That Hideous Strength* was, for example, the fictional expression of his book published two years before, *The Abolition of Man*, in which Lewis warned of the dangers of some approaches to education. It is certainly an attack on three peculiarly modern superstitions: that scientific endeavour can never be corrupted; that the newspapers are always to be believed; and that anything with the word 'national' in front of it must be benign.

The works of H. G. Wells and others had established the popular image of 'aliens' as superhumanly intelligent and robotically unfeeling. They had nothing to learn from us and no intention of teaching us. We were to see them as killers, for they would undoubtedly see us as vermin. But need it be so? In *Out of the Silent Planet*, Lewis presents other possibilities. He was determined to pour as many themes into that complex novel as it could contain; the result is surfeit and spillage, but it is not principally for its narrative that the book should be prized. It is notable for the prophetic strain that is occasionally to be found in his writing, a visionary quality that leaves us feeling that Lewis knows something he could not and cannot know.

A fellow Inkling, Nevill Coghill, described Lewis at this time as 'a largish, unathletic-looking man, heavy but not tall, with a roundish florid face that perspired easily . . . he had a dark flop of hair and rather pouched eyes; those eyes gave life to the face, they were large and brown and unusually expressive,' giving the impression of 'a mild, plain powerfulness'. Lewis had already adopted the persona of a plain man who faced the world with brusque common sense, who liked beer and boisterous fun, and who avoided any display of feeling or sentiment. Despite his roots in Ireland, he had become very English. He had told Greeves to 'keep clear of introspection, of brooding, of spiritualism, of everything eccentric. Keep to work and sanity and open air – to the cheerful and matter of fact side of things.' These may have been lessons that Lewis felt obliged to administer to himself, since he managed successfully to disguise his intense sensitivity and the acute sense of loss and longing he always nourished.

Lewis's 'powerfulness', however, was not necessarily mild at all, since he had acquired the reputation for being loud and bellicose in argument. He still had the temperament of a bluff Ulsterman who could turn debate into conflict, and he seems to have nurtured a desire to dominate or humiliate others. Some of the undergraduates who suffered in his Oxford tutorials never became accustomed to his sarcastic rebukes. Yet his kindness, to the bereaved, the widowed and the childless, to whom he gave two-thirds of his considerable income (anonymously), was rarely doubted. The critic Kenneth Tynan was one among many who remained grateful for his 'muscular' capacity for consolation. And his claim to ordinariness had its virtues. He always addressed himself to the general reader in prose that is as simple as it is elegant; he was plain, succinct and sensible.

This is nowhere more evident than in *The Problem of Pain*, published in 1940, in which Lewis put forward a simple argument that, if you are to invoke this problem, you can 'judge' God's actions only by God's standard and not by one you find congenial. The book begins with Lewis's contention that religion started not as an explanation, but as an awed response to the numinous, which is itself the guardian of moral law. There is the supplementary argument that numinous awe is a 'jump' by which 'a man goes beyond anything that can be "given" in the facts of experience'.

Lewis's summary of the question of pain is that 'if God were good, He would wish to make His creatures perfectly happy, and if God were almighty He would be able to do what He wanted. But the creatures are not happy. Therefore God lacks either goodness, or power, or both.' At this point a difficulty arises: 'Try to exclude the possibility of suffering which the order of nature and existence of free wills involve, and you find that you have excluded life itself.' He also considers the nature of divine love. Is such love 'tolerant'? Not on the available evidence. However, a tolerant, even indulgent, love is the type that humankind would prefer. But, in short, 'to ask that God's love should be content with us as we are is to ask that God should cease to be God.' Lewis adds, memorably, that 'all the days of our life we are sliding, slipping, falling away as if God were, to our present consciousness, a smooth inclined plane on which there is no resting.' This is his intuitive sense of the Fall. He expresses also his understanding of 'Adam'. 'Adam' was a race of men who existed in total and joyful dependence on God. Something then whispered to this man, or race, that it could do all this on its own, without God. The consequence of man's rebellion was the opposite of what was intended; in seeking autonomy, he lost power. Lewis can construe the Fall, then, only as a primeval assertion of self-will and thus as an act of self-mutilation.

Lewis also raises a question that many people have, quite properly, asked. Why is it so often the good, decent, kindly, ordinary people who suffer so much? In his answer, he reminds us once again that Christianity is supernaturalist. It is just such good, kindly people, more than some sinners, who most need to have the illusion of self-sufficiency prised from them. It is a hard saying, but, as he argues, no harder than that which Christ so often said. There is then the problem of eternal punishment. Lewis writes, 'what is cast (or casts itself) into hell is not mankind. It is "remains".' What goes into hell is what once had been a soul, or what might be termed spiritual flotsam. He observes in this context, 'you will remember that in the parable, the saved go to a place prepared for them, while the damned go to a place never made for men at all.' Damnation, Lewis suggests, is 'the state of *having been* a human soul'.

✠

DURING THE SECOND World War Lewis continued his career of Christian exposition in a different fashion with *The Screwtape Letters* (1942), which, more than any of his other quasi-theological works, has proved the most enduring and the most popular. It concerns the advice given to a junior devil, Wormwood, from his uncle, who is also one of his satanic superiors; it concerns a proposed human victim, or 'patient' as Screwtape calls him. In an interview towards the end of his life, Lewis would claim that *The Screwtape Letters* was the only one of his books that he did not enjoy writing. This is a pity, for it is certainly the wittiest, and arguably the most entertaining, of all his apologetics.

As Lewis recalled, the world of Screwtape is 'all dust and itch'. It could hardly be otherwise, for Screwtape is a demon, an 'under-secretary' of a department and thus respectably, if not impressively, deep 'in the lowerarchy' of hell. Wormwood is a young, eager, inevitably amateurish tempter whose human 'patient' is the subject of the letters. These letters are elegant, and subtle, and of course wholly evil. They allow Lewis to survey the fallen world of humankind by means of satire and close observation, so that he might be seen as the Samuel Richardson of sin. It is epistolary fiction with a purpose. Of the Second World War, then raging, Screwtape writes,

> How much better for us if *all* humans died in costly nursing homes amid doctors who lie, nurses who lie, friends who lie, as we have trained them, promising life to the dying, encouraging the belief that sickness excuses every indulgence . . . And how disastrous for us is the continual remembrance of death which war enforces. One of our best weapons, contented worldliness, is rendered useless. In wartime not even a human can believe that he is going to live forever.

At the time of the composition of *The Screwtape Letters*, Lewis was preparing short talks on religious subjects for the men billeted at various Royal Air Force stations throughout the country. This effort was followed by a series of radio broadcasts on 'The Christian Faith as I see it – by a Layman'. Three series were published in book form, as *Mere Christianity*, and proved to be the most powerful and influential of all Lewis's contributions to religious debate. He was then merely an Oxford don with some small reputation as a Christian apologist and science-fiction writer. *The Pilgrim's Regress* had aroused little interest and *The Problem of Pain*, although widely admired, had not really increased his reputation. Yet he had been asked to give some broadcasts on the radio and he chose to speak about his faith. His experience of conversion was recent, and he had been an atheist for most of his life. He had to start very simply, then, in the elegantly plain style that was to become his trademark. He had to begin where all begin.

Granted that there is a moral law, recognized by all and obeyed in its fullness by none, where did it come from? Surely science, or natural philosophy, can provide an answer? Yet Lewis argues that if there is a power creating and informing this law, science is in fact helpless, 'since that power, if it exists, would be not one of the observed facts but a reality which makes them, and no mere observation of the facts can find it'. As he suggests elsewhere, a novel will of course tell you something about the author, but you will never 'find' the author in the novel.

In these broadcasts Lewis construes the Fall as a suggestion from 'the enemy' on the understanding that men could 'set up on their own as if they had created themselves'. From this all else proceeds in 'the long terrible story of man trying to find something other than God which will make him happy'. In our attempt to run on the wrong fuel, as he puts it in the argot of the day, we find that 'the machine conks'. On the nature of Christ, he argues to his radio audience that you must make your choice. Either this man was, and is, the Son of God: or else a madman or something worse. You can shut Him up for a fool, you can spit at Him and kill Him for a demon; or you can fall at His feet and call Him Lord and God. But let us not come with any patronizing nonsense about His being a great human teacher. He has not left that open to us. He did not intend you to work out your own salvation with fear and trembling, for it is God who works within you.

All our 'work' consists in allowing God to work within us. Here, then, is mere Christianity. The broadcasts were simple in manner but not in matter. In another contribution, for example, he remarked, 'if I find in myself a desire which no experience in this world can satisfy, the most probable explanation is that I was made for another world.'

In 1947 Lewis's disquisition *Miracles* was published. Some claim it to be his most difficult work. While most of his apologetics address themselves to those – educated and uneducated alike – who were unconvinced of religious faith, this book seems directed to a sceptic who is both highly intelligent and highly educated. Lewis devotes the first part to an explanation of why one should accept the supernatural, or, rather, why one cannot accept naturalism. He goes on to investigate the miracles of the Old and New Testaments, showing in each case how they fit within a divine, and perhaps even natural, order. The question 'Can miracles occur?' depends for its answer on a priori belief. He asserts that 'if naturalism is true, then we do know in advance that miracles are impossible: nothing can come into nature from the outside because there is nothing outside to come in, nature being everything.' But he adds that

a strict materialism refutes itself for the reason given long ago by Professor [J.B.S.] Haldane [the geneticist and physiologist]: 'If my mental processes are determined wholly by the motions of atoms in my brain, I have no reason to suppose that my beliefs are true . . . and hence I have no reason for supposing that my brain is composed of atoms.'

If reasoning is derived from a non-rational cause, it has no validity. Lewis goes on to remark that

The Supernatural is not remote and abstruse: it is a matter of daily and hourly experience, as intimate as breathing. Denial of it depends on a certain absent-mindedness . . . A miracle is by definition an exception. How can the discovery of the rule tell you whether, given a sufficient cause, the rule can be suspended? . . . belief in miracles, far from depending on an ignorance of the laws of nature, is only possible in so far as those laws are known.

✠

OTHER WORK, OF a quite different nature, would prove to be Lewis's most enduring legacy. He had begun a short novel for children at the close of 1939 but, in the conditions of the time, could not proceed with it. He started work again on *The Lion, the Witch and the Wardrobe* in 1948 or 1949; he made up for the long hiatus by working rapidly and finishing seven instalments of the story by 1953. They became known collectively as the Chronicles of Narnia. It was not that he forced religion into his story, or that he wished to create an allegory of Christianity; it was simply the shape and direction his imagination took. The name Narnia itself is now as familiar as a wardrobe. It has become a metonym for any fantasy land, more particularly for a land to which one would like to escape. It is a world that perhaps only a northern imagination could have conceived, with its lush valleys, its mighty mountains, its thundering rivers and its fresh, cold seas. And it is a world peopled by creatures that will nurture it – talking beasts, fauns, centaurs, dryads, Marsh-wiggles, naiads, giants and dwarfs – rather than human beings, the instinctive despoilers. But only humans can rule this land. The Pevensie children discover this when they are made kings and queens of Narnia. The story of how they found this land, through a wardrobe, has in turn become an image for any escape from the troublesome or mundane.

Over this land stands its creator and sustainer, Aslan the Great Lion, son of the Emperor-over-sea, who in the first volume of the chronicles gives his life for a traitor. Lewis himself always denied that Narnia was created, or born, as Christian allegory – and, as an expert in allegory, he should have known. The lion was not at first intended to mirror the story of Christ; rather, as Lewis once put it, 'Aslan bounded in' and stayed. But he asked 'what might Christ become like if there really were a world like Narnia, and He chose to become incarnate and die and rise again in that world as He actually has done in ours?'

It is significant that Lewis chose 'world' and not 'land'. In Narnia there are many races and many worlds. Long before the term 'multiverse' was coined, Lewis had introduced us to the idea that by leaping into a puddle one could enter another cosmos and another time. That is what happens in *The Magician's Nephew*. And all these different races, from different regions and mythologies, rub shoulders without the static of spite. Indeed, they are essentially innocent. They have never known a Fall, but they certainly know the passions. Unlike many Christian traditionalists, Lewis believed that there was a place for the passions, even the darkest; anger could be justified and hatred could be merited.

As he often maintained, Lewis believed in hierarchy. But by this he did not mean the rule of might or, especially, the rule of a priesthood; rather, he held that everyone had their proper niche. So in Narnia. The talking beasts are the keepers of the flame, the chroniclers, the centaurs predict the future from the stars, the dwarfs are the warriors, the naiads the singers, and the fauns are graceful, kind, strange and silly – and that is enough.

We realize that Narnia has no capital. While the mighty empire of Calormen to its south has the magnificent but horrible city of Tashbaan, Narnia has only Cair Paravel, the citadel of the ancient kings, with its fairy-tale turrets and the mermaids who sing in the surrounding bay. Beyond Cair, there are places of awe, such as Aslan's How and Lantern Waste, but no great conurbations. Narnia needs none. By the last book, the reader cannot help noticing that Narnia has become ominously sparse, that whole races seem to have vanished. The miserable Narnians summoned to the bonfire to hear the commands of the 'anti-Aslan' or 'Tashlan' include no giants, no talking panthers, no tree spirits. And there is only one unicorn. Narnia is already in decline before her final eclipse. 'All worlds come to an end,' as Roonwit the centaur says, an arrow in his side. But it is not the end, not quite.

✠

IN 1954 LEWIS was appointed to take the chair in English medieval and Renaissance literature at Magdalene College, Cambridge. Despite his manifest ability and status he had not been promoted by his alma mater, but the move from Oxford to a rival university was still difficult. He had tribulations of a more private nature, too, when his lifelong companion, Janie Moore, became a victim of dementia and his brother Warnie a prey to alcoholism. By 1963 his own health was fading fast, with weakness to his heart, his prostate and his kidneys. After lunch on Friday 22 November, he lay upon a downstairs bed, which had been set up for him, and there he died. Four days later he was buried in the churchyard of Holy Trinity in the Oxford suburb of Headington.

Twenty-Two

Religion as Contemporary
Evangelicals, Pentecostalists, Charismatics

In recent years two complementary but quite distinct move-ments, evangelicalism and Pentecostalism, have acquired many adherents within the Anglican Communion and else-where. Contemporary English evangelicals are not at all like their nineteenth-century predecessors. They do not pursue social reform, and they are not committed to political action. They do not establish clubs or institute societies. They are likely to have been educated by state provision rather than by private meditation on the Bible. That is why it is impossible to understand modern English evangelicalism without reference to the universities. In this, as in so many other ways, the movement in England differs strikingly from that in America. Tertiary education lies, if not at its core, then certainly at its root.

English evangelicalism, for example, owes a vast and even vital debt to the spirit and doctrine of the Universities and Colleges Christian Fellowship (formerly the Inter Varsity Fellowship). The spirit is to be considered before the doctrine. It is hard to overstate the enthusiasm and even exhilaration of the evangelical life for those who are committed to it. It is a world of spiritual combat and of passionate intensity in which the evangelicals believe themselves to be winning souls, lifting hearts and battling Satan. Without embarrassment or reservation, they assert that God has given them direct instruction through scripture or during prayer; he may even become manifest as a voice. Earnest debate and enraptured singing accompany this sense of mission in a manner that would have been familiar to Wesley and to Bunyan. Nothing has changed or, rather, nothing has changed but the world outside, with its altered values, its competing religions and its sceptical or indifferent populace.

The emergence of the Christian Fellowship may be placed at the beginning of 1919, when several members of the Student Christian Movement believed that their organization, which had been founded in 1889, was insufficiently evangelistic; it did not rest its faith sufficiently on the Crucifixion and Christ's atonement for the sins of the world, which was for them the lightning rod of belief. The Fellowship therefore seceded from the Movement while increasing in strength and numbers. The doctrinal basis of the Fellowship will in large part explain the extraordinary self-confidence encountered among evangelical students, since it has its roots in a very clear if narrow summary of the gospel. One of its tenets holds that 'Those who believe in Christ are pardoned all their sins and accepted in God's sight only because of the right-eousness of Christ credited to them; this justification is God's act of undeserved mercy, received solely by trust in him and not by their own efforts.' Faith, and not works, is the key. It is also stated that 'The church [is] the body of Christ both local and universal, the priesthood of all believers given life by the Spirit and endowed with the Spirit's gifts to worship God and proclaim the gospel, promoting justice and love.' These evangelical Christians are in fact living the Reformed gospel at its most austere. For all the joy, warmth and optimism they so often exude, they stand on the stoniest and sharpest of doctrinal foundations.

Their mission is now generally composed of a series of public events. Plain evangelism of the type practised in the New Testament is not considered feasible. One of their number spoke for the whole movement by explaining that 'we could all go outside and tell people nice parables, but no one would listen. The principles of evangelism haven't changed; the methods – I believe – have.' There are performances, talks, short films, mini-concerts and public discussions. Christianity is to be youthful, new, exciting, at ease with contemporary culture; it is, in a sense, uncassocked. When approaching non-Christians the evangelicals would often emphasize the fact that they also had no time for 'religiosity'. Christianity had nothing to do with religion; it was a personal relationship with God. In the context of the English soul, here was a mysticism for the 'man in the street'. There will even be dramatic performances so that contemporary entertainment becomes the gateway to religious truth. The entertainment is often cerebral, and even provocative, but it is entertainment nonetheless. The author of the *Tretise of Miraclis Pleyinge*, the fifteenth-century Lollard text against the dramatic rendition of religious scenes, may not have approved.

Public evangelism is also a frequent occurrence, but not in the conventional or familiar manner. It is not necessary to envisage a solitary figure taking up a soapbox and hectoring passers-by. Door-to-door evangelism is also surprisingly rare. Something else is needed.

A common method of attracting bystanders, for example, is to perform a little sketch involving two or three, usually young, evangelists. When the sketch is over another actor, or 'preacher', steps forwards and begins a talk. The approach, so described, might seem startlingly childish, but in many ways this format was devised to counter the impression – all too often given by solitary and spontaneous street preaching – of a hectoring bigot who is self-regarding and even unhinged. There is indeed a childlike strain within contemporary evangelicalism. It has always encouraged simple faith, while academic theology has been deprecated and Christian history generally ignored. It is a rare evangelical who knows much of Wyclif or Hooker, or even Tyndale.

Evangelicals are by no means latter-day Puritans, but they share certain obvious parameters. You will rarely if ever find an evangelical drunk; smoking is very rare; and no one, naturally, has sexual intercourse unless he or she is married. Indeed, on all matters sexual evangelicals tend to conservatism. But they cannot be described as bigots, and attitudes to contraception, abortion and homosexuality vary from group to group. One area to which no latitude is extended, however, is the occult or anything that can be associated with the New Age spiritualism that emerged in the early 1970s. There was a profound conviction that even the most apparently innocuous expressions of neo-paganism led inevitably to devil-worship.

The evangelical understanding of the gospel is established on the doctrine of penal substitution, by which Christ suffered instead of humankind, with the natural inference from the doctrine that justification comes from faith alone and not from any human endeavour. There is another distinction from secular moralists. For the evangelical, visiting someone in prison is a good Christian deed, but an attempt to reform prison conditions is considered to be 'worldly'.

It would be wrong to suggest that today's evangelicals regard Roman Catholics as 'non-Christians' by definition, but it is not unusual to hear Catholicism mentioned in the same tone as Mormonism. This attitude is not so much arrogant as parochial, but there can be something deliberate and even defiant to this parochialism. It is based on the unspoken assumption that there is no need to understand other traditions, since it is enough to know that they are wrong.

While the belief that only evangelicals are 'really' Christians is widespread among themselves, it is by no means universal and should not be misunderstood. They are claiming not that only those who share their principles will be saved but, rather, that all true Christian traditions are in fact evangelical in spirit. They often speak of a golden thread running through Christian history by which they are led; it is composed of adherence to the Bible, a belief in personal faith, conversion and the atonement on Golgotha. They profess that the foundation of their belief is to be found in the Bible, and many still consider that text to be 'inerrant', without fault. Even in early twentieth-century England, many evangelicals maintained that divine inspiration entailed factual truth. Although strict creationism is rare, it is not uncommon to hear two evangelicals agonizing over a minor discrepancy between two scriptural versions of an event.

For such evangelicals, the Bible is entirely self-sufficient; it provides its own context and its own commentary. If a verse appears confusing or problematic, another can be found with which to interpret it. A common refrain will be that 'the Bible is clear about everything that matters.' Luther's painstaking reinterpretation of the gospel might as well be forgotten, with the untroubled assumption that the letters of Paul to Romans, Galatians and Ephesians are enough for the truth to be revealed. The fact that this truth spent 1,500 years in hibernation, before the Protestants revealed it, is a problem that is rarely addressed. The principal purpose of Bible study for the evangelical, however, is not so much to uncover eternal verities as to see what can be applied to contemporary lives; everything – however abstruse, antiquated or arcane – is held to have direct application to the individual living in the modern world.

✠

THERE HAVE BEEN Pentecostals, according to the Christian Bible, since the day of Pentecost itself, when the Holy Spirit entered the Apostles. That divine afflatus has been celebrated, and copied, by many of the faithful over the succeeding centuries, but its first significant expression accompanied the advent of Wesleyanism in the eighteenth century; subsequently, it became an aspect of 'entire sanctification' and the 'Holiness Movement' with its belief in the 'second blessing'. Its most recent renewal in England came at the end of the nineteenth century, when Pentecostalism sprang up outside the major denominations.

In turn, contemporary Pentecostals believe that the miraculous gifts of the Holy Spirit mentioned by St Paul can, and should, still be experienced today. They believe, moreover, that these gifts are bestowed when, as Christ promised, the Holy Spirit descends upon them, filling them with his grace and granting them a second baptism both ecstatic and cleansing. This is known as 'baptism in the Spirit'. Pentecostals claim by this sacred blessing to possess the gifts of healing ('faith healing', as it is popularly known) and of prophecy, of discernment of spirits and deliverance from possession, of miracles and of *agape* or holy love. Of the blessings bestowed, the most striking and controversial is 'the gift of tongues', the technical term for which is 'glossolalia'. An outsider hearing someone speaking in tongues will recognize something like a language, with all the intonations and rhythms that would entail, but they will neither understand it nor be able to identify it except as a form of prophesying. Christ promises the Holy Spirit and 'new tongues', but says little more. They are mentioned throughout the Pauline epistles, however, and hints are found in the Old Testament, particularly in the second chapter of the short Book of Joel, where it is written:

> And it shall come to pass afterward, that I will pour out my spirit on all flesh; and your sons and your daughters shall prophesy, your old men shall dream dreams, your young men shall see visions: and also upon the servants and upon the handmaids in those days will I pour out my spirit. (28–9)

No traditional denomination or confession has ever doubted the reality of the gifts as described in the New Testament. The question was, and in certain quarters still is, whether the powers claimed by Pentecostals are the same as those given to the early Church, and it is asked most persistently of 'the gift of tongues'. When first bestowed on the Apostles, it was said to be a plurality of languages, each perfectly recognizable, but when manifested among present-day Pentecostals it seems to many only a confused cataract of syllables, strangely beautiful but completely obscure.

✛

THE 'FATHER OF English Pentecostalism', as he has been termed, was gentle and gentlemanly, gracious and meek – the pattern, perhaps, of a Victorian Anglican clergyman. There was little in him to suggest that he would become the channel of a revivalist river, still less the wildest that England had known since Wesley. In 1884 Alexander Boddy was sent by the Bishop of Durham to minister to the parishioners of All Saints in Monkwearmouth, Sunderland. This was the area where Bede wrote and lived, where English Christianity itself had had its first great revival more than twelve hundred years earlier. Perhaps Boddy knew of the ancient significance of the town and its name, perhaps not. He seems to stand at a slight angle to the conventional image of the parson; he was at heart a mystic, earnestly, even desperately seeking the depths and heights of Christian faith. He had heard of the 'Welsh Revival' of prayer and song in 1904, and of similar gatherings in Denmark and Norway, where the gift of tongues was vouchsafed. He travelled to these countries in search of the experience and, sufficiently convinced by what he saw and heard, returned to Monkwearmouth with the same missionary purpose. He wrote that 'on one occasion I received a special witness from the Lord of my sanctification. It was when we were adoring the Lamb that the power of God overwhelmed me, and caused me to sink helplessly to the floor.'

This was the first sign of true and instantaneous conversion, and the example was followed by others who believed themselves to be saved in similar fashion and who spoke in tongues.

Alexander Boddy (first from right, standing) among Pentecostal pioneers from the Sunderland Convention, 1913.

The *Daily Chronicle* reported, 'Mr Boddy informs me that about twenty are to be found in his parish . . . boys and girls, after the strange Pentecostal baptism, start up and sing in sweet, silvery, unearthly voices.' His became known as the Sunderland Mission, attracting adherents from all over the country and in turn inspiring other Pentecostal assemblies. The news, for example, might spread from town to town by means of local newspapers, regional preaching or simple rumour. The first three groups were Elim Pentecostal Church, the Assemblies of God and the Apostolic Church. They were founded by different people, but did not essentially differ in faith or practice and were all guided in their meetings by prayer, song, dance and individual testimony. Many of their votaries shared the belief that theirs was the last revival before the coming of the Lord, when all human hope and endeavour would be consummated in 'the Rapture'.

The experience of baptism 'in the Spirit' was exemplary and, as one Pentecostal recorded, 'the fire fell and burned in me till the Holy Spirit clearly revealed absolute purity before God.' The experience of speaking in tongues was almost a communal one, or at least one encouraged and expected within the community. 'I found myself beginning to utter words in a new tongue,' as one pastor put it. 'I was in a condition of spiritual ecstasy and wholly taken up with the Lord.' Most visitors to Pentecostal services would attest that when people speak in tongues, only the timbre of their voice is their own. Beyond that, the language sounds nothing like their native tongue, and is spoken with an emphasis and a velocity that their voices habitually lack.

There is, however, an inconvenient fact. The phenomenon of tongues, while predominantly Christian, is not peculiar to Christianity, let alone to Protestant Christianity; religious groups in Africa, East Asia and Indonesia speak in tongues, or something very similar, in their own rituals. Mormons speak in tongues and so, alas, do Satanists. On the other side, early Quakers spoke in that way and Edward Irving, a clergyman of the Church of Scotland, recalled a woman speaking 'to her own great edification and enjoyment'. Certain evangelicals, however, have objected to the wilder manifestations of sacred speaking. They assert that an appearance of drunkenness or madness is entirely unbiblical. Like many evangelical judgements, this is in fact contradicted by scripture. In the Book of Acts, we read of how the Apostles were mocked for drunkenness as they spoke in tongues. And we should note also that 'singing in the spirit' is entirely biblical. Paul refers to 'spiritual songs' or 'songs from the spirit'. It is the same music. Many Pentecostals were described as 'continuationists', since they accepted that their gifts were directly inherited from the moment of Pentecost; the Spirit is still in operation and still represents the fire within. Others, termed 'cessationists', believe that the gifts of the Spirit were a first-century phenomenon and that *all* such gifts ceased with the end of the apostolic age.

The Pentecostal movement has no discrete denomination. It was often assumed that those baptized in the Spirit would return to their own churches and inspire the members of their congregation. But that was not often their experience. They went back to their own churches and found themselves greeted by strong opposition and in danger of being ostracized. From the first, it was not the enthusiasm, or the signs and wonders, that proved the stumbling block but specifically the gift of tongues. The critical refrain would become familiar: it was a first-century phenomenon, not intended by God to endure. They were informed that 'these things are not for today, but for the early church.' Consequently, their experiences were unscriptural and to be rejected. Yet here it was, alive again, inspiring faith as well as a measure of distrust. As a result many resorted to the Pentecostal churches that now began to emerge as the home for spiritual exiles. Other assemblies were conducted on a small scale with what was called 'the tiny little circle: our church, our home, our family and me'. They were sometimes known as 'house churches'.

The future of the English Church, whether Anglican, Roman Catholic or Nonconformist, might well be Pentecostal. In London, particularly, attendance in 'the churches of the spirit' is increasing. This is in large measure owing to the influx of African and Caribbean people. Their churches tend to be Pentecostal in emphasis, and their pastors or elders take seriously the business of caring for all in their community. For all the rapture offered in the services, the Black Pentecostal church is solid, sober, morally austere and coolly critical of what used to be called 'the ways of the world'. Its members are happy in Jerusalem; Babylon holds no allure.

✝

THE PENTECOSTALS, HOWEVER, may not have been fully prepared for the emergence of the charismatic movement in the 1960s. Where before the Pentecostalists tended to be working class and largely self-taught, the charismatics were middle class and relatively well educated. It was the difference between generations. The charismatics also placed great emphasis upon speaking in tongues, prophecy and healing, together with greater freedom for individual manifestations of piety, such as the revelation of 'words from God' and the attendance of 'worship meetings' beyond the boundaries of Sunday, meetings that included manifestations of ecstatic behaviour among the celebrants. Intimacy and 'otherness' were part of the same moment of awakening. The divine was immanent, rather than transcendent, and was revealed in the participation of those assembled. They elected to praise God incarnate, the human aspect of Christ, rather than God transcendent. They did not wait for the Spirit to descend in places of worship or celebration, but practised direct intervention with prayer and the laying on of hands. They tended to work within, rather than outside, the conventional denominations, so that an Anglican or a Catholic charismatic was not a contradiction in terms. Charismatic faith sprang from individual spiritual experience and not from any dogmatic system. The fire fell wherever it found entrance. It therefore represented an ecumenical vision, with the whole Church invoked as the 'body of Christ'.

The charismatics raised their hands, palms upwards, in song, and performed mime or dance as a token of grace. They were 'empowered by the Spirit'. It was no longer the rehearsed drama of a priest or minister separated in front of a congregation. The communal act of worship, in the company of fellow believers, was thought to offer redemption as well as transformation. It has been compared to the removal of masks at a ritualized masked ball.

The charismatics were in love with music. Songs and ballads, 'pop' and jazz, rap and hip hop were an indispensable part of their services, together with choruses and communal singing. They were aligned with the youthful vitality, the energy and optimism, and the other values popularly associated with the mixed culture of contemporary English society. Whether this was a true impression or not is open to debate, but it is appropriate that the charismatic movement has its origins in the 1960s. It is certainly true that the charismatics tended to remain apart from the Pentecostal movement, which was considered to be too entrammelled in its past. Yet the law of change is inexorable and, in recognition of its growing power and influence, the Pentecostal movement began to accept the charismatic movement as its natural companion. It was a question of fellowship and a common witness. To some the charismatics became known as the 'restoration movement'.

✠

THERE TEND TO BE two services in the charismatic church, one on a Sunday and another in the middle of the week. The Sunday service is not a liturgy in the conventional sense, since there is little or no formal structure. 'Church' itself may be the wrong word. Partly because of space, and partly for traditional reasons, these services tend to be held in halls, whether community halls or church halls. If charismatics worship in buildings of their own, these in turn are shaped like halls and not churches.

It is certain that the hall will be full, comprising people of all ages. Sunday is traditionally the day of 'big church', when a congregation of more than a thousand is not unusual. The pastor may stride across the platform and 'work' his congregation with pleas, prayers and injunctions. The doctrine is in essence still Protestant and evangelical. There will be children, moving about unattended or indeed participating. There will be babies everywhere, and it is not unusual to see mothers breastfeeding.

Obviously there are no vestments, and even a suit is rare. At length, and unprompted, someone starts singing a chorus, and soon all will join in, some standing, some sitting, some dancing. The song will be repeated, over and over. The effect would be hypnotic, even boring, except for the strange waves and oscillations in the atmosphere that keep the congregation alive and awake. For all the ease and joy in evidence, a charismatic service is not relaxing. As likely as not someone will begin to 'sing in the Spirit', slowly or briskly, and often in tongues. The participants tend to sway as they sing, their palms upturned to the roof, smiling sleepily or with a kind of yearning frown, lips parted and eyes half closed. The singing is unearthly, but, for all its loveliness, it is often too eerie to be exhilarating. To be lifted up, another must reach down, and these songs do not reach down to the listener. They are heard in a kind of hushed, uneasy awe.

But if that church is heeding St Paul's injunctions, the singers are neither 'performing' for the rest of the congregation nor forgetting its needs. Someone will stand up to interpret what has been sung, if all are to be edified. For the visitor, it comes as something of a relief to hear words of explanation after all that unsettling beauty. In the song, one learns, lay a message – either for the congregation as a whole or for a particular, and particularly errant, member of it.

The service then moves to familiar ground. One of the elders will deliver a sermon. Charismatics have no priests, nor do they always have 'pastors'. A typical opening question might be, 'Who here *knows* that they've been baptised in the Holy Spirit?' Most hands will dart up. The elder might continue with the proposal, 'May I suggest that those of you who don't have not?' The sermon itself is typically long, by formal standards rambling, and is invariably intended to stimulate self-reflection and stir to action. It is a fine preacher indeed who can make a sermon more exciting than the service. For those who prize the liturgical element in worship, a charismatic service can be surprisingly rewarding. In the repetition of words, and in the accumulation of phrases and prayers and songs, we hear a hint of the origins of all liturgy, see a glimpse of the rushing stream before it became frozen into sculpture.

The midweek meeting is held in a member's home and therefore feels more like a 'house church'. It is small and intimate where, in contrast, the charismatic congregation attending a Sunday service might seem less welcoming. The 'structure' is approximately the same but there is no sermon, and very little speaking in tongues. It consists almost entirely of song, and the group of worshippers tends to be intelligent, good-humoured and, above all, remarkably at ease. There is little evidence of intensity, either about faith or about life; the charismatic Christian could not be more different from the received image of the members of other cults. It might be said, in fact, that charismatics often have a certain gentleness. They feel, justly or not, that they know the truth, not as one knows a formula but as one knows a person. Naturally they will be more relaxed about their faith than those who find solace in chapters and verses.

At the end of the previous century, charismatic churches were the fastest growing in the United Kingdom. So they remain, while the congregations of Methodist, Baptist and Congregational churches, for example, have diminished by some 40 per cent over the last sixty years.

THIS ACCOUNT OF contemporary movements leads, indirectly, to the consideration of the last three primates of England. When George Carey became Archbishop of Canterbury in 1991, an evangelical revival had already begun. Many explanations for that early revival have been offered, but perhaps it can be considered as a reaction to the acquisitive and self-regarding decade of the 1980s. Christians everywhere were encouraged to pray for 'Archbishop George'. Stolidly conservative, he was a supernaturalist who believed without reservation 'in Christ buried and Christ resurrected', and he stood in sharp relief to the liberal intellectuals who had dominated Anglican discourse. To many evangelicals his predecessor, Robert Runcie, had seemed altogether too 'Anglican', mild, ecumenicist and liberal. Runcie was in fact a far more robust figure than was generally allowed, but to evangelicals he was proceeding in the wrong direction. Carey, on the other hand, was one of their own. He presided over both the Lambeth Conference of 1991, which accepted the ordination of women, and the Conference of 1998, which reaffirmed the Church's traditional teaching on homosexuality as 'incompatible with Scripture'. His stance on both questions was informed by evangelical belief.

When Carey was succeeded in 2002 by Rowan Williams, it seemed that the evangelical period was over. 'Liberal' was the word most often used of Williams, and not always flatteringly. But in truth, although gentle and courteous in address, Williams was and is as fervent a believer as Carey or any evangelical. This learned, otherworldly Welshman should be considered, if anything, to be a mystic. His theological preferences – the Fathers and the esoterica of East and West – display that in abundance, as do his beautiful and unsettling religious poems.

Justin Welby succeeded him in 2013, as an evangelical but also as a charismatic. There is little in Welby's manner or persona to betray his private convictions. Polished, urbane and politically engaged to an extent that is still rare among evangelicals, he was baptised in the Spirit and prays in tongues. This is simply part of his daily life and not, as he has put it, something 'to make a song and dance about'. This is impeccably Anglican, since 'song and dance' might be seen as the heart of the charismatic movement. Yet, in true English spirit, Welby is a spiritual ecumenicist whose director in faith, Father Nicolas Buttet, is a Roman Catholic.

Twenty-Three

Religion as Theology

John A. T. Robinson (1919–1983), John Hick
(1922–2012), Don Cupitt (1934–)

Twentieth-century English theology had not been concerned with creating great systems of thought, or polemical and didactic works; it had rested on the empirical and the experienced, and on a direct response to the changes within modern spirituality. John Arthur Thomas Robinson was born in the precincts of the cathedral at Canterbury on 15 June 1919; as he said later, 'you can't get much nearer than that to the heart of the establishment.' He came from a thoroughly clerical family; his father had been a canon of that cathedral, and several uncles had been prominent clergymen. He was set to be an instinctively pious and orthodox child – or, perhaps, he could have become the exact opposite. But orthodoxy prevailed. He attended Marlborough College, where he did not excel but where he did win the divinity prize, and in October 1938 he was admitted to Jesus College, Oxford. During his first long vacation he joined the Student Christian Movement, and in these years as an undergraduate he seems to have immersed himself in the reading of theology. His first prize essay was on 'Kant's Ethics and the Christian Moral Ideal', before he eventually gained a first-class degree in the theological tripos. His future now seemed secure; he attended Westcott House, an Anglican theological college in Cambridge, specifically to prepare for his ordination, and in June 1943 he was admitted to Trinity College, Cambridge, in order to prepare the dissertation for his PhD in divinity. In the pursuit of higher learning as a career, it was inevitable that he, like other contemporaries, would fit within the enlightened, rational and liberal consensus of the time.

The title of Robinson's dissertation, 'Thou Who Art', introduced a thesis that covered some six hundred pages and gave the final lie to any impression of Robinson as some enthusiastic amateur. It is concerned with 'the notion of personality and its relation to Christian theology'. He follows the Austrian theologian Martin Buber in emphasizing that 'the different relationships into which a man enters are not additional to the essence of personality but constitutive of it.' There is no 'I' in or for itself, but only 'I' in relation to others. The most fundamental relation of all is 'that between man and the eternal person "Thou" of God'. He also states that 'every contact of an "I" with a finite "Thou" points beyond itself to [an] encounter with an infinite "Thou",' so that every glance or word, contact or meeting 'can be an occasion in which the eternal is recognised as present'. That truth must take the place of any belief 'in an "It-God", a "God of the third person", between whom and the "Thou" of religious faith an impassable gulf is fixed'. This is the ground of Robinson's theology. In common with other English theologians, he adduces his evidence from human experience rather than from dogma or abstract principle.

He served as deacon and then as priest for the parish of St Matthew, Moorfields, in the east of Bristol before his marriage to Ruth Grace in 1947. In 1948 he became chaplain for the theological college attached to Wells Cathedral, and three years later he was appointed dean of Clare College, Cambridge, as well as a lecturer in divinity at the university. There he wrote studies of eschatology and of Eucharistic ritual. A third book, *Jesus and His Coming: The Emergence of a Doctrine*, followed in 1957. He was often assumed to be one who had come upon matters of faith as a result of his vocation; in truth he was already a trained, as well as a highly skilled and formidable, theologian.

John A. T. Robinson, 1963, photograph.

In 1959, after an invitation from Mervyn Stockwood, the Bishop of Southwark, Robinson became the suffragan bishop of Woolwich. It was there that he entered into public debate. In 1960 a collection of his essays and addresses was published, *On Being the Church in the World*, which earned him much attention. In the autumn of that year he was asked to take part in the court case against *Lady Chatterley's Lover* by D. H. Lawrence. Its publishers were intending to issue an unexpurgated edition of the novel, but were forbidden to do so under the terms of the Obscene Publications Act. The Bishop of Woolwich agreed to be called in the book's defence. As part of his cross-examination, Robinson stated that 'what Lawrence is trying to do is to portray the sex relationship as something essentially sacred.' This caused a small furore; the bishop was described by the tabloid newspapers as the 'notorious bishop' or the 'Lady Chatterley bishop', with the insinuation that he was advocating sexual promiscuity.

This was only the prelude to the misunderstanding of Robinson's purpose. In the late autumn of 1961 he began to suffer from debilitating back pain. He was forced to take to his bed, and in that period he began to consider and contemplate the theories and presuppositions concerning the God he celebrated; this was the origin of his most popular book, *Honest to God*. It was published in March 1963, and was perhaps unfortunately previewed in an article for *The Observer*. Its heading, 'Our Image of God Must Go', may have misled some into thinking the bishop was perilously close to atheism.

In fact Robinson was eager to build on the foundation laid by other contemporary theologians, by denying that God was Being beyond or outside human experience. God was in truth 'the ground of all being', an intrinsic part of all consciousness and all relations. He was not Other but Thou. This is in part an extension or enlargement of the faith propounded in Robinson's doctoral dissertation. He wrote in *Honest to God* that 'the word "God" denotes

the ultimate depth of all our being, the creative ground and meaning of all our existence.' In the opening chapter he notes that 'the
signs are that we are reaching the point at which the whole conception of a God "out there" . . . is itself becoming more of a hindrance
than a help.' It is not compatible with individual experience or
with the witness of the New Testament. The transcendent is not
above or beyond us, 'but is encountered in, with, and under the
Thou of all finite relationships as their ultimate depth and ground
and meaning'. God is in change, transformation and movement.
He is in doubt and in certainty. He is in the transaction and the
journey. He is in the kiss and in the blow. It is a question not of
belief or non-belief, of theism or atheism, but rather of a readiness or unreadiness to 'the openness to the holy, the sacred, in
the unfathomable depths of even the most secular relationship'.
There God might dwell. This stance was not unfamiliar to contemporary theologians, but it delivered a shock to many English
Christians who were not accustomed to such speculations. There
ensued a bitter controversy, in which the Bishop of Woolwich was
accused of blasphemy, of heresy, even of atheism. But he had done
what he considered to be his religious duty, and that was enough.
Theologians characteristically write for other theologians, with
an increasingly specialized vocabulary, but Robinson wished to
address a wider audience.

He was by no means confined to the study of theism, however,
and in the years before *Honest to God* he had published a number of
New Testament studies in which he proposed clear and convinc-
ing interpretations of the biblical texts in moral and eschatological
settings. In his elucidation of the Gospel of John and of Pauline
theology, he was neither 'liberal' nor 'conservative', but based his
accounts on close textual reading; as a result, he was recognized as
one of the most significant New Testament scholars of the time.
After ten years at Woolwich, he returned in 1969 to Cambridge as
fellow, dean of chapel and lecturer in theology at Trinity College.

Despite his range of duties, he continued writing and lecturing. *The Human Face of God*, in which he considered once again the question of 'transcendence within immanence', was published in 1973. His biblical studies came to a conclusion with *Redating the New Testament* three years later. Throughout this period he was also engaged in lecture tours to other parts of the world, from South America to South Africa. But his mission was coming to an end. In the early summer of 1983 he was diagnosed with cancer of the pancreas, and by the close of that year he died.

✠

JOHN HICK WAS BORN on 20 January 1922 in the Yorkshire seaside town of Scarborough, with which his family had a long association. After a period in a preparatory school, then with a private tutor, at the age of fifteen he was sent to a Quaker boarding school, Bootham in York, where he spent two years. He then returned to Scarborough to work as a clerk in his father's law firm. But his real work was just beginning. He was educating himself, and his principal interest lay in Western philosophy, with especial concern for the work of Immanuel Kant. It was perhaps fortunate that his great-uncle Edward Hirst taught ethical theory at Manchester University; it was Hirst who encouraged Hick to pursue philosophical studies even while the young man was studying law. He was still attending lectures on legal matters at University College, Hull, in 1940, when he experienced a revelation.

Hick wrote later,

> I underwent a powerful evangelical conversion under the impact of the New Testament figure of Jesus. For several days I was in a state of intense mental and emotional turmoil, during which I became increasingly aware of a higher truth and greater reality pressing in upon me.

He became aware of 'the ultimate divine Reality'. This represented for him the opening of the gate. His reaction was so powerful that he gave up the profession of law and began training for the Christian ministry in Hull and then in Edinburgh. His early studies, however, were interrupted by the coming of war, in which, as a conscientious objector, he served with the Friends Ambulance Unit in Greece, Italy and Egypt.

On his return to Edinburgh University Hick became immersed in his philosophical studies, directing his interest particularly to Kant and that philosopher's 'critical realism', which assumed, in Hick's own words, that 'there is indeed a world, indeed a universe, out there existing independently of us, but that we can only know it in the forms provided by our human perceptual apparatus and conceptual systems.' The danger lies in mistaking our interpretation for objective truth. This, in truncated form, was a key to Hick's later theology. He was a successful scholar and, having received a First from Edinburgh in 1948, he moved on to Oriel College, Oxford, where he completed his doctoral thesis.

After receiving his doctorate, Hick began training for a ministry in the Presbyterian Church at Westminster College in Cambridge, and on finishing that course in the summer of 1953 he was inducted as minister for the Presbyterian church in the parish of Belford, Northumberland. He stayed there for three and a half years, engaged in traditional pastoral work, before being approached by Cornell University in Ithaca, New York, to take up an assistant professorship. He started work there in the spring of 1956, and in the following year he published his first theological work, *Faith and Knowledge*.

In this Hick puts forwards the proposition that 'while the object of religious knowledge is unique, its basic epistemological pattern is that of all our knowledge.' He then enlists Kant's theory of knowledge in which the individual perceives things not in themselves, as they really are, but as appearances that conform to a priori assumptions and conceptions. This in turn invites the possibility that any one interpretation will differ from another, so that the recognition or understanding of God will take many forms. He had come to the conclusion that faith did not require the assent to certain dogmas or propositions, but rather what he termed 'experiencing-as', which might be taken to represent the process of living and becoming part of the life of the spirit. The experience of faith was infinitely more significant than concepts of it. In this sense he affirms that 'our apprehension of the divine is *mediated* through our apprehension of values,' so that human experience can help us to seek and find grace. This is in one sense a very English emphasis. He goes on to state that

> the primary religious perception, or basic act of religious interpretation, is not to be described as a reasoned conclusion or unreasoned hunch that there is a God. It is, putatively, an apprehension of the divine presence within the believer's human experience. It is not an inference to a general truth, but a 'divine–human encounter', a mediated meeting with the living God.

The world is experienced as the creation of the Divine Being. In a later book, *The New Frontier of Religion and Science* (2006), he argues that 'it is the teaching of each of the world faiths that the divine reality does not force itself upon us, but leaves space for an uncompelled response on our part.'

In the autumn of 1959 Hick left Cornell and became professor of Christian philosophy at Princeton Theological Seminary in New Jersey, attached to American Presbyterianism. He then returned to England for a fellowship at Gonville and Caius College in Cambridge, where he completed work on his book *Evil and the God of Love* (1966). In his argument he proposes that human beings had been created in the image of God but not yet in the likeness of God. For that further change the individual has to pass through what John Keats called 'the vale of soul-making'. Hick discounts the presence of original sin and suggests in its place a journey through the buffets of time and circumstance, of sin and failure, towards an ultimate good. Suffering is an inalienable part of this process. There was no mythical Fall but rather a distant perception of future grace to which we must proceed by means of faith. This was very far from the Presbyterianism of his younger days, and is in itself a testimony to his belief in a journey.

In 1967, after three years at Cambridge, Hick was appointed professor of theology at the University of Birmingham, where he remained for fifteen years. It was there that he clarified his position on the possible and various interpretations of the divine. He described in *An Autobiography* (2002) how, in Birmingham, 'As I spent time in the mosques, synagogues, gurdwaras and temples as well as churches something very important dawned on me . . . it seemed evident to me that essentially the same thing was going on in all these different places of worship.' In his theology he tested the compatibility of Christianity with other religions, such as Sikhism or Hinduism, and, more pertinently, its resemblance to them. This became known as the 'pluralist hypothesis', which simply means that all faiths lead in the same direction. As he put it in *God and the Universe of Faiths* (2008), 'it involves a shift from the dogma that Christianity is at the centre to the realization that it is God who is at the centre and that all the religions of mankind, including our own, serve and revolve around him.' In this context he elucidates the meaning of Jesus Christ. If Jesus was indeed the Son of God, and therefore himself divine, Christianity would have an immense significance over other religions. But it would be unwarranted. He was 'a metaphorical son of God' rather than 'a metaphysical God the Son', a man 'intensely and overwhelmingly conscious of the reality of God', who could command such spiritual authority that he possessed miraculous powers. The alternative is beyond any hypothesis, 'for to say, without explanation, that the historical Jesus of Nazareth was also God is as devoid of meaning as to say that this circle drawn with a pencil on paper is also a square.' He would later clarify his notion of God by substituting the 'Real'.

From Birmingham Hick moved on to become professor of the philosophy of religion at Claremont Graduate University near Los Angeles, where he remained for a further ten years. In 1992, at the age of seventy, he retired from that institution and returned to Birmingham as 'home', but he continued to travel widely, for conferences and lectures, and published a number of theological studies. In one of these later books, *An Interpretation of Religion* (1989), he notes that 'religious experience takes different forms within different religio-cultural traditions,' and suggests that 'in order to make sense of this variety we have to postulate an ultimately ineffable (or transcategorial) Real whose universal presence is humanly experienced in these different ways.' He died on 9 February 2012, three weeks after his ninetieth birthday.

✠

DON CUPITT WAS BORN in Oldham, Lancashire, on 22 May 1934. His father was a successful manufacturer, and determined that his four children should be educated privately in order to favour their chances in the world. Cupitt was despatched to Charterhouse School in London, where he duly accepted the orthodox creed of Anglicanism, although he disliked the nationalist and militaristic exposition of its beliefs in the school. He was more convinced by the arguments of Plato and of Platonism in the course of his classroom study, and he also became acquainted with the theories of Charles Darwin. In 1952 he was accepted at Trinity Hall, Cambridge, to study the natural sciences; he was soon converted to evangelical Christianity there, while at the same time pursuing a profound interest in theology ancient and modern. In his third year at university, in fact, he moved from the natural sciences to a degree course in theology. He may have tried to cram too much learning into one year, and as a result received a disappointing upper second in his final examinations. The obligatory national service then intervened, and he was despatched to Cyprus as a member of the Royal Corps of Signals.

On his return to Cambridge Cupitt decided to train for the Anglican ministry at Westcott House, as John Robinson had done, and he received a first-class degree at the conclusion of his studies. He was ordained in early June 1959 and served his curacy in the inner-city district of Salford, less than 10 miles from his birthplace; he was part of the diocese of Manchester, from which came the request that he continue his theological writing. His curacy expired after three years, and he returned to Westcott House as vice-principal. His academic career then took a customary path. After three years at Westcott House he was appointed dean of Emmanuel College, Cambridge, with the additional task of directing undergraduate and postgraduate studies in theology; in 1968 he received a university post as an assistant lecturer in the philosophy of religion.

In these years Cupitt took leave of his early evangelicalism, in part through his reading of the English mystics, Walter Hilton and Richard Rolle among them. In this tradition God is unknowable and inexpressible, and is celebrated by the mystic as the void, the abyss, the silence and 'the shoreless sea'. In his first book, *Christ and the Hiddenness of God*, published in 1971, Cupitt argued that in the presence of the transcendent the only recourse is to the contemplation of Jesus as a token of the divine. He elucidated this Christian example as one of 'utter purity of heart, disinterestedness, and commitment to the way of love'. Cupitt's most significant book, *Taking Leave of God*, was published in 1980, to the dismay of some of his more orthodox readers. In it, he asserted that 'there may be beyond the God of religion a transcendent divine mystery witnessed to in various ways by the faiths of mankind. But we

cannot say anything about it.' If an objective God is also a hidden
God (to use the traditional vocabulary), the individual must find
a way towards faith and grace by means of right conduct rather
than right belief. God is then interpreted as a moral idea or an ideal
standard of perfection.

Cupitt notes in *The World to Come* (1982) that religious belief
is expressed in 'a body of ideals and practices that have the power
to give ultimate worth to human life'. We may worship our idea
of God but He, or It, is unfathomable and therefore unknowable. Cupitt has a vision of the 'Ineffable', close to Hick's notion
of 'Ultimate Reality'. Even the idea of Being is provisional and
uncertain. He argues, therefore, that we must have recourse to
the human world, since 'it is all there is for us, and outside there is
nothing at all, not even nothingness.' There is no 'outsideness'. It
has become apparent that Cupitt's books in sequence are stages in
his exploration of his initial experience, or conception, of a hidden
and unknowable God. In *Life Lines* (1986) he states the need 'to
rehabilitate the spiritual life, as being a pilgrimage through a long
series of truths . . . this pilgrimage has no great destinations and is
never complete.' Being is Becoming. No final goal can be discovered, which some have taken to mean 'no God', only a recognition
of the provisional and uncertain status of all our judgements and
perceptions. He seeks a religion appropriate for the contemporary
world and, as a result, his theology is always in movement.

Cupitt charts the growth of understanding in *Creation out of
Nothing* (1990) by suggesting that faith may be discovered in the
embrace of this 'nothingness'. This may be experienced in the
manner of the fourteenth-century English mystics, although he
does not allude to them. He suggests further, in *The Time Being*
(1992), that it is necessary to have a religion 'without absolutes,
without perfection, without closure, without eternity'. The path
to salvation lies in the affirmation of 'time, language, the passions
and death'. To participate fully in the life of the world is to come

closer to the divine. In his later work he studies, in that precise context, the waves and ripples of ordinary speech in the 'Now-moment', in which 'multiplicity, becoming and chance are objects of pure affirmation,' and contemplates the 'solar efflux of pure contingency'. He invokes the idea of the 'pure' a great deal, as if in homage to an older theology. But he suggests by it that life itself, in all its transience and instability, is sacred.

That notion of 'solar efflux' is part of Cupitt's understanding of what he calls 'solar ethics' in a world that has gone beyond the measure of orthodox religion. Of course it takes its meaning from the nature of the sun, since 'we should live as the sun does . . . it simply expends itself gloriously, and in so doing gives life to us all,' so that 'the process by which it lives and the process by which it dies are one and the same.' In the process of our own living and dying, we should bring light and warmth to those others with whom we share our being. 'I need to forget about myself,' he wrote, 'and to pour out my life into the human world.' It is the spiritual obligation to which he most powerfully assents, and he asserts elsewhere that 'we find happiness by plunging ourselves into and identifying ourselves with the outpouring flux of existence – of which we are indeed just parts so that we are lost in life, burning, rapt.' Cupitt has returned us to the fourteenth-century English mystic Richard Rolle, who composed *The Fire of Love*. We may note here the constancy of the English soul, as it has been described in this book.

Further Reading

Ankarsjö, Magnus, *William Blake and Religion* (Jefferson, NC, 2009)

Bebbington, D. W., *Evangelicalism in Modern Britain* (London, 1995)

Beer, Frances, *Women and Mystical Experience in the Middle Ages* (Woodbridge, 1995)

Brown, G. H., *A Companion to Bede* (Woodbridge, 2010)

Daniell, David, *William Tyndale: A Biography* (New Haven, CT, 2001)

Davies, Michael, and W. R. Owens, eds, *The Oxford Handbook of John Bunyan* (Oxford, 2021)

DeGregorio, Scott, ed., *The Cambridge Companion to Bede* (Cambridge, 2010)

Dickens, A. G., *The English Reformation* (New York, 1964)

Fanous, Samuel, and Vincent Gillespie, eds, *The Cambridge Companion to Medieval English Mysticism* (Cambridge, 2011)

Faught, C. Brad, *The Oxford Movement: A Thematic History of the Tractarians and Their Times* (University Park, PA, 2003)

Glasscoe, Marion, *English Medieval Mystics: Games of Faith* (London and New York, 1993)

Hill, Christopher, *The World Turned Upside Down: Radical Ideas during the English Revolution* (London, 1973)

Hudson, Anne, *Wyclif, Political Ideas and Practice: Papers by Michael Wilks* (Oxford, 2000)

Kennedy, Philip, *Twentieth-Century Theologians: A New Introduction to Modern Christian Thought* (London and New York, 2010)

Ker, Ian, and Terrence Merrigan, eds, *The Cambridge Companion to John Henry Newman* (Cambridge, 2009)

Knowles, David, *The English Mystical Tradition* (New York, 1961)

Laurence, Anne, W. R. Owens and Stuart Sim, eds, *John Bunyan and His England, 1628–88* (London, 1990)

Levy, Ian C., ed., *A Companion to John Wyclif: Late Medieval Theologian* (Leiden, 2006)

McAvoy, Liz Herbert, *A Companion to Julian of Norwich* (Cambridge, 2015)

MacCulloch, Diarmaid, *Reformation: Europe's House Divided, 1490–1700* (New York, 2004)

—, *The Later Reformation in England, 1547–1603*, 2nd edn (New York, 2001)

McGrath, Alister, *The Twilight of Atheism: The Rise and Fall of Disbelief in the Modern World* (New York, 2004)

Melnyk, Julie, *Victorian Religion: Faith and Life in Britain* (Westport, CT, 2008)

Moorman, J.R.H., *A History of the Church in England* (London, 1958)

Mozley, J. F., *Coverdale and His Bibles* (Cambridge, 2005)

Nichols, Aidan, *G. K. Chesterton, Theologian* (London, 2009)

Norman, Edward R., *Church and Society in England, 1770–1970: A Historical Study* (Oxford, 1976)

Reardon, Bernard M. G., *Religious Thought in the Victorian Age: A Survey from Coleridge to Gore* (New York, 1995)

Rectenwald, Michael, *Nineteenth-Century British Secularism: Science, Religion and Literature* (London, 2016)

Rix, Robert, *William Blake and the Cultures of Radical Christianity* (Aldershot and Burlington, VT, 2007)

Tayler, John James, *A Retrospect of the Religious Life of England* (London, 1876)

Ward, W. R., *The Protestant Evangelical Awakening* (Cambridge and New York, 1992)

Acknowledgements

I would like to express my gratitude to my two research assistants, Thomas Wright and Murrough O'Brien, for their invaluable help in the progress of this narrative.

Photo Acknowledgements

The author and publishers wish to express their thanks to the sources listed below for illustrative material and/or permission to reproduce it. Some locations of artworks are also given below, in the interest of brevity:

From *The Bookman*, XXVI/152 (May 1904): p. 267; Boston Public Library: p. 278; The Donald Gee Centre for Pentecostal and Charismatic Research, Doncaster: p. 343; Evening Standard/Hulton Archive via Getty Images: p. 353; Fitzwilliam Museum, University of Cambridge: p. 156; Flickr: p. 24 (photo Haydn Blackey, CC BY-SA 2.0); Houghton Library, Harvard University, Cambridge, MA: p. 142; Lewis Walpole Library, Yale University, Farmington, CT: p. 218; Library of Congress, Prints and Photographs Division, Washington, DC: pp. 192, 245, 297, 310; Los Angeles County Museum of Art (LACMA): p. 46; National Gallery of Art, Washington, DC: p. 232; National Portrait Gallery, London: pp. 187, 205; Nationalmuseum, Stockholm: p. 134; private collection: p. 108; Scottish National Portrait Gallery, Edinburgh: pp. 79, 94; Stiftsbibliothek Engelberg (Cod. 47, fol. 1v): p. 10; The Wenceslaus Hollar Collection, Thomas Fisher Rare Book Library, University of Toronto: p. 84.

Index

Page numbers in *italics* refer to illustrations.